American Crossings

American Crossings

Border Politics in the Western Hemisphere

Edited by Maiah Jaskoski,
Arturo C. Sotomayor,
and Harold A. Trinkunas

Johns Hopkins University Press
Baltimore

© 2015 Johns Hopkins University Press
All rights reserved. Published 2015
Printed in the United States of America on acid-free paper
9 8 7 6 5 4 3 2 1

Johns Hopkins University Press
2715 North Charles Street
Baltimore, Maryland 21218-4363
www.press.jhu.edu

Library of Congress Cataloging-in-Publication Data

American crossings : border politics in the Western Hemisphere / edited by
Maiah Jaskoski, Arturo C. Sotomayor, and Harold A. Trinkunas.
        pages cm
    Includes bibliographical references and index.
    ISBN 978-1-4214-1830-8 (pbk. : acid-free paper) — ISBN 1-4214-1830-4
(pbk. : acid-free paper) — ISBN 978-1-4214-1831-5 (electronic) —
ISBN 1-4214-1831-2 (electronic) 1. Boundaries—America. 2. Borderlands—
America. 3. Boundary disputes—America. 4. Geopolitics—America.
5. America—Foreign relations. I. Jaskoski, Maiah, 1977– II. Sotomayor,
Arturo C. III. Trinkunas, Harold A.
    JC323.A58 2015
    320.1'2—dc23   2015006254

Special discounts are available for bulk purchases of this book. For more
information, please contact Special Sales at 410-516-6936 or
specialsales@press.jhu.edu.

Johns Hopkins University Press uses environmentally friendly book
materials, including recycled text paper that is composed of at least
30 percent post-consumer waste, whenever possible.

Contents

Acknowledgments

As we began to assemble a list of those who contributed to this book, we realized that we had acquired a very large intellectual debt. This volume has benefited greatly from the generous funding of the Naval Postgraduate School (NPS) Center for Contemporary Conflict and the Defense Threat Reduction Agency at the US Department of Defense; this agency provided a seed grant for a brainstorming workshop held at Stanford University's Center for International Security and Cooperation (CISAC), in June 2012.

We also received financial support from the International Studies Association's (ISA) Venture Research Grant program, which offered additional resources to convene for a second workshop held in San Francisco during the 2013 Annual Convention of the International Studies Association. We also wish to acknowledge the Center for Inter-American Policy and Research at Tulane University for providing Arturo C. Sotomayor with initial research support in 2008 to explore territorial dispute settlements in Latin America.

Harold A. Trinkunas is grateful for the generous support of the late Charles W. Robinson and his family, whose contributions to the Brookings Foreign Policy Program enabled the completion of this book. The book's findings are in keeping with the Brookings Institution mission: to conduct high-quality and independent research and, based on that research, provide innovative recommendations for policy makers and the public. The conclusions and recommendations of any Brookings research are solely those of its authors and do not reflect the views of the institution, its management, or its other scholars.

We received especially valuable and constructive feedback at the CISAC and ISA workshops, and at a panel ("Latin American Borders and Borderlands: Conflicts and Harmonies") that we organized for the 2013 International Congress of the Latin American Studies Association in Washington, DC. Those offering feedback included Anne Clunan, Mariano-Florentino Cuéllar, Kent Eaton, George Gavrilis, Chappell Lawson, Benjamin Lessing, David Mares, David Scott Palmer, David Pion-Berlin, Jessica Rich, Viridiana Rios, and Edith Sheffer. These events were also enriched by presentations by C. J. Alvarez, Jorge Bustamante, Emmanuel Brunet-Jailly, Sarah Chartock, Cristina Eguizábal, Tasha Fairfield, José Antonio Lucero, Covadonga Meseguer, Rodrigo Nieto Gómez, Salvador Raza, Nicolás Rodríguez Games, Gustavo Vega, and Phil Williams. We would like to thank Ryan French at the NPS Center for Contemporary Conflict, whose superb organizational skills were essential to the success of the Stanford workshop. Diego Esparza thoroughly read and provided valuable feedback on the full manuscript. Emily Miller at the Brookings Institution provided both editing and valuable suggestions for improving chapters 6 and 11.

At Johns Hopkins University Press, Catherine Goldstead enthusiastically supported this project and offered encouraging editorial guidance, and Sheila Ann Dean provided excellent assistance at the copyediting stage. Finally, we are indebted to an anonymous reviewer, whose incisive feedback improved the manuscript.

The findings and any errors in this volume are those of the authors alone, and not of the other individuals, or the organizations, that supported the project.

American Crossings

Chapter One

Borders in the Americas

Theories and Realities

Maiah Jaskoski, Arturo C. Sotomayor,
and Harold A. Trinkunas

By the summer of 2014, it had become clear that the United States was witnessing an unprecedented surge in the number of children attempting to cross its southern border; many of them were traveling alone. These children, taking the same routes that are used to transport illicit goods and undocumented adults, were especially remarkable because they voluntarily turned themselves over to border patrol agents once they crossed into the United States. Although historically less than 20,000 unaccompanied minors were apprehended per year at the United States–Mexico border, these numbers climbed steadily beginning in 2011, to reach over 60,000 between January and August 2014. In a notable change, most originated in Central America rather than Mexico, as had been the previous pattern. A surge in violence in Central America's Northern Triangle (El Salvador, Guatemala, and Honduras) and misinformation about changes in US immigration policies had led many Central American parents—both in the region and residing illegally in the United States—to conclude that the risky, unaccompanied trip was preferable to their children remaining in their countries of origin. In the United States, the Department of Health and Human Services, which was normally charged with the care of illegal migrant minors, was overwhelmed, and the armed forces assumed responsibility for housing and caring for the detainees.[1] The public, and many in Congress, reacted with alarm to the apparent unpreparedness of government agencies to deal with unaccompanied minors crossing US borders, and some even used the issue to call attention to what they saw as the country's vulnerability to covert entry by threatening actors, such as international terrorists.

The human tragedy of this surge in unaccompanied children entering the United States from Mexico highlights the complexity of borders, even in a region as peaceful and integrated as the Americas. In particular, this case of migrant children demonstrates how questions of economics, security, governance, and identity can interact to produce unintended consequences. The long period of peace between the United States and Mexico has created a border that is largely free of military tensions but is paradoxically becoming ever more heavily securitized, with an increased presence of US Border Patrol agents and drones; this has been in response to the September 11, 2001, terrorist attacks on the World Trade Center in Manhattan and a growing anti-immigrant sentiment. It was in this context that many Central Americans traveled to the United States in pursuit of economic opportunities, and since they faced a highly restrictive visa regime barring legal entry, an infrastructure to facilitate illicit border crossings flourished. In addition, Central America has experienced a recent surge in criminal violence as a result of a shift in illicit drug trafficking routes across the Americas. Increased drug interdiction efforts in South America, particularly in Colombia and Peru, led transnational criminal organizations to shift their operations toward Central American countries, principally Honduras, where sea and air boundaries are more weakly enforced. In the last few years, human traffickers increasingly spread deceptive rumors, leading many in Central America to believe that a change in US immigration policy allowed women and children easier border crossings. Faced with the ever more violent reality of the Northern Triangle, parents assessed the risk of unaccompanied children traveling to the United States through illicit trafficking networks to be lower than that of remaining at home, thus producing the surge.[2] In response, the United States, the Inter-American Development Bank, and the Northern Triangle governments have recognized the multidimensional causes for the recent migration of children northward; in November 2014, they announced a plan to improve cross-border cooperation and governance in Central America that would address public safety and create economic opportunities in the region.[3]

As this case shows, in a globalized world, borders still matter. In fact, borderlines demarcating international boundaries, and borderlands—that is, the physical spaces near those boundaries—can become increasingly salient precisely because of peace and more open trade policies among states, both of which have existed for decades between the United States and Mexico. This book examines the Western Hemisphere, where dramatic political and economic shifts have taken place with important implications for borders. The end of the Cold War and widespread democratization from military rule in Latin America provided strong incentives for governments to resolve international territorial disputes and demilitarize borders. Simultaneously, countries shifted from state-led to liberal economic models, opening borders to trade. This opening has created challenges for the state, which has been historically weak in Latin America, to regulate the legal transit of people and goods, reduce illicit crossings, and offer border security. In some cases nonstate actors operating in borderlands may be the only providers of order, albeit not the type national governments would prefer.

Through rich analyses of borders in the Americas, this book develops and builds on existing scholarship. It includes broad analyses that span important historical periods (Andreas) and cover cases across the Americas (Thies, Sotomayor). The volume also contains in-depth research on crucial borderlines and borderlands that are renowned for extreme and, in some cases, varying insecurity, international conflict, and/or dynamic trade relations: the United States–Mexico border (Isacson), the Tri-Border Area connecting Argentina, Brazil, and Paraguay (Aguiar, Kacowicz), and the Argentina-Chile (Mani), Colombia-Venezuela (Trinkunas), and Colombia-Ecuador (Jaskoski) borders.

Traditionally, border research has focused on cases from Europe and North America, treating borders as (1) external limits demarcating sovereignty (geopolitics), (2) boundaries of internal security and the rule of law (policing), (3) spaces of economic transactions, or (4) lines or areas defining imagined communities (identity). In those regions, the effect of globalization and liberalization as trends has been overdetermined. Recent research on Europe, which enjoys a surplus of regional institutions (i.e., NATO and the European Union) and consolidated democracies, has tended to analyze borderlines as mostly peaceful delimitations between liberal, democratic states with a low predisposition for domestic conflicts.[4] By contrast, this book analyzes a region that includes borders that vary across space and time in terms of degree and trajectory of international border disputes, level of illegal trafficking and smuggling and their implications for international trade and border security, and how illicit practices affect political and economic stability. Using key cases from the Western Hemisphere, this volume reveals the complex interplay among border components and its consequences for security, international relations, and borderland inhabitants. Added to its focus on interactions among border features, this book also highlights the influence of domestic factors—most prominently, limited state capacity—on borderlines and borderlands.

This chapter elaborates on the four features of borders mentioned above, and then draws on the contributing authors' analyses to highlight how a focus on important borderlines and borderlands in the Americas deepens our understanding of borders by revealing surprising interactions among the border characteristics and by demonstrating the particular roles of the state regarding Latin American borders. The chapter concludes by outlining the rest of the volume.

Borders in Theory

As a "physical demarcation allowing territorial divisions to be secured and marked on a map,"[5] borders separate states from one another. This definition of borders enables scholars not only to identify "the state," but also to define an area of state administrative organization and control. Borderlines delineate this space, either topographically (e.g., rivers or mountains) or geometrically. These borderlines and surrounding borderlands are sites for the convergence of four domains of concern to states and their inhabitants: national security, police security, economic development, and identity construction.

Borders as Geopolitics

In the field of international relations, classic realism has analyzed borders to understand conflict, stressing the importance of territorial competition, in which "borders are strategic lines to be militarily defended or breached."[6] As such, traditionally borders have been seen as a source of tension; conflict arises when borders are contested, and belligerents share borders. Territorial and border conflicts are exponentially costly.[7] As Paul F. Diehl argues, "conflicts over territory are more likely to involve military force and escalate to war than are disputes over other issues . . . not only are territorial concerns significant in generating militarized conflict, they also play a role in the dynamics of conflict behavior between disputants."[8] For example, international tensions in the forms of security dilemmas, arms races, and spirals are often caused by troop movements that take place along contested borders. The main insight of this perspective is that cooperation among states will be limited as long as border and territorial disputes remain unresolved.

Borders as Economic Institutions

By contrast, liberals often see international frontiers as sources of cooperation and wealth. It is through borders that states interact and engage in economic transactions.[9] Logically, the natural geography and human-made infrastructure associated with borders establish the basic parameters of the costs associated with transactions across borders. However, borders are also sites where states regulate cross-border flows of goods, borderland markets, and human migration, thus imposing their own costs and perhaps creating opportunities for profit. State agencies might even respond to the market by seeking to shut it down, particularly in the case of cross-border flows based on the supply and demand of illicit goods in different countries.[10] At the other end of the spectrum, the state itself may compete as a market actor, such as when security forces sell their services to the private sector in border zones.[11]

The confluence of states' different rules, procedures, taxes, and definitions of legality creates the opportunity for market actors—licit and illicit—to profit from jurisdiction shopping, locating their activities in the zones where they can realize the greatest gains. It is noteworthy how it can be highly lucrative to participate in crossings precisely where they are illegal; when states define certain activities as illegal, they create a risk premium for undertaking the activity.[12] The opportunity for increased gain naturally leads actors engaged in both legal and illicit transactions to seek to influence the politics of border control, and thus rules governing economic exchanges.

BORDERS AS POLICE JURISDICTIONAL BOUNDARIES

Overlapping with but distinct from the economic dimension, borders can also be analyzed in terms of internal security and police control. For example, Malcolm Anderson argues that as institutions, borders mark and delimit state sovereignty and rights of individual citizens.[13] As institutions, borders entail specific state practices that have become institutionalized over time: passport controls at official crossing points, policing, restrictions on imports and exports, and the collection of customs duties. In so doing, borders organize political and public life and define the scope and domain of sovereignty.

By marking the limits of the state's jurisdiction over individuals and territories, the border is a potential site of coercion and extraction.[14] Peter Andreas argues: "As territorially demarcated institutions, states have always imposed entry barriers, whether to deter armies, tax trade and protect domestic producers, or keep out perceived 'undesirables.' All states monopolize the right to determine who and what is granted legitimate territorial access."[15] Within this paradigm, the borders that separate states are an institution that signals, in George Gravilis's words, "the point at which a state's authority ends and provides officials and populations with a point of reference beyond which their activities are not authorized."

Gravilis goes on to say: "Borders, in short, are local manifestations of the claims of a state's authority. They enable coercion and extraction and signal ownership."[16]

Borders as Imagined Communities

Borders can also be understood as makers of identity that have played a key role in the construction of national cultures.[17] For example, constructivists and anthropologists often see borders beyond their material dimension by focusing on how frontiers help establish identity narratives that distinguish between the "in group" and the "out group." Jean-Pierre Cassarino argues:

> The boundary has a significance which results from the interaction between two social systems or between an individual and a group . . . borders carry a heavy weight of symbolism which impacts on the ways in which the individual lives the border, as well as the entry and exit of the bordered area. The most important analytical breakthrough may lie in understanding the subjective meaning that is attached to the boundary and whether it coincides with the material border that is designed by the state.[18]

That is, the process of identity formation not only produces difference between those who live on each side of the border, but also between border inhabitants and those residing in the core of their respective states.

The More Things Change: Maritime and Air Borders

For thousands of years, evolving technology, first extending humankind's reach across oceans, then below them, and finally above into the atmosphere, has made sea and air boundaries comparably important to traditional land borders and borderlands. But while technology produces new borders, many of the theoretical considerations first developed to understand land borders may extend to other boundaries as well. For example, geopolitical tensions arising from competing maritime boundary claims among states bordering the South China Sea threaten a conflict that could quickly become global, and they are leading even relatively poor states, such as the Philippines, to invest in their navy and air force.[19] The renewal of long-range Russian air force bomber patrols along the boundaries of NATO countries suggests that air borders, too, can be used for geopolitical signaling.[20] In addition, air and sea boundaries are of critical economic importance for the flow of goods and persons, far more so than land borders in many parts of the world. Airports and seaports, precisely because they are choke points, are sites of intensified police presence and government control,

for strong and also weak states. Finally, sea borders are crucial in the formation of national identity, contributing to a maritime identity for countries such as
Portugal and Great Britain; and, by their absence, to landlocked Bolivia's national obsession with recuperating its access to the Pacific Ocean that it lost in
war to Chile. Although this volume focuses largely on land borders, we will
touch upon the role of maritime and air borders where they become relevant for
understanding dynamics in the Americas.

Borders in the Western Hemisphere

Looking across the Western Hemisphere, we see the four facets of borders—
geopolitical limits, policing boundaries, economic transaction points, and spaces
defining imagined communities—interacting in ways not anticipated in traditional studies. From a policing perspective, several borders in the hemisphere
experience great insecurity, which has intersected with international relations; in
many cases conflicts in borders zones have escalated amid border banditry and
the smuggling of people, drugs, and guns, creating tensions both between countries and among actors in borderlands. Other border zones are peaceful precisely
because of the actions of illegal actors that establish and maintain order.

From a geopolitical perspective, though there are multiple international territorial and maritime border disputes in the Western Hemisphere, few states are
willing to fight militarily over contested boundaries, and some highly tense, long-
standing disputes have been resolved through surprisingly smooth and brief bilateral processes. Cameron G. Thies shows in his chapter that it is not militarized
border conflict but identity-based nationalist sentiment that keeps international
territorial rivalries alive in Latin America. Yet nationalist sentiment appears to be
limited in important ways. As illustrated by Kristina Mani's analysis of Argentina-
Chile territorial disputes, state actors focused more on technocratic questions
than on nationalist sentiment have, through regular cross-border interactions,
depoliticized and resolved border conflicts. More broadly, in a context in which
technical expertise often overrides nationalism, many Latin American territorial
disputes have been historically settled without the use of force, relying on diplomatic as well as judicial means.[21]

The relative infrequency of international warfare in the Western Hemisphere
has significantly influenced border relations more broadly. That states can peacefully settle their boundary disputes suggests they may also be able to resolve other
conflicts, including those related to trade and finances. Following this line of argument, Beth Simmons has argued that in Latin America, the peaceful resolution

of territorial conflicts has improved the terms of trade, thus allowing for regional and economic integration. Her finding implies that territorial dispute settlement via international arbitration can set precedents to solve outstanding economic issues. Borders then become the source of cooperation by allowing states to overcome their mutual distrust.[22] At the same time, the realities of the Western Hemisphere's borders push us to problematize this association of reduced border conflict in terms of militarized conflict on the one hand, and international trade on the other. As the chapter by Harold A. Trinkunas shows, in the case of the Venezuela-Colombia border rivalry, escalated border tensions have been accompanied by increasing economic openness between the two countries.

If the relationship between international border conflict and international trade is multifaceted, linkages between border openings and illegal activities also prove difficult to pin down. As Arie M. Kacowicz vividly demonstrates in this volume, when international peace and increased trade do occur together, a potential consequence is the rise of different kinds of conflicts, including security challenges in borderlands posed by smugglers and transnational terrorist organizations. And yet, in contrast to the Tri-Border Area, other borderland violence may not follow increased economic trade. Adam Isacson and Peter Andreas emphasize in their respective chapters that, in fact, illicit actors using open borders to transport their illegal shipments depend on and enforce peace in borderlands as a means of ensuring smooth economic transactions. Maiah Jaskoski shows how armed guerrillas relying on regular passage across the international borderline for economic as well as military strategic reasons also may enforce that international border, as in the Ecuador-Colombia case.

Just as problematic as the relationship between open borders and borderland security is the assumption that economic liberalization results in open borders at all. Focusing on the supposedly open borders caused by liberal economic reforms across the region can blind us to the new regulatory structures that necessarily emerge to monitor legal exchange and prevent illegal crossings. José Carlos G. Aguiar's analysis of the Tri-Border Area shows how, in the neoliberal context, a new regulatory regime has been constructed to formalize and regulate much of what previously had been considered illegal smuggling.

The State

The Western Hemisphere serves as a rich setting for studying borders not only because of the complex interactions among border features, but also due to the particular characteristics of the state and its functions with regard to borderlines and borderlands. Most prominently, the contributing authors emphasize two overlapping themes: the role of the armed forces and weak state capacity.

Latin American militaries emerge as central players when it comes to studying borders. Mani writes of the delicate issue of civilians taking over border conflicts where the armed forces have historically wielded substantial political influence. In her analysis of the Argentina-Chile case, the military became a "veto" player; without military support, border resolutions could not move forward. Sotomayor argues that Latin American leaders increasingly utilize international legal mechanisms to resolve border disputes because doing so allows them to wrest political power from the military. And yet, as he points out, demilitarizing borders encourages the armed forces to move into internal security functions, which can politicize the military. This finding is consistent with Alfred Stepan's "new professionalism" paradigm for understanding why in the 1960s Latin American militaries took over governments.[23] Indeed, for the Tri-Border Area, Kacowicz notes that one factor contributing to insecurity is that posttransition governments have been reluctant to bring the military back into internal affairs by calling on it to provide security in the borderlands.

The issue of whether and when to use the military for security on borders and in borderlands looms large in Latin America, where the armed forces often offer the only possibility for establishing state border presence. As Mani writes, militaries are the "actors literally at the frontier of their territories." Jaskoski demonstrates that the main state presence near the Ecuador-Colombia border is provided by the Ecuadorian army. Trinkunas emphasizes that the Venezuelan military was handed an important border security mission in the 1980s to control cross-border flows between Venezuela and Colombia, and that the armed forces on the ground have been important in that case for providing governance on the border. Sotomayor shows that as border disputes are demilitarized, fewer military forces are devoted to the border, reducing border security.

Although the armed forces may be the main state presence on borders, they may not embody independent state interests. In fact, one indication of weak state capacity is corruption within state security forces, including the military. Trinkunas describes how the Venezuelan armed forces have extracted rents from licit and illicit cross-border trade. Andreas analyzes social relations between smugglers and law enforcers, and the resulting corruption of the latter, along the United States–Mexican border in the late nineteenth and early twentieth centuries. Jaskoski describes the ongoing interactions, including economic exchanges, between Colombian guerrillas and the Ecuadorian military.

The implications of weak state capacity go beyond the question of corrupt state security forces. Thies argues that a crucial implication of intermediate state capacity is a region characterized by unresolved border disputes among governments that do not seek to conquer one another. For Andreas, weak state capacity is a key ingredient for ongoing smuggling across the United States' international borders in that law enforcement's "successes" in intervening with smuggling have merely led smugglers to innovate, developing more sophisticated methods.

In a context of borders that have increasingly been opened to trade through liberal economic reforms, weak state regulatory capacity has meant that border openings have brought illegal as well as legal trade, as noted by Andreas and others. Trinkunas writes that illegal actors have taken advantage of the relatively open Colombia-Venezuela border, and that in fact the income of those actors through their illegal transactions has been so important to the Venezuelan economy that it has contributed to continued open borders for trade more broadly. As noted above, Kacowicz writes that open borders brought not only illegal trade to the Tri-Border Area but also insecurity, through the rise of transnational criminal organizations. In contrast, Andreas and Isacson's chapters depict a different picture amid limited state capacity. Powerful actors involved in smuggling often move their goods peacefully and reliably across the border without spurring violence and, in fact, ensure the peace, precisely to facilitate smooth cross-border economic transactions.

Though there is much to be said about weak states in the Americas and implications for borders, a final way that the volume addresses questions of the state is by concentrating on an element of valuable state, and specifically bureaucratic, capacity. This element involves how international tensions over borders have been reduced through the shifting of territorial disputes away from the oversight of politicians and military personnel focused on nationalist interests and reputations, to the jurisdiction of expert bureaucrats. Sotomayor highlights that Latin American foreign ministers traditionally have been trained in economics or law, and this can help move border disputes to international judicial arenas where external, impartial rulings stand. Mani emphasizes how productive regular interactions between Chilean and Argentine technical experts depoliticized border discord, facilitating dispute resolution. Trinkunas observes a similar phenomenon with regard to military personnel in the case of Venezuela-Colombia border tensions.

Overview

This book is organized according to three crucial outcomes: the geopolitics of borders, national policies for border security and cross-border trade, and licit and illicit behaviors of borderland actors.

PART I. GEOPOLITICS OF BORDERS

Chapters in part I analyze the foundations and evolution of longstanding international border rivalries, taking seriously the implications of democratization following military rule, as well as increased economic opening, for conflict continuity and resolution. In chapter 2, Thies presents a broad overview of international conflict over territorial boundaries, tracing how border conflicts have led to interstate rivalries—which also rest in important ways on nationalist territorial sentiment—and how those rivalries have contributed to state building. Contrary to expectations, his quantitative analysis suggests that overall interstate warfare has not contributed to state building in Latin America. However, rivalries have strengthened states, as measured by the extraction of revenue through taxation, possible in a context in which territorial threats are "especially salient to rulers and their citizen subjects." At the same time, there are limits to how strong states can become amidst rivalries; this situation leads to an uneasy equilibrium, though not a full-scale war that would lead to strong states. But lacking full peace, the rivalries mean that states "struggle to maintain internal sovereignty at times."

In chapter 3, also delving into the troubled peace among Latin American countries, Sotomayor argues that in seeking resolutions to territorial disputes, governments frequently turn to international legal structures, especially the International Court of Justice (ICJ), due to a combination of three factors. These include the bias in favor of legalistic approaches in Latin America, especially among ambassadors and foreign affairs ministers trained in economics and law; the ICJ's place as the most trusted and neutral international judicial structure that also sits at the highest level in the hierarchy of international judicial systems; and the fact that legalizing disputes removes political power from militaries in post-transition settings.

Like Sotomayor's analysis, in chapter 4 Mani places importance on the technical training of state officials charged with handling international territorial disputes. She argues that the resolution of the border dispute between Argentina and Chile was the result of "technocratization" of security cooperation; this involved institutionalized communications between civilian and military bureaucrats from the two countries who had technical expertise with regard to defining the international borderline.

PART II: NATIONAL POLICIES FOR BORDER SECURITY AND CROSS-BORDER TRADE

Part II of the volume examines the relationship between border security and cross-border economic flows. The main focus is on how national governments in the Western Hemisphere have sought to open borders to legal commerce in the contemporary neoliberal economic context at the same time that they confront ongoing and perhaps increasing mandates to provide security, and thus controls, along those same frontiers. An important commonality across all three analyses is the salience of cross-border economic disparities, which encourage smuggling, illegal migration, and asymmetric international relations governing security and economic transactions.

In chapter 5, Kacowicz traces the deeply intertwined phenomena of international peace and economic regionalism that opened the Tri-Border Area. An unintended outcome of international peace and borders newly opened to trade has been the emergence of new security threats very different from the traditional international territorial conflicts that predated the opening. These threats involve trading in illicit goods, which has been diverted in some instances to generate financial support for transnational terrorist groups.

In chapter 6, through a close examination of Colombia-Venezuela relations from the late 1990s to the present, Harold Trinkunas challenges the expectation that increased territorial conflict between two countries will reduce trade. In this case, substantial trade continued even as international tensions over security at the border escalated. Trinkunas points to domestic politics to explain the rise in economic interdependence, and in particular, to both powerful Colombian business coalitions that relied on exporting consumer goods to Venezuela, and high demand from Venezuelans for Colombian goods.

In chapter 7 Isacson emphasizes a strictly economic logic driving cross-border flows between Mexico and the United States, and how stronger illicit economic actors can actually result in fewer security threats to the border. On the basis of these observations, Isacson asserts the ineffectiveness of US border security policies, which have not countered the more powerful economic forces at play. At a more fundamental level, Isacson illustrates that current misconceptions of the border produce a mismatch between policy and reality.

PART III: LICIT AND ILLICIT BEHAVIOR BY BORDERLAND ACTORS

Part III of the volume shifts the level of analysis to borderlands. In chapter 8, Andreas presents historical examples of a high level of porosity of borders in the Americas, with a focus on the very borders we would expect to be the most well defined—those of the United States. He stresses in particular how smuggling formed the foundation of early US trade relations in the hemisphere; this funded, for example, the American Revolution and the Confederate side of the Civil War. The analysis further emphasizes that US efforts to halt smuggling have historically failed, as exemplified by large inflows of unauthorized Chinese immigrants and the smuggling of alcohol into the country during Prohibition. Against this historical backdrop, Andreas notes that alarm over illicit trafficking into the United States, especially of illegal drugs, is unwarranted; borders are no more porous than they were historically, because sufficient state capacity has never existed to seal US borders.

In chapter 9, Jaskoski argues that weak—but existent—state presence on Ecuador's borderline, and in the Ecuadorian borderlands abutting Colombia, helps us to understand the logic of the Ecuador-Colombia border. An intermediate level of Ecuadorian state presence has triggered efforts by nonstate actors to directly define the border; in response to limited Ecuadorian military presence, Colombian guerrillas have enforced the international borderline to facilitate their easy crossings.

In chapter 10, Aguiar demonstrates how neoliberalism promotes lowering of old national trade barriers, which in turn promotes the rise of new and different barriers in the Tri-Border Region. Through a close anthropological view of the political economy of smuggling in the borderlands, Aguiar examines how open borders in fact have led to greater controls, for certain populations, in the form of stringent regulations of what was previously considered tolerable illegal smuggling.

In a concluding chapter to the volume, we reflect on the interactions across levels of analysis, observing how international and domestic factors, as well as organization-level dynamics—and especially tensions between agencies operating at the border and national-level policymakers—help to explain the three outcomes of interest. The chapter closes with potential solutions for borderline and borderland conflicts and recommendations for further research.

NOTES

1. Peter Mayer, Claire Ribando Seelke, Maureen Taft-Morales, and Rhoda Margesson, *Unaccompanied Children from Central America: Foreign Policy Considerations* (Washington, DC: Congressional Research Service, August 28, 2014).

2. Julia Preston, "Hoping for Asylum, Migrants Strain U.S. Border," *New York Times*, April 10, 2014, http://www.nytimes.com/2014/04/11/us/poverty-and-violence-push-new-wave-of-migrants-toward-us.html.

3. "Presidents of El Salvador, Guatemala and Honduras Outline Plan to Promote Peace and Prosperity in their Region," Inter-American Development Bank, Washington, DC, November 14, 2014, http://www.iadb.org/en/news/news-releases/2014-11-14/northern-triangle-presidents-present-development-plan,10987.html.

4. See, for example, Emmanuel Brunet-Jailly, ed., *Borderlands: Comparing Border Security in North America and Europe* (Ottawa, Canada: University of Ottawa Press, 2007).

5. Jean-Pierre Cassarino, "Approaching Borders and Frontiers: Notions and Implications," in *Cooperation Project on the Social Integration of Immigrants, Migration, and the Movement of Persons*, Research Report 2006 / 03 (European University Institute and the European Commission at the Robert Schuman Center, 2006), http://cadmus.eui.eu/bitstream/handle/1814/6274/CARIM-RR_2006_03.pdf?sequence=1, 2.

6. Peter Andreas, *Border Games: Policing the U.S.-Mexico Border* (Ithaca, NY: Cornell University Press, 2009), 81.

7. See, for example, Jack Child, *Geopolitics and Conflict in South America: Quarrels among Neighbors* (New York, NY: Praeger, 1985), 5.

8. Paul F. Diehl, "Territory and International Conflict: An Overview," in *A Road Map to War: Territorial Dimensions of International Conflict*, ed. Paul F. Diehl (Nashville, TN: Vanderbilt University Press, 1999), x.

9. See, for example, Robert O. Keohane and Joseph S. Nye, *Power and Interdependence: World Politics in Transition* (Boston, MA: Little, Brown, 1977); and John Gerard Ruggie, "Territoriality and Beyond: Problematizing Modernity in International Relations," *International Organization* 47, no. 1 (winter 1993): 139–74.

10. Andreas, *Border Games*, 15–28.

11. Maiah Jaskoski, "Public Security Forces with Private Funding: Local Army Entrepreneurship in Peru and Ecuador," *Latin American Research Review* 47, no. 2 (2012): 79–99.

12. On this risk premium as it applies in the transport of illegal drugs into the United States, see the analysis of Bertram et al. of the "profit paradox." Eva Bertram, Morris Blachman, Kenneth Sharpe, and Peter Andreas, *Drug War Politics: The Price of Denial* (Berkeley, CA: University of California Press, 1996), 20–21.

13. Malcolm Anderson, *Frontiers: Territory and State Formation in the Modern World* (Oxford: Polity, 1996), 1–3, referenced in Hastings Donnan and Thomas M. Wilson, *Borders: Frontiers of Identity, Nation and State* (New York, NY: Berg, 1999), 5.

14. See Charles Tilly, *Coercion, Capital, and European States, AD 990–1992* (Cambridge, MA: Blackwell, 1990).

15. Peter Andreas, "Redrawing the Line: Borders and Security in the 21st Century," *International Security* 28, no. 2 (autumn 2003): 78–111.

16. George Gavrilis, *The Dynamics of Interstate Boundaries* (New York, NY: Cambridge University Press, 2008), 6.

17. Donnan and Wilson, *Borders*, 5.

18. Cassarino, "Approaching Borders," 12.

19. See Martin Fackler, "To Counter China, Japan and Philippines Will Bolster Maritime Cooperation," *New York Times*, January 10, 2013, http://www.nytimes.com/2013/01/11/world/asia/japan-and-philippines-to-bolster-maritime-cooperation.html.

20. See Associated Press, "Russian Bomber Patrols to Reach Gulf of Mexico," *New York Times*, November 12, 2014, http://www.nytimes.com/aponline/2014/11/12/world/europe/ap-eu-russia-military.html.

21. A large amount of literature explores this empirical puzzle. See, for example, Arie M. Kacowicz, *The Impact of Norms in International Society: The Latin American Experience, 1881–2001* (Notre Dame, IN: University of Notre Dame Press, 2005); Jorge Domínguez, "Boundary Disputes in Latin America," Peaceworks 50 (Washington, DC: United States Institute of Peace, 2003), 1–44; Miguel Angel Centeno, *Blood and Debt: War and the Nation-State in Latin America* (University Park, PA: Pennsylvania State University Press 2002), 33–100; David R. Mares, *Violent Peace: Militarized Interstate Bargaining in Latin America* (New York, NY: Columbia University Press, 2001), 28–51; Felix E. Martin, *Militarist Peace in South America: Conditions for War and Peace* (New York: Palgrave-Macmillan, 2006); and Beth A. Simmons, "Territorial Disputes and Their Resolution: The Case of Ecuador and Peru," Peaceworks 27 (Washington, DC: United States Institute of Peace, 1999).

22. Beth Simmons, "Capacity, Commitment, and Compliance: International Institutions and Territorial Disputes," *Journal of Conflict Resolution* 46, no. 6 (December 2002): 832–36.

23. Alfred Stepan, "The New Professionalism of Internal Warfare and Military Role Expansion," in *Authoritarian Brazil: Origins, Policies, and Future*, ed. Alfred Stepan (New Haven, CT: Yale University Press, 1973), 47–65.

PART I / Geopolitics of Borders

Chapter Two

Borders, Rivalries, and the Racketeer State

An Alternative Theory to State Development in Latin America

Cameron G. Thies

Borders have played a central role in the development of state capacity, regional peace, and security in Latin America throughout the post-independence period.[1] In this chapter, I knit together a larger story about the interrelationship of these factors that draws on my larger body of work on state building.[2] This story, like all theoretical accounts, is somewhat stylized. By drawing on specific cases, statistical analyses, and larger bodies of theories, this chapter explores territorial conflicts and their effects on interstate rivalry, state building, and regional security dynamics. There is still more work to do to fully flesh out the theoretical connections as well as to determine more specifically the empirical scope of the argument.

This chapter presents a straightforward argument that is consistent with other explanations found in the literature on state development and territorial consolidation. I argue that territorial conflicts became central to state building in many Latin American states relatively early in their post-independence years. In these cases, territory became a salient and contentious issue that led to the institutionalization of conflict between states in the form of interstate rivalries. Rivalries provided states with some means to increase their capacity over time since they could be used instrumentally when needed by rulers as a kind of protection racket.[3] Yet, the long-term effect of the institutionalization of unresolved conflict has produced a limited form of state building and a regional negative or cold peace.[4] The net effect of this long-term historical dynamic is that Latin American states are unlikely to engage in serious interstate conflict with each other, yet they are also limited in their ability to manage internal conflict and exercise effective control over the entirety of their territory.

The analyses presented in this chapter draw on a mixture of qualitative and quantitative methods in order to test this theoretical argument. The use of statistical modeling is particularly important given that the theoretical argument is quite general—it is not specific to Latin America or even to particular states in the region. Statistical analysis allows for the comparison of data on border and territorial conflicts as well as data on the capacity of the state and regional security. I supplement these general statistical claims with case study evidence. The case study analysis also allows me to look back further in time than the statistical analyses, due to a lack of data prior to the start of the twentieth century.

I begin with an overview of territorial conflicts to demonstrate their importance as salient, contentious issues in Latin America. The broad picture of conflict in the region is then fleshed out with illustrations from the Argentine-Chile case. This case demonstrates the development of contention over territory within Argentina and Chile; it helps to explain the formation of an interstate rivalry consisting of a number of interlinked territorial disputes. I suggest that if contentious territorial issues motivate rivalry, then rivalry (like war) may be used by state rulers to augment their extractive capacity. Statistical analysis from Latin America is used to show that rivalry has allowed rulers to run a type of protection racket. Yet, the increase in tax extraction is nowhere near the levels generated by total war among European states. The kind of state building observed as a result is rather limited. Latin America's regional culture of cold or negative peace is the result of interstate rivalries between states that are neither perilously weak nor exceptionally strong. Statistical analyses of the region are again used to show this result. I conclude with some thoughts on future work needed to fully develop both the argument and the empirical analysis of territorial conflict state building and regional peace and security.

The Salience of Border and Territorial Issues in Latin America

Territorial conflict has been a salient feature of Latin America since independent states formed in the region in the nineteenth century. Conflict scholars have approached the measurement of conflict in several ways that are informative to understanding the territorial struggles in the region. A lot of the quantitative literature on conflict relies on the Correlates of War (COW) Project's militarized

Table 2.1   Militarized interstate disputes (MIDs) in Latin America, 1826–2001

Time period	All MIDs	Territorial MIDs	Great power MIDs
1826–1899	122	39 / 122 = .32	77 / 122 = .63
1900–1945	164	56 / 164 = .34	82 / 164 = .50
1946–2001	190	65 / 190 = .34	67 / 190 = .34
Total	476	160	226

Source: Correlates of War Project, http://www.correlatesofwar.org/.

interstate dispute (MID) dataset. A militarized interstate dispute refers to "cases in which the threat, display or use of military force short of war by one member state is explicitly directed toward the government, official representatives, official forces, property, or territory of another state."[5] As such, MIDs are a useful proxy for militarization of interstate interaction, since they code the full array of state action from threats to the use of force.

Table 2.1 summarizes the history of MIDs in Latin America across three broad time periods: the 1800s, 1900–1945, and 1945–2001. There were a total of 476 MIDs across the three periods with a general increase over time, largely reflecting the increasing number of independent states in the region along with enhanced abilities to communicate threats and project force. We can also see that the great powers have been less actively involved in the MIDs that occurred in the region over time. In the nineteenth century, over 60 percent of the MIDs involved at least one great power, whereas that proportion dropped to a little over a third in the post–World War II period. What remained virtually constant was the percentage of all MIDs that were territorial in nature; this was usually at around one-third for each time period and for the overall series. Latin American states have clearly been concerned with territory to the point that they routinely engaged in the militarization of their interactions with each other over it.[6] As table 2.1 shows, this fact is not solely a function of external intervention given the declining involvement of great powers in the region's MIDs; it also is not a function of a specific time period.

MIDs do not contain information on wars per se, but the Correlates of War (COW) Project also provides coding for interstate wars. An interstate war is defined as "sustained combat, involving organized armed forces, resulting in a minimum of 1,000 battle-related fatalities"[7] within a twelve-month period between members of the interstate system.[8] Latin America's interstate wars are listed in table 2.2. The table contains the COW name for the war, the participants, the

Table 2.2   Interstate wars in Latin America

Interstate war	Participants	Years	Battle deaths
Mexican-American	Mexico, US	1846–1847	6,000 MEX; 13,283 USA
La Plata	Argentina, Brazil	1851–1852	800 ARG; 500 BRA
Franco-Mexican	Mexico, France	1862–1867	12,000 MEX; 8,000 FRA
Ecuadorian-Colombian	Ecuador, Colombia	1863	700 ECU; 300 COL
López / War of the Triple Alliance	Argentina, Paraguay, Brazil	1864–1870	10,000 ARG; 200,000 PAR; 100,000 BRA
Naval/Guano	Chile, Peru, Spain	1865–1866	100 CHL; 600 PER; 300 SPN
First Central American	Guatemala, El Salvador	1876	2,000 GUA; 2,000 SAL
War of the Pacific	Chile, Peru, Bolivia	1879–1883	3,276 CHL; 9,672 PER; 920 BOL
Second Central American	El Salvador, Guatemala	1885	200 SAL; 800 GUA
Third Central American	Honduras, El Salvador, Guatemala	1906	300 HON; 300 SAL; 400 GUA
Fourth Central American	Nicaragua, El Salvador, Honduras	1907	400 NIC; 300 SAL; 300 HON
Chaco	Bolivia, Paraguay	1932–1935	56,661 BOL; 36,000 PAR
World War II	Brazil	1944–1945	1,000 BRA
Korean	Colombia	1951–1953	140 COL
Football	Honduras, El Salvador	1969	1,200 HON; 700 SAL
Falklands/Malvinas	Argentina, United Kingdom	1982	746 ARG; 255 UKG
Cenepa Valley	Ecuador, Peru	1995	550 ECU; 950 PER

Source: Correlates of War Project, http://www.correlatesofwar.org.

duration in years, as well as the approximate battle deaths for each participant. Many of these wars (especially those between neighbors) had a territorial component, including some that resulted in large territorial losses for some and gains for others. The losses (or perceived losses) are likely candidates for the source of ongoing, contentious issues surrounding borders and territory. This is especially true given that most wars (and MIDs) over territory occur between neighbors.

Finally, conflict scholars have also considered how conflicts, whether MIDs or interstate wars, may be serially connected to produce interstate rivalries. Rivalries have been conceptualized and operationalized in slightly different ways, but the main features revolve around the identification of long-term, hostile relationships. For example, Paul Diehl and Gary Goertz suggest that:

> what characterizes a rivalry relationship is not military force, but conflict over one issue or set of issues. Issue constancy over time thus permits one to say that all the competition in the rivalry belongs to the "same" relationship. The advantage of issue conceptions is that they make one more certain that the

various incidents in a rivalry belong together as part of the same relationship. Because the issue or issues remain constant, one can link the various disputes of a rivalry. In addition, this approach makes it easier to code the beginning and end of rivalries. Once the issue or issues have been resolved, the rivalry is over.[9]

Yet, the actual operationalization of this issue-based approach is only partially incorporated in the most recent iteration of their work.[10] The rivalry concept in this latest version adds a requirement for linked conflict, in which "the interrelation of issues primarily determines whether disputes belong to the same rivalry"; but they primarily identify rivalries based on the number of MIDs that occur in a certain time period.[11]

William Thompson's conceptual approach requires that strategic rivals must view each other as "(a) competitors, (b) the source of actual or latent threats that pose some possibility of becoming militarized, and (c) enemies."[12] Operationally, he reviews the historical record to identify when the principal decision makers in each country mutually identified each other as rivals. Finally, Sara Mitchell and Cameron Thies (2011) focus on geopolitical issues, such as territorial, maritime and riparian, as the basis for interstate rivalry.[13] Their approach has two dimensions.

The first dimension, issue rivalry, captures the number of contested geopolitical issues in an interstate dyadic relationship. The second dimension, militarized rivalry, encapsulates the way in which specific issues are handled. Pairs of states that experience multiple geopolitical issue claims at the same point in time are considered to be issue rivals. Pairs of states that experience repeated militarized disputes over a single geopolitical issue are considered to be militarized rivals.

Operationally, Mitchell and Thies identify the start of a rivalry when the issue is first raised diplomatically between states and the end as when an issue is officially settled between two states. This approach provides a much more precise way of dating the beginning and end of rivalry than others in existence.

In this chapter, I emphasize the issue-based approach to regional and global politics since it challenges the traditional realist notion that states are guided only by the pursuit of power.[14] In this approach, states compete over specific issues, including matters like border disputes, regime survival, and economic interests. Issues comprise both tangible and intangible dimensions, such as security and wealth for the former, and identity and status for the latter. Issues that are highly salient along both the tangible and intangible dimension, such as border and territorial disputes, are more likely to result in MIDs, rivalries, or wars in the attempt to settle the issue at stake.

Table 2.3 compares "issue" and "militarized" rivalry approaches that focus on issues as the linkages across serial conflicts with the enduring rivalries and the strategic rivalries.[15] Territorial issues are central to most of the rivalries identified by each approach, especially those that occur between neighbors or in the region. Thompson actually refers to these as spatial rivalries, as opposed to positional rivalries that occur between great powers jockeying for status and power. Regardless of the precise operational or conceptual definition of interstate rivalry, it is clear from table 2.3 that Latin America has always been rife with interaction in the form of rivalries over borders and territory.

I have argued elsewhere that territory has been incorporated into the nation-building projects of a number of Latin American states.[16] A large body of literature has in fact documented the manner in which territorial conflicts gave rise to a form of territorial nationalism in the Argentina-Chile case.[17] The desire for tangible resources and wealth from neighboring territory, as well as the nationalism associated with the identity and status intangibles both should help to drive the development of a stronger, more capable state apparatus.

The Argentina-Chile case was an ideal choice for theory development surrounding the relationship among territorial conflicts, the tangible and intangible dimensions of these contentious issues, and interstate rivalry. Table 2.4 demonstrates that Argentina and Chile completed one rivalry cycle during the period 1873–1909 (with ten MIDs) and entered a second period of rivalry in 1952 that ended in 1984 (with seventeen MIDs). Many of these conflictual episodes were serial in nature. The conflicts centered on two main sources of territorial contention—the demarcation of the border in the Andes Mountains and competing claims for territory in Patagonia. Despite the gap between the two periods of rivalry, since the issues under contention were the same they are considered a single rivalry rooted in territorial issues. Mitchell and Thies date the rivalry from 1841–1998 based on the first issue of a territorial claim and the resolution of the last outstanding claim. Thompson identifies a similar time period (1843–1991) for the Argentine-Chilean spatial rivalry. Kristina Mani's chapter in this volume analyzes the bilateral rapprochement in the 1990s.

While this is described in more detail in my article mentioned earlier ("Territorial Nationalism in Spatial Rivalries") one can find evidence of (1) belligerent press accounts arguing for border resolutions in favor of the journalists' native country, (2) school children being taught to view their country through the lens of huge losses, (3) public opinion often becoming more belligerent than the leadership of both countries, and (4) military training and planning that emphasized

Table 2.3   Interstate rivalries in Latin America

Rivalries	Issue	Militarized
United States–Haiti	1859–present	
United States–Mexico	1831–2001	1831–1848 / 1835–1848
United States–Honduras	1899–1972	
United States–Nicaragua	1900–1928, 1965–present	
United States–Panama	1924–1995	
United States–Colombia	1890–1972	
United States–Ecuador		1952–present
United States–Peru		1947–present
Haiti–Dominican Republic	1894–1935	
Trinidad & Tobago–Venezuela		1962–present
Belize-Guatemala	1981–present	1981–present
Belize-Honduras	1981–present	
Guatemala-Honduras		1899–1933
Guatemala–United Kingdom	1868–1981	1868–1981
Honduras–El Salvador	1899–present	1899–1992
Honduras-Nicaragua	1900–present	1912–1961 / 1912–present/
		1999–present
Honduras-Colombia	1982–1986	
Honduras–United Kingdom	1981–1981	
Nicaragua-Colombia	1900–1930 / 1979–present	1979–present
Colombia-Venezuela	1951–present	1951–present / 1955–present
Colombia-Peru	1839–1935	1839–1922 / 1932–1935
Venezuela-Guyana	1966–present	1966–present
Venezuela–United Kingdom	1841–1966	1841–1899
Venezuela-Netherlands	1850–1866	1854–1866
Guyana-Suriname	1975–present	1975–present
Guyana-Netherlands	1966–1975	
Ecuador-Peru	1854–1998	1854–1945 / 1947–1998
Ecuador-Brazil	1854–1922	
Peru-Bolivia	1848–1936	1848–1912
Peru-Chile	1879–1929	1879–1884 / 1884–1929
Peru-Spain		1864–1866
Brazil-Paraguay	1846–1929	1846–1874
Brazil-Argentina	1972–1998	
Brazil–United Kingdom	1826–1926	1838–1926
Brazil-France		1826–1900
Bolivia-Paraguay		1878–1938
Bolivia-Chile	1848–present	1848–1884 / 1884–present
Paraguay-Argentina	1941–1983	
Chile-Argentina	1841–1998	1841–1903 / 1904–1985 /
		1900–1985
Chile–United Kingdom		1940–present

(continued)

Table 2.3   (continued)

Rivalries	Issue	Militarized
Argentina-Uruguay	1882–1973	1882–1973 / 1900–1973
Argentina–United Kingdom	1841–present	1841–present / 1940–present / 1966–present
Argentina-Russia		1967–1986

Notes: This table is adapted from Sara Mitchell and Cameron G. Thies, "Issue Rivalries," *Conflict Management and Peace Science* 28, no. 3 (2011): 230–260. Rivalries in bold are those that experience one or more militarized disputes over the contested issues. An issue rivalry exists if the dyad experienced two or more territorial, maritime, or river claims simultaneously. The rivalry starts when the first issue claim begins, and ends when the last issue claim is resolved. A militarized rivalry exists if the dyad experienced two or more MIDs over a specific issue. The rivalry begins when the issue claim begins, and ends when the issue claim is resolved.

geopolitical thinking to back up the eventual reclamation of disputed territory. Leaders found themselves on the brink of war on multiple occasions. The contentious issues surrounding territory therefore formed the glue that held together a series of twenty-seven territorial conflicts, such that an interstate rivalry formed. The interstate rivalry therefore became an institutional feature of the two countries' relations, in which unresolved territorial conflicts shaped both the development of state apparatus and foreign policy decision-making. Even periods of joint democratic governance did not constrain the militarization of territorial conflicts, as proponents of the democratic peace would have us believe, and public opinion often pushed for war when governments urged restraint.[18] Only periods of global war, and Argentina's ill-fated attempt to retake the Malvinas from Britain coupled with the end of its military dictatorship seem to have restrained a territorially rooted impulse for each country to engage in conflict with their chief rivals.

If the contentious issue of territory became institutionalized in the form of interstate rivalries in Argentina and Chile, and those rivalries helped to drive the development of the state, where else might this argument apply? The next steps for this research program are to identify other likely candidates where territorial conflict is a common, ongoing feature of interstate relationships in the region. The relationship between Ecuador and Peru seems a likely candidate based on previous analyses.[19] Monica Herz and João Pontes Noguiera note the same kind of problem in Ecuador and Peru that has been faced by Argentina and Chile with *uti possidetis juris* (the principle that post-independence boundaries should match those of the colonial period); that is, as long as undemarcated borders were inter-

Table 2.4   Militarized interstate disputes (MIDs) between Argentina and Chile

Year	Rivalry period I	Year	Rivalry period II
1873	Patagonia	1952	Alto Palena incursions
1876	Jeanne-Amalia Affair	1955	Alto Palena II
1877	Río Negro	1958	Alto Palena III
1878	Seizure of the *Devonshire*	1958	Isle of Snipe
1879	Occupation of Patagonia	1959	Isla Nueva
1891	Río Gallegos	1960	Alto Palena IV
1897–1898	Puna de Atacama	1963	Alto Palena V
1900–1902	Ultima Esperanza	1964	Alto Palena VI
1905	Navarino Island Beacon	1965	Laguno del Desierto
1909	Navarino Island Beacon II	1967–1968	Ushuaia
		1977–1978	Beagle Channel I
		1978–1979	Beagle Channel II
		1980–1981	Interocean II
		1981	Los Andes Incident
		1981–1982	Beagle Channel III
		1983	Islet of Hermanos
		1984	Shelling of Beagle Channel

Source: Adapted from Cameron G. Thies, "Territorial Nationalism in Spatial Rivalries: An Institutionalist Account of the Argentine-Chilean Rivalry," *International Interactions* 27, no. 4 (2001): 399–431, 408) and Correlates of War MID Dataset.

preted quite differently in each country and among neighbors, it led to "considerable resentment among those who suffered disproportionate losses, such as Peru and Ecuador."[20] They also indicate that "cartographic discourse" associated with the teaching of history in schools in Ecuador was part of the construction of "Ecuadorianness."[21] Thus, at first glance, the same building blocks for territorial nationalism appear to have been in place in the Ecuador-Peru rivalry. This suggests that many of the aforementioned rivalries presented in table 2.3 are also likely rooted in contentious territorial conflicts with salient tangible and intangible dimensions.

The Impact of Border and Territorial Conflict on State Building

If the aforementioned work as well as a long stream of research on territory is correct in identifying territorial threats as especially salient to rulers and their citizen subjects, then rivalries produced by these contentious threats should provide rulers with an effective tool to extract revenue from their citizens to build the modern state.[22] In previous work on both Central America and South America, I have demonstrated this effect in statistical analyses.[23] The general argument draws on a long-established literature on bellicose or predatory theory developed out of the experience of early modern European states.[24] While some may draw directly on this literature to suggest that the absence of war in the contemporary world is the primary reason for the emergence of relatively weak states, my argument is that the changed global circumstances have led states to pursue other means of running a kind of protection racket. War, especially major power war, is becoming increasingly rare in the post-World War II era—perhaps even unthinkable.[25] The norm of "territorial integrity" or norm "against conquest" has been enshrined by states in many of their treaties and international organizations.[26] Latin America was the earliest region to make claims based on *uti possidetis*. This practice then went on to become an enduring feature of African interstate relations through the Organization of African Unity (OAU). While Latin America has had its share of wars, their prevalence has declined dramatically since 1945. Yet, as we know, militarized territorial conflict persists and may have been woven into the fabric of national identity and ritualized/institutionalized in the form of interstate rivalries. Those rivalries may be a means through which the state can augment its extractive capacity in a manner akin to the role warfare played in earlier periods of interstate history.

My statistical analyses of the region indicate that interstate war and civil war both diminished the extractive capacity of Latin American states in the twentieth century.[27] Table 2.5 illustrates the effects of different forms of conflict on state capacity measured in fiscal terms.[28] The measure of state capacity included as the dependent variable is the tax ratio (taxes as a share of gross domestic product). This is a standard way of measuring state capacity from a fiscal capacity perspective.[29] The argument for such a measure is that without tax revenue, no other large-scale government activity is possible. Thus, growth in the tax ratio should produce a stronger state apparatus.

The interstate war and strategic rivalry variables are not included in the same model, because strategic rivalries also include many of the interstate wars. Model 1 on the left-hand side of table 2.5 looks at the effect of interstate and civil war on state capacity. Wars reduce taxation as a percentage of GDP, as indicated by the coefficient in table 2.5, by nearly 4.5 percent during the years they are experienced and throughout the subsequent decade. Civil wars reduce taxation by nearly 3 percent. This finding is consistent with larger, cross-national statistical studies.[30] Model 2, with results on the right-hand side of table 2.5, examines the

Table 2.5   The negative effect of war and the positive effect of strategic rivalry on the tax ratio in Latin America

Independent variable	Coefficient	PCSE	Coefficient	PCSE
Interstate war	−4.47***	1.39		
Strategic rivalry			1.92**	.40
Civil war	−2.64***	.50	−.00	1.01
Democracy	.23**	.09	.18	.10
External debt	−8.24***	2.16	−13.05***	2.39
GDP per capita	1.64***	.53	2.58***	.60
Inflation	.26***	.05	.26***	.05
Trade openness	8.66	7.77	10.84	8.28
Agriculture	−23.76***	3.19	−19.75***	3.49
Time-trend	.08***	.02	.11***	.02
Constant	.44	3.24	−9.14*	4.16
N	653		653	
Adj. R^2	.51		.52	
Wald X^2	614.70***		531.72***	

Source: Adapted from Cameron G. Thies, "Territorial Nationalism in Spatial Rivalries: An Institutionalist Account of the Argentine-Chilean Rivalry," *International Interactions* 27, no. 4 (2001): 399–431.

Note: All significance tests are two-tailed: *$p < .05$, **$p < .01$, ***$p < .001$. PCSE stands for panel-corrected standard error.

effect of strategic rivalries using Thompson's 2001 measure on state capacity.[31] Here we find that rivalry has a positive effect on state capacity. Depending on the measurement used for rivalry (recall the aforementioned different measures in the previous section), the effect is between 1 and 2 percent increase during rivalry years. Thus, interstate rivalries allow state rulers to increase their extractive capacity, but their effect is not nearly as strong as war had been in previous historical periods. While Miguel Centeno is correct in his conclusion that limited wars in Latin American produced limited state building, the mechanism for this limited state building (at least in the twentieth century) was rivalry, not interstate war.

The analyses for Central America, conducted in a very similar fashion, show the same results for that region.[32] We can also make several other observations about state building in the region from the aforementioned results in table 2.5. First, Centeno was correct in his assertion that states often turned to debt rather than taxation to finance their wars; thus, the state-building impact of external conflict was truncated. Second, states that were democratic were able to raise more revenue through taxation than their autocratic counterparts. Finally, the same sorts of structural factors that affected state building elsewhere in the developing world, such as gross domestic product per capita, share of the agricultural sector in the national economy, and inflation, operated similarly in Latin America (as identified in table 2.5). We should therefore not view Latin America as somehow an exception to the factors that generate state fiscal capacity. The positive effect of interstate rivalry on fiscal state capacity has been demonstrated in Africa and the Middle East.[33] What also emerges from these analyses is that for the purpose of revenue extraction—a contemporary version of Tilly's "protection racket"—rulers often manipulate interstate rivalries.[34] For example, Aaron Schneider argues that after independence from Spain and the breakup of the Central American Federation, El Salvador and Guatemala increased their taxation efforts to build military power as a result of their rivalry, which continued through the 1930s.[35] Kurtz documents the ability of the Chilean state to increase revenue extraction during its rivalry with Peru, especially as a result of the War of the Pacific; although this was not the case for Peru due to internal domestic turmoil.[36] Centeno points to the case of Paraguay, which in its early conflict-ridden history had to fund itself through expanded domestic extraction.[37] Yet, if the tangible and intangible dimensions of territorial conflict link a series of conflicts to an interstate rivalry that could then be used to increase state capacity to a limited extent, how has this long-term process affected regional peace and security?

State Building and Regional Peace and Security

What are the regional consequences of territorial conflict that generate interstate rivalry? Rivalry institutionalizes unresolved territorial conflict, which then can be used instrumentally by rulers to produce modest increases in their extractive capacity. A region full of rivalries, as is the case for Latin America, is one in which states that are neither feeble nor exceptionally strong engage in routinized conflict over territory. At best this has produced a kind of cold peace or zone of negative peace. Arie Kacowicz's comparative work on zones of negative peace in West Africa and Latin America identifies one crucial factor in the maintenance of negative peace and movement toward stable or positive peace: the resolution of territorial conflicts.[38]

In my own quantification of Kacowicz's general propositions about the sources of a zone of negative peace, I linked the zones of peace argument with Alexander Wendt's concept of cultures of anarchy.[39] According to Wendt, international society can be comprised of several basic cultures of anarchy, based on the type of role that predominates among a group of states. If states primarily occupy the

Table 2.6   Factors affecting the zone of negative peace in Latin America

Variables	Coefficient	Standard error
Rival role relationship	.25***	.04
US hegemonic role	.83***	.03
US capabilities	−.39***	.01
US intervention	.16***	.02
US cumulative intervention	−.16***	.01
US economic dependence	−.01	.02
Regional balance of power	−1.32***	.03
System shock	−.60***	.02
Domestic shock	.07***	.01
Distance	.02**	.01
Regional polity average	−.09***	.01
Regional economic development	.01***	.00
Regional trade agreement	.17***	.02
Joint satisfaction	−5.86***	.52
Negotiated territorial issues	−.18***	.04
N	5,791	
R^2	.64	

Source: Adapted from Cameron G. Thies, "The Construction of a Latin American Interstate Culture of Rivalry," *International Interactions* 34, no. 3 (2008): 231–257, 245.
Note: All significance tests are two tailed; *$p<.05$, **$p<.01$, ***$p<.001$.

enemy role, then a Hobbesian culture of anarchy akin to a zone of conflict prevails—a war of all against all. A zone of negative peace is much like a Lockean culture of anarchy, in which there is competition (often over territory), but the aim of states is not the elimination of others as in the Hobbesian culture. Instead, the foundational role of a Lockean culture of anarchy is that of the rival. A society of states who are largely friends would create a Kantian culture of anarchy akin to a zone of stable peace.

Given the similarity between the zone of negative peace and the Lockean culture of anarchy, I used the number of interstate rivalries present in any given year as an indicator of Latin American regional culture in a previously published article.[40] This allowed me to operationalize the zone of negative peace argument for statistical analysis. The result of this half of a simultaneous regression analysis (the other half being the factors that produce rivalry) is presented in table 2.6. Positive signs on the coefficients represent variables that support the negative peace, and negative signs represents movement away from the negative peace though we cannot tell whether this is in the direction of a zone of stable peace or a zone of conflict. Most of the factors identified by Kacowicz as affecting the negative peace have the expected effects in the statistical analysis of Latin America presented in table 2.6, lending additional credence to his qualitative case studies. I will interpret here the findings from table 2.6 below by walking through the variables and the direction of effects they have on the Lockean culture of anarchy (or zone of negative peace).

Obviously, since the rival role is the constitutive element of the Lockean culture of anarchy, one finds that the formation of a rival role relationships helps to bring about the zone of negative peace. Let me highlight a few more findings about regional peace and security from this analysis shown in table 2.6. The US hegemonic role in Latin America also has a positive effect on the negative peace, which is expected by Ronald Ebel, Raymond Taras, and James Cochrane, and Arie Kacowicz, who argue that a strong, but benevolent hegemon protects states from the uncertainties of international life.[41] Yet, higher ratios of United States to Latin American capabilities threaten to undermine the regional culture, perhaps reflecting "overlay" by a great power that dominates regional interaction.[42] There is obviously some tension between the ideational component of regional hegemony reflected in the perception of the US hegemonic role and the material component reflected in US military capabilities vis-à-vis the region. United States interventions in the affairs of Latin American countries support a negative peace, but the overall cumulative effect of such interventions moves the region away from negative peace and possibly toward a zone of conflict. Economic dependence on the United States is not significantly related to the zone of negative peace, in contrast to the arguments of Ebel, Taras, and Cochrane who suggest that the United States, in its role as patron, has provided markets and capital to the region. Overall, these findings about the political-military and economic exercise of US hegemony seem to challenge David Mares's claim that US hegemonic activity is inconsequential to the region.[43]

Arie Kacowicz argues that a community of liberal democracies is required to sustain the negative peace, but he also recognizes that historically, Latin America has been a community of autocracies existing in a zone of negative peace.[44] Movement away from the community of autocracies, or toward the formation of a mixed community of autocracies and new democracies, appears to have worked against the zone of negative peace. Higher levels of economic development and regional trade agreements have a positive, significant effect on the negative peace. Joint satisfaction with the status quo, reflecting an underlying normative consensus in the region, is negatively related to the negative peace, though we cannot infer if this means a move toward more positive peace or toward conflict. Negotiated territorial issues significantly undermine the negative peace in Latin America. Kacowicz expects neither of these findings, though if the move is toward more stable peace, then it is a positive thing for the region.

In general then, if Latin America is properly characterized as a zone of negative peace (or Lockean culture of anarchy in Wendt's terms), then the plethora of overlapping interstate rivalries support such a regional culture. The interstate rivalries formed out of a series of territorial conflicts allow for the development of states with limited capacity. The conduct of their interstate relationships thus produces a regional culture characterized by negative peace. Such states are unlikely to engage in full-scale conflict or war with each other, and as a result, struggle to maintain internal sovereignty at times. Thus, according to this stylized story, a chain leading from territorial conflicts to interstate rivalries, to state capacity, and ultimately to a regional negative peace is the long-run product of the interstate system in Latin America. It is the current negative peace that is evolving in the democratic period. As subsequent chapters illustrate, regional integration, international adjudication, and security cooperation represent the new frontier of border relations.

Concluding Thoughts

The basic building blocks for understanding the role of borders and territory on state building, regional peace, and security are in place. My argument is that territorial conflicts (at least in some key locations) are a highly salient, contentious issue. The tangible and intangible dimensions of territorial issues link separate territorial conflicts to interstate rivalries that condition future conflicts and foreign policy decision making. Once created, rivalries can be used instrumentally to increase the fiscal capacity crucial to state building. Rivalries, as institutionalized repositories for unresolved territorial conflict, also helped create the fabric of Latin American interstate culture, best characterized as a zone of negative peace or Lockean culture of anarchy. The result for most Latin American states for most of the twentieth century is limited state building in a region characterized by a cold peace. This situation quite likely will endure, since most states do not have the capacity to challenge the regional status quo, nor are they able to resolve territorial conflicts that are woven into their nation-states. Most of the active conflict experienced by states tends to be internal now, yet their historically limited state building has left them ill equipped to handle internal challenges.

Future work should flesh out the theoretical connections between territorial conflict, interstate rivalry, state building, and regional peace and security. I believe the outlines of this argument are in place, but more theoretical work remains. Additionally, the empirical scope of this argument needs to be more properly identified. Which countries does this argument apply to, and what time period does it best explain? This could be interrogated more carefully in the Latin American system, since it is comprised of several fairly distinct subsystems. We might also attempt to transport this argument to other parts of the world. As previously noted, many of the processes associated with contemporary state building are not unique to Latin America. Filling in missing empirical gaps in Latin America and around the world could further enhance theoretical development.

NOTES

1. I would like to thank Maiah Jaskoski, Arie Kacowicz, David Mares, Arturo Sotomayor, and Harold Trinkunas for their helpful comments on previous versions of this chapter.

2. Cameron G. Thies, "State Building, Interstate and Intrastate Rivalry: A Study of Post-Colonial Developing Country Extractive Efforts, 1975–2000," *International Studies Quarterly* 48, no. 1 (2004): 53–72; Thies, "War, Rivalry, and State Building in Latin America," *American Journal of Political Science* 49, no. 3 (2005): 451–65; Thies, "The Political Economy of State Building in Sub-Saharan Africa," *Journal of Politics* 69, no. 3 (2007): 716–31; Thies, "Public Violence and State Building in Central America," *Comparative Political Studies* 39, no. 10 (2006): 1263–82; Thies, "National Design and State Building in Sub-Saharan Africa," *World Politics* 61, no. 4 (2009): 623–69; and Lingyu Lu and Cameron G. Thies, "War, Rivalry and State Building in the Middle East," *Political Research Quarterly* 66, no. 2 (2013): 239–53.

3. See Charles Tilly, *The Formation of National States in Western Europe* (Princeton, NJ: Princeton University Press, 1975) suggested that states, like a Mafioso, run a protection racket because they essentially charge individuals and groups for protection that they need in part because of the very existence of competition between states (or between rival mafia in the case of a Mafioso).

4. Negative peace is defined by Kacowicz as "the absence of systematic, large-scale collective violence between political communities." Negative peace is largely synonymous with what Benjamin Miller labels his "ideal type" of cold peace. See Arie Kacowicz, *Zones of Peace in the Third World: South America and West Africa in Comparative Perspective* (Albany, NY: SUNY Press, 1998), 7; and Benjamin Miller, "When and How Regions Become Peaceful: Potential Theoretical Pathways to Peace," *International Studies Review* 7, no. 2 (2005): 231–32.

5. Daniel M. Jones, Stuart A. Brember, and J. David Singer, "Militarized Interstate Disputes, 1816–1992: Rationale, Coding Rules, and Empirical Patterns," *Conflict Management and Peace Science* 15, no. 2 (Fall 1996): 163.

6. Paul R. Hensel, "One Thing Leads to Another: Recurrent Militarized Disputes in Latin America, 1816–1986," *Journal of Peace Research* 31, no. 3 (1994): 281–97.

7. Meredith Reid Sarkees, "Extra-state Wars (Version 4.0): Definitions and Variables," The Correlates of War Project, Pennsylvania State University, State College, Pennsylvania, http://correlatesofwar.org/data-sets/COW-war/extra-state-wars-codebook; and Meredith Reid Sarkees and Frank Wayman, Resort to War: 1816–2007 (Washington, DC: CQ Press, 2010).

8. Miguel Angel Centeno disagrees with some of the COW Project interstate war coding (see *Blood and Debt: War and the Nation-State in Latin America* [University Park, PA: Pennsylvania State University Press, 2002], 44–46). He includes Brazil's participation in World War I, the Leticia War (1932–33) between Colombia and Peru, and the border disputes between Ecuador and Peru in 1941 and 1981, but does not include Colombia's participation in the Korean War (1951–53). See Thies for a comparison of the Centeno and COW coding ("War, Rivalry," 456, table 1). Note that the COW Project upgraded the 1995 Cenepa Valley dispute between Ecuador and Peru to a war after the publication of Centeno's book and Thies's article.

9. Paul F. Diehl and Gary Goertz, *War and Peace in International Rivalry* (Ann Arbor, MI: University of Michigan Press, 2000), 23–24.

10. James P. Klein, Gary Goertz, and Paul F. Diehl, "The New Rivalry Dataset: Procedures and Patterns," *Journal of Peace Research* 43, no. 3 (2006): 331–48.

11. Ibid., 337.

12. William R. Thompson, "Identifying Rivals and Rivalries in World Politics," *International Studies Quarterly* 45, no.4 (2001): 56.

13. Sara Mitchell and Cameron G. Thies, "Issue Rivalries," *Conflict Management and Peace Science* 28, no. 3 (2011): 230–60.

14. For examples, see Richard W. Mansbach and John A. Vasquez, *In Search of Theory: A New Paradigm for Global Politics* (Ithaca, NY: Cornell University Press, 1981); John A. Vasquez, *The War Puzzle* (Cambridge, UK: Cambridge University Press, 1993); and Paul R. Hensel, "Contentious Issues and World Politics: The Management of Territorial Claims in the Americas, 1816–1992," *International Studies Quarterly* 45, no.1 (2001): 81–109.

15. Vasquez, *War Puzzle*, 247–50.

16. Cameron G. Thies, "Territorial Nationalism in Spatial Rivalries: An Institutionalist Account of the Argentine-Chilean Rivalry," *International Interactions* 27, no. 4 (2001): 399–431.

17. Carlos Escude, *La Argentina: Paria Internacional?* (Buenos Aires, Argentina: Editorial de Belgrano, 1984); Escude, *La Argentina vs. las Grandes Potencias* (Buenos Aires, Argentina: Editorial de Belgrano, 1986); Escude, "Argentine Territorial Nationalism," *Journal of Latin American Studies* 20, no. 1 (1988): 139–65; Manuel Ugarte, *The Destiny of a Continent* (New York, NY: Alfred A. Knopf, 1925); and Susan Calvert and Peter Calvert, *Argentina: Political Culture and Instability* (Pittsburgh, PA: Pittsburgh University Press, 1989).

18. Bruce Russett and John Oneal, *Triangulating Peace: Democracy, Interdependence and International Organizations* (New York, NY: W. W. Norton, 2001).

19. Beth Simmons, "Territorial Disputes and Their Resolution: The Case of Ecuador and Peru," Peaceworks 27 (Washington, DC: United States Institute of Peace, 1999); and

Monica Herz and João Pontes Noguiera, *Ecuador vs. Peru: Peacemaking amid Rivalry* (Boulder, CO: Lynne Rienner, 2002).

20. Herz and Pontes Noguiera, *Ecuador vs. Peru*, 27.

21. Ibid., 24–25.

22. For example, see Paul K. Huth, *Standing Your Ground: Territorial Disputes and International Conflict* (Ann Arbor, MI: University of Michigan Press, 1996); Douglas M. Gibler, *The Territorial Peace: Borders, State Development, and International Conflict* (New York, NY: Cambridge University Press, 2012); Douglas M. Gibler, Marc L. Hutchison, and Stephen V. Miller, "Individual Identity Attachments and International Conflict: The Importance of Territorial Threat," *Comparative Political Studies* 45, no. 12 (2012): 1655–83; and John A. Vasquez, *War Puzzle* (Cambridge, UK: Cambridge University Press, 1993).

23. Cameron G. Thies, "Public Violence and State Building"; and Thies, "War, Rivalry."

24. Charles Tilly, *Coercion, Capital, and European States, AD 990–1992* (Cambridge, MA: Blackwell, 1992); Tilly, "War Making and State Making as Organized Crime," in *Bringing the State Back In*, ed. Peter Evans, Dietrich Rueschemeyer, and Theda Skocpol (Cambridge, UK: Cambridge University Press, 1985), 169–91; Douglass C. North, *Structure and Change in Economic History* (New York, NY: W.W. Norton, 1981); and Margaret Levi, "The Predatory Theory of Rule," *Politics and Society* 10, no. 4 (1981): 431–65.

25. John Mueller, *Retreat from Doomsday: The Obsolescence of Major War* (New York, NY: Basic Books, 1989).

26. Mark W. Zacher, "The Territorial Integrity Norm: International Boundaries and the Use of Force," *International Organization* 55, no. 2 (2001): 215–50; and Tanisha M. Fazal, *State Death: The Politics and Geography of Conquest, Occupation, and Annexation* (Princeton, NJ: Princeton University Press, 2007).

27. Unfortunately, a lack of comparable tax and other economic data prevents testing for the role of warfare in state building in the nineteenth century when war was more common and states were emerging from the colonial era.

28. Thies, "War, Rivalry." The data on interstate and civil wars comes from the aforementioned Correlates of War Project, and the strategic rivalry data is from William Thompson ("Identifying Rivals and Rivalries"). The control variables include covariates normally associated with variation in state capacity measured in fiscal terms. The sources and measurement of these data are described more fully in Thies's article.

29. Ideally, we would be able to separate direct (e.g., income) and indirect (e.g., customs) taxes, so that we could assess the willingness of individuals to directly relinquish their income to the state in exchange for protection. Unfortunately, the availability of more fine-grained tax data is sparse. That is why the tax ratio has become the standard in the literature—it is an aggregate measure that is widely available across countries and over time.

30. Cameron G. Thies and David Sobek, "War, Economic and Political Development in the Contemporary International System," *International Studies Quarterly* 54, no. 1 (2010): 267–87.

31. Thompson, "Identifying Rivals," 56.

32. Thies, "Public Violence and State Building."

33. Thies, "Political Economy of State Building"; and Lu and Thies, "War, Rivalry and State Building."

34. Tilly, "War Making and State Making."

35. Aaron Schneider, *State-Building and Tax Regimes in Central America* (New York, NY: Cambridge University Press, 2012).

36. Marcus J. Kurtz, *Latin American State Building in Comparative Perspective: Social Foundations of Institutional Order* (New York, NY: Cambridge University Press, 2013).

37. Centeno, *Blood and Debt*, 162.

38. Kacowicz, *Zones of Peace*; and Kacowicz, *The Impact of Norms in International Society: The Latin American Experience, 1881–2001* (Notre Dame, IN: University of Notre Dame Press, 2005).

39. Alexander Wendt, *Social Theory of International Politics* (New York, NY: Cambridge University Press, 1999).

40. Cameron G. Thies, "The Construction of a Latin American Interstate Culture of Rivalry," *International Interactions* 34, no. 3 (2008): 231–57. See this article for a full description of the sources of data and measurement of the variables, as well as a discussion of the statistical modeling technique.

41. Ronald H. Ebel, Raymond Taras, and James D. Cochrane, *Political Culture and Foreign Policy in Latin America* (Albany, NY: SUNY Press, 1991).

42. Barry Buzan and Ole Waever, *Regions and Powers: The Structure of International Security* (Cambridge, UK: Cambridge University Press, 2003).

43. David R. Mares, *Violent Peace: Militarized Interstate Bargaining in Latin America* (New York, NY: Columbia University Press, 2001).

44. See Kacowicz, *Zones of Peace*.

Chapter Three

Legalizing and Judicializing Territorial and Maritime Border Disputes in Latin America

Causes and Unintended Consequences

Arturo C. Sotomayor

L atin America has witnessed a large number of territorial and maritime disputes, some of which have been settled through institutional arbitration. According to Beth Simmons, Latin America has the highest degree of territorial arbitration when compared to other regions, with as many as twenty cases documented in the past two centuries.[1] After centuries of experimenting with different forms of third-party intervention, an increasing number of Latin American countries are turning to international tribunals, like the International Court of Justice (ICJ), to resolve border disputes. In fact, all pending Central American territorial and maritime disputes, with the exception of the ongoing Guatemala-Honduras border conflict, have been submitted to the ICJ in The Hague. There is thus an increasing trend to legalize and judicialize border disputes in the region. What factors explain this choice? Why is judicial settlement of border disputes preferred over other means of settlement? What are the effects of using judicial means to settle border disputes? I argue that judicialization is a function of civilians trying to increase their power vis-à-vis the military in new democracies.

Countries willing to settle border disputes politically can work (1) bilaterally toward a mutual solution; (2) trilaterally through third-party intervention; (3) regionally via the mediation of a regional organization; (4) multilaterally through the assistance of global organizations such as the United Nations (UN) or (5) judicially, using legal tools, such as judicial settlement or arbitration. The first four methods involve diplomatic means and can occur in formal or informal forums.

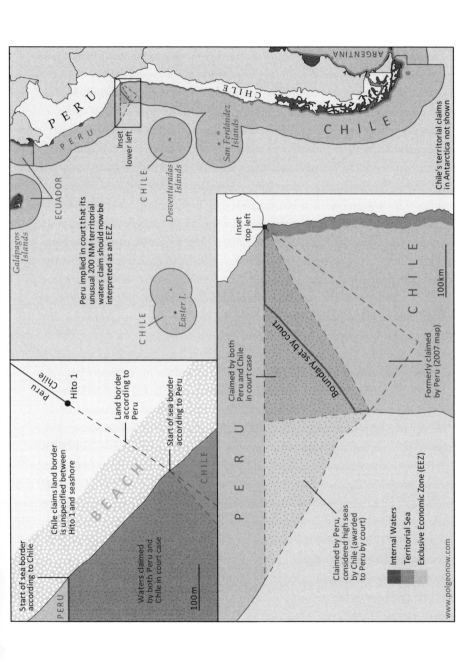

Map 3.1. Peru and Chile's sea dispute settled in court
Courtesy of Evan Centanni of Political Geography Now (www.polgeonow.com).

The last, however, requires states to agree to a binding decision, usually on the basis of international public law. It can involve the ICJ or some other standing international tribunal.[2] However, while the ICJ is one of the most authoritative and legitimate international tribunals to date, resorting to it entails high costs. The proceedings are expensive. Judges take years (if not decades) before issuing a ruling. It is also an inflexible forum, allowing states very little control over the cases and procedures involved. In The Hague, disputants can only choose one ad hoc judge; the rest are determined by rigid legal rules. Additionally, proceedings are made public, the UN Charter sets the powers of the tribunals, the arbitration itself takes place in the Netherlands, and public international law is the only applicable law. The outcomes are uncertain due to lack of judicial precedence to inform new cases, as in common-law systems.

This situation in Latin America is perplexing. In recent years, an increasing number of Latin American countries have taken their border disputes to the highest legal world body at The Hague. Why have Latin American states taken the judicial path to resolve pending territorial disputes? This chapter illustrates that the choice to legalize border disputes is influenced by domestic factors and collective perceptions about neutrality and impartiality. Dispute settlement through judicial means literally legalizes a border dispute by making it a matter of law rather than politics or military strategy. In so doing, legalization is an attempt to depoliticize and demilitarize a border dispute by transforming it into a legal conflict. Such a choice decreases the risks of arms spirals and security dilemmas among neighboring countries with conflictive border relations, leading to a deescalation of interstate conflict. Nevertheless, legalization creates domestic challenges of its own, because it diverts the attention of the armed forces away from their traditional sovereignty missions and inadvertently contributes to civilian attention deficits in defense matters. By removing the armed forces from their main role of protecting borders, civilians who have relied on judicial settlement of territorial disputes have assigned nontraditional missions and roles to soldiers, such as public security and law enforcement, ultimately undermining military readiness and border security.

In order to develop my argument, this study is divided into four sections. The first section analyzes the patterns of border dispute settlement in Latin America by focusing specifically on the posttransition to democracy (post-1980s) and post–Cold War (post-1992) eras. This allows me to control for important variables in the analysis by holding the collapse of the Soviet bloc and the wave of democratization that swept the region as two constants. The second section examines the domestic, normative, and cognitive rationales behind Latin America's increased interest in judicial settlement of border disputes. The third section analyzes the unintended consequences of such actions, including the demilitarization of border disputes and the civilian attention deficits it generates on defense policy. Finally, section four offers a brief empirical analysis of the Peru-Chile maritime case, for which the ICJ issued a ruling in 2014, after the dispute was brought within its jurisdiction.

Patterns of Border Dispute Settlement in Latin America Post-1990

As table 3.1 illustrates, Latin American countries have shopped among various international forums to resolve their disputes, ranging from diplomatic to quasi-judicial and judicial methods at the bilateral, trilateral, regional, and global levels. While the regional mechanisms available to resolve territorial and maritime conflicts have varied over time, certain general patterns can be identified.

To some extent, all Latin American states with border disputes have resorted to bilateral mechanisms, given their geographic proximity. Every unresolved territorial dispute that is not under the offices of a mediator or third party can be subject to bilateral negotiations. As of today, there are at least eleven cases pending resolution in Latin America that are not under any form of bilateral or third-party negotiation.[3]

Surprisingly, some prominent disputes have been settled bilaterally. As indicated in table 3.1, at least five sets of countries have relied on bilateral mechanisms to try and solve their territorial claims, including Chile-Argentina (discussed in this volume by Kristina Mani), Venezuela–Trinidad and Tobago, Bolivia-Chile, and Peru-Chile. Yet, only Chile-Argentina and Venezuela–Trinidad and Tobago have been able to fully settle their disputes.[4]

The failure to solve a dispute bilaterally is the reason why a third party is often called on to help. As Page Fortna observes, third parties help disrupt the causal pathways to war and make peace agreements more durable by increasing the costs of attack, reducing uncertainty about actions and intentions, and preventing and controlling accidental violations and skirmishes.[5] Within the Latin American region, countries have relied on ad hoc regional mediators, regional institutions, global organizations, and world tribunals to overcome their mutual suspicions of each other while attempting to solve territorial and maritime claims.

For example, the most successful regional mediation effort took place between 1995 and 1998, when Argentina, Brazil, Chile, and the United States effectively

Table 3.1 Country choice of forum settlement in Latin America, 1990–2013

Countries	Issue	Forum	Year	Resolution
Ecuador-Peru	Cenepa Valley	Regional	1995–1998	Resolved
Guatemala-Belize	Guatemala's claim of 1/3 of Belize's territory, including access to the Atlantic through the Caribbean	Regional	2000–2007	Unresolved
Chile-Argentina	23 boundary disputes	Bilateral	1988–1991	Resolved
Venezuela–Trinidad and Tobago	Jurisdiction over Gulf of Paria	Bilateral	1990	Resolved
Bolivia-Chile	Bolivia's access to the Pacific	Bilateral	1990–1999	Unresolved
Peru-Chile	Maritime dispute over Pacific frontier	Bilateral	1990–1999	Unresolved
Argentina-UK	Falklands/Malvinas	Bilateral	2001	Unresolved
Venezuela-Guyana	Venezuela's claim over parts of Guyana's territory	Multilateral: UN Secretary General	1984, 1991–2000	Unresolved
Honduras–El Salvador	El Salvador's refusal to comply with 1992 ICJ ruling on border dispute	Multilateral: UN Security Council	2003	Unresolved
Argentina-Uruguay	Pulp mill dispute in the Argentine-Uruguayan border	Judicial: ICJ	2006	Resolved
Argentina/UK	Falklands/Malvinas	Multilateral: UN Decolonization Committee	2004	Unresolved
Honduras–El Salvador	Border dispute	Judicial: ICJ	1992, 2002	Resolved
Nicaragua-Honduras	Border dispute	Judicial: ICJ	1999	Resolved
Nicaragua-Colombia	San Andrés Islands in the Caribbean	Judicial: ICJ	2001	Partially resolved, pending implementation of ICJ ruling
Costa Rica–Nicaragua	Navigational rights over the San Juan river	Judicial: ICJ	2005	Pending
Peru-Chile	Delimitation boundary in the Pacific Ocean	Judicial: ICJ	2008	Partially resolved, pending implementation of ICJ ruling
Bolivia-Chile	Chile's obligation to negotiate access to the Pacific Ocean with Bolivia	Judicial: ICJ	2013	Pending

helped Ecuador and Peru settle their dispute over the Cenepa Valley; the two countries had already fought two wars over the valley. The process yielded a binding bilateral boundary agreement subject to international public law, and followed by a peacekeeping mission.[6] However, this successful case of ad hoc mediation is also unique, essentially because it relied on a regional forum that was outside the inter-American system and which, in fact, bypassed the Organization of American States (OAS) altogether. No other such ad hoc mediation forum has been put in practice since then.

Belize and Guatemala have attempted to solve their dispute through a regional mechanism as well, but more formally through the OAS Fund for Peace. On November 8, 2000, the heads of the delegations of both countries signed an agreement to enter a comprehensive set of negotiations, mediated by the OAS, to resolve their territorial *differendum*. The dispute originated two centuries ago when Britain and Spain argued over their colonial territories in Central America. This disagreement survived Guatemala's independence from Spain in 1839 and Belize's from the United Kingdom in 1981. Basically, Guatemala wants to gain greater access to the Atlantic Ocean through the Caribbean by claiming almost two-thirds of Belize's territory. At the core of the dispute lies what Guatemala sees as the inability of the UN General Assembly to reach a satisfactory solution to the country's unresolved territorial claims against Britain, as laid out in November of 1980. Like previous bilateral and UN efforts, the OAS's attempt at mediation failed in 2007 when Guatemala rejected the proposals on the table. The two countries' legal teams are now preparing to initiate proceedings at the ICJ, pending a referendum on the matter in Guatemala.[7] This territorial dispute remains the only case ever brought before the OAS forum for resolution by a Latin American state.[8]

Countries in the region have also relied on third-party mediation by global organizations. For example, the UN has been called upon several times to mediate between Venezuela and Guyana, Honduras and El Salvador, and Argentina and the United Kingdom.[9] Yet, talks in the UN forum have not led to substantive settlements.

This leads us to our final form of conflict resolution; namely, adjudication by an international tribunal as opposed to an arbiter, guarantor, or mediator. Interestingly enough, the number of cases turned over to this type of court has increased. On September 20, 2007, the Guyana-Suriname Arbitral Tribunal, established under the UN Convention on the Law of the Sea, released its findings on the long-standing maritime controversy between these two countries.[10] This has

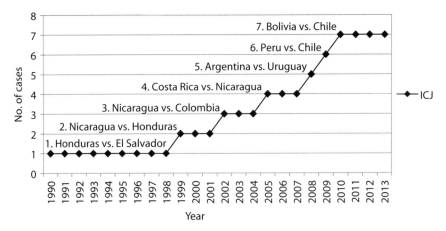

Figure 3.1. S-shaped curve of Latin American territorial disputes brought to the International Court of Justice (ICJ).

so far been the only maritime dispute brought forth by a country in the Western Hemisphere under the Law of the Sea Convention.

More readily used has been the ICJ in The Hague. Historically, the court was never the preferred forum for dispute settlement among Latin American countries. From 1948 to 1990, The Hague delivered only a single ruling dealing with a Latin American territorial and frontier dispute: El Salvador vs. Honduras (with Nicaragua's involvement). In 1986 the court held a ruling in favor of Honduras, thus obligating El Salvador and Nicaragua to concede.[11]

More than three decades would pass before the ICJ would deliver another ruling involving a Latin American territory. The trend of turning to courts and judicial arbitration, as opposed to political and diplomatic mediation, began late in the Cold War. As depicted in figure 3.1, the number of times the ICJ has been embraced as the preferred forum resembles a wave, containing both an S-shaped curve and a bell-shaped pattern that resemble typical diffusion-based behavior. In fact, since the 1990s all Central American territorial and maritime disputes, with the exception of the Guatemala-Belize conflict, have been forwarded to The Hague. The ICJ wave began in 1986 with a joint Honduras–El Salvador commission, which requested the court's intervention to delimit parts of the land frontier and to determine the legal situation in the islands and maritime area surrounding the Golf of Fonseca. On September 12, 1992, seven years after the first request was made, the presidents of both countries met at the border to receive the final decision on a long-term dispute that had included the infamous 1969 Soccer War between these two neighbors. The decision favored Honduras more than El Salvador, with the former being granted the right to two-thirds of the disputed territory. Although officially accepted by both states, this judgment has failed to lower border tensions and has even prompted Honduras to approach the UN Security Council to solve the issue, while El Salvador requested the ICJ for a revision of the judgment in 1992 and again in 2002. In 2003, the court vindicated its previous rulings and awarded most of the disputed territory to Honduras, forcing both countries to sign a border demarcation treaty to implement the terms of The Hague's judicial decree.[12]

Since then other Latin American countries have continued to invoke the power of the court. Nicaragua turned to the ICJ twice, in 1999 and again in 2001, to resolve its border disputes against Honduras[13] and Colombia, respectively; and Costa Rica brought a case against Nicaragua in 2005 to delineate navigational and related rights on the San Juan River. Interestingly enough, the "IJC wave" spread first in Central America, among small and neighboring states with symmetrical military capabilities. These states also share a common history, having experienced similar patterns of colonization, independence, civil wars, and conflict resolution processes. The wave eventually reached South America in 2006, when Argentina began proceedings in The Hague against Uruguay for allegedly violating international public law by allowing the construction of pulp mills across the border. Similarly, in 2008 Peru instituted proceedings against Chile to delimit its boundary on the Pacific Ocean. Finally, in 2013 Bolivia also began legal proceedings against Chile to reclaim its sea outlet.[14]

Legalizing Disputes in Latin America: Arguments and Sources of Explanation

Why is judicial settlement of border disputes now the preferred means of settlement? Why are other alternatives discarded? In the following sections I discuss four possible explanations: (1) domestic legal traditions, (2) legalistic norms and biases, (3) perceptions of impartiality and neutrality, and (4) civil-military relations and domestic politics.

Domestic Legal Approaches

Domestic legal scholarship offers a theoretical explanation for the selection of a forum. Both legal scholars and political scientists are often inclined to explain forum preference by focusing on the characteristics of a country's domestic legal structure. That is, states are usually more willing to trust international organizations that reflect their own domestic institutions than those that do not. According to Andrew Moravcsik, a domestic legal system that embodies societal preferences, interests, and ideas, can influence a state's behavior toward other states and international institutions.[15] For example, states with civil law systems are more likely to accept the compulsory jurisdiction of international courts than states with other types of legal systems, such as common or Islamic law. This is because international public law most closely resembles civil law in its use of bona fides and because of its disregard for the use of precedents. By virtue of sitting in The Hague, the ICJ is exposed to a predominantly civil law tradition of continental Europe. The institutional similarity between international public law and civil legal systems encourages civil law countries to approach international courts for arbitration. As noted by Emilia Powell and Sara Mitchell, "civil law states accept similar legal principles domestically, which makes it easier for them to correlate their behaviors, and the adjudicator and civil law disputants will converge naturally on the same outcomes."[16]

This approach, however, only partially explains why the ICJ has recently become the preferred venue for settling territorial disputes in Latin America. Most countries are ruled by civil law traditions, yet Latin America has the highest propensity to submit to legal rulings vis-à-vis other regions, including continental Europe where civil law was founded. According to a study by Beth Simmons, there have "never been a legally constituted third-party ruling on a land border in Europe, there have been two between independent countries in Africa, two in the Middle East, three in Asia, the Far East and the Pacific, and twenty in Latin America!"[17] In fact, in 2008 fully one half of the ICJ's docket was made up of Latin American cases, including four centered on territorial and maritime border disputes.[18]

Moreover, if the legal tradition determines the forum, then we should have seen more cases adjudicated by the ICJ historically, since most Latin American countries have been ruled by civil law for centuries, long before the IJC came into being. Yet, interest in The Hague is a relatively recent trend in Latin America. Furthermore, The Hague is not the only international tribunal mandated by international public law. Other regional and global courts use similar procedures, yet they are not invoked as often as the ICJ by countries with civil law traditions. In addition, the fact that countries as diverse as Guyana, Surinam, and perhaps even Belize, are pursuing settlements via an international tribunal, despite their common law traditions, casts some doubt on how domestic law influences the choice of a forum. At best, the domestic legal tradition is a necessary but insufficient condition to explain why states prefer international tribunals to other ways of settling border disputes.

INTERNATIONAL LEGITIMACY AND IMPARTIALITY

Constructivist explanations offer an alternative approach that focuses on the role of international legitimacy. Seen from this perspective, plaintiffs are not only concerned about maximizing material gain; they share a number of concerns about the moral power and authority of the institution that they are invoking.[19] As Ian Hurd points out, international legitimacy is a subjective quality and is determined by an actor's perception of the institution.[20] International legitimacy emerges from an organization's complex of symbols, authority, and history. From this perspective, a specific forum will be preferred when its actions, statements, and resolutions have been recognized as representing the collective sentiment of the international community. For Hurd, in addition to this general affirmation, a decision often acquires enhanced legitimacy when the forum's utterances carry more force than had individual members made them.[21]

A constructivist approach can account for the apparent Latin American bias toward the ICJ. The Hague is not only the highest international court available, but its relatively neutral composition, as well as its reputation for delivering impartial rulings, provide strong incentives to christen it as a preferred option. Indeed, a forum with high international legitimacy raises the costs of noncompliance by affecting the reputation of those who decide to ignore its ruling and authority.

In fact, the perception of impartiality and neutrality plays a key role in explaining why Latin American countries seem to prefer legally binding and judicial global forums. First, countries in the region have reasons to be concerned about the impartiality and neutrality of regional forums. There certainly is the fear that most regional institutions tend to reflect the interests and preferences of regionally powerful actors.[22] As David Mares observes, the United States is the country that has traditionally dominated the geopolitics of the Western Hemisphere.[23] Even when the United States is not the major source of influence, other regional powers and organizations can still affect outcomes. Bolivia initially supported bringing the OAS into its dispute with Chile, but then had a sudden change of heart when José Miguel Insulza—a native of Chile—became the OAS secretary general in 2005. Likewise, diplomatic discussions about revitalizing the Central American Court of Justice were opposed by most of Nicaragua's neighbors, especially Honduras, in part because this regional tribunal is headquartered in Managua.

Second, alternative forums of settlement, such as regional organizations, may actually make accommodation more difficult by providing incentives for cheap talk. Going regional imposes a policy dilemma because there will always be the temptation to go to a higher, more authoritative and legitimate court (such as the ICJ). Countries in the Americas know that regional forums are not the last resort. If things go wrong regionally, they can still appeal to global courts without undermining their reputation by ignoring regional rulings. Ultimately, if an agreement negotiated under regional auspices seems unfavorable or unlikely to win ratification, then the states involved can simply reject it and turn to a global tribunal for a "second opinion." This enables rival states to win time or freeze a conflict while pretending they are looking for a settlement. As one lawyer working for a legal firm that provides international legal counseling explains: "going regional is often merely a strategy used by the counterpart to win time to prepare the case in the ICJ."[24] For this reason, jurists like J. G. Merrills believe that while boundary disputes are almost always intraregional, regional organizations generally have little to contribute. In his view, regional mechanisms often provide "the antagonists with the diplomatic and material support necessary to continue the struggle."[25]

Certainly, the ICJ's neutral composition makes it particularly appealing vis-à-vis other forums. Beth Simmons recognizes the benefits of having access to a neutral legal authority, observing that "even if an arbitration panel produces the same terms as did political compromise, some domestic groups will find it more attractive to make concessions to a disinterested institution than a political adversary."[26] Perceptions of international legitimacy and reputation costs can play a role, especially when states anticipate that they will pay a higher cost in the long run if they break their commitments. States willing to solve their disputes might be tempted to turn to forums that increase those costs in order to ensure enforcement and commitment.[27] Yet a variety of forums can help increase reputation costs and enhance the legitimacy of a ruling. For example, Argentina accepted the Vatican's mediation and decision in 1978 over the Beagle Channel dispute, in part because the military junta perceived the Papacy as having moral authority.[28] Rejecting the Pope's judgment would thus have incurred prestige costs. Interestingly enough, Guatemala and Belize also considered the Papal path when OAS negotiations failed to resolve their case in 2007; but in the end The Hague option was preferable to all others. Hence, evidence from the above cases suggests that settling disputes via a legal means is not exclusively about strategic bargaining; prestige, authority, and legitimacy matter too. But the ICJ is not the only legally binding institution with legitimate authority; states can still rely on other equally legitimate bodies (the Pope or other international tribunals). Hence, we still have to explain why Latin American states have recently developed a preference to legalize border disputes and then use specific international courts, such as the ICJ.

LEGAL BIAS AND NORMATIVE BEHAVIOR

Normative biases provide additional sources of explanation. Latin American foreign policy has been ruled by a collective and normative understanding that favors legal obligations among regional neighbors. This common regional understanding is based on the expectation and practice that countries from the Americas will resort to pacific settlements whenever conflict emerges.[29] For that purpose, they have relied on international public law to regulate their external behavior by appealing to various regional norms, such as nonintervention, sovereignty, good offices, mediation, and arbitration.[30] At the same time, they have behaved as norm entrepreneurs by encouraging and spreading regional norms that applied exclusively to them.[31] For example, jurists from the southern continent formulated laws at the turn of the twentieth century designed to limit the ability of nations to use force in protecting the interests of their citizens in foreign countries. These principles are widely known as the Calvo and Drago Doctrines. Additionally, the legal principle of *uti possidetis juris*[32] was devised by Latin American republics as a relief measure against having to use treaties to limit the international boundaries of several adjoining states. Through these doctrines, most boundaries between former Portuguese and Spanish colonies were accepted as they were in 1810 for South America, and 1821 for Central America.[33] Latin American states have relied on these common regional and normative understandings in their mutual interactions, and have even developed their own diplomatic culture that emphasizes the legalization of dispute settlement.

This trend of relying on normative and legal biases is reinforced by the fact that a small cohort of foreign policy experts advises most presidents, and in Latin America this group tends to be dominated by lawyers or economists. As Kalevi J. Holsti argues, Latin America has a strong legalistic culture and tradition in which territorial claims are often based on legal interpretations instead of strategic arguments: "Lacking other commanding doctrines such as "manifest destiny," a civilizing mission, world revolution, or anticommunism, legalism helps establish the worth, reputation, and prestige of small countries on the margins of the central international system."[34]

Legalism is seen not only in the approach that countries use to deal with each other, but also in the practice of putting lawyers and economists in charge of supervising and implementing foreign policies. In Latin America ambassadors and foreign affairs ministers overwhelmingly tend to be lawyers or economists.[35] In other words, jurists are de facto the regions' diplomats. These historical practices have reinforced the idea and perception that foreign policy in Latin America is essentially a legal or economic matter more than a political or military one.

This legalization of foreign policy then compounds decisions to go to the ICJ since a rather small cohort of individuals, who share a similar legal view of world affairs and have similar normative and judicial biases, makes most foreign policy decisions. This legal bias increases policy cohesion, which ultimately leads decision-makers to reject certain forms of settlement in favor of legal and judicial forms of arrangement.[36] Thus, the nature of Latin America's foreign policy making, with its emphasis on international public law and economic development, provides a strong impetus to favor judicial settlement via the UN system. This translates into a conviction that the ICJ is the only logical and legal option available, even if there are, in fact, other available options.

LEGALIZATION AS MEANS TO NEUTRALIZE THE MILITARY: THE DOMESTIC POLITICS OF JUDICIALIZATION

Finally, domestic politics plays an important role in explaining forum selection for border dispute settlement. In particular, Latin American states have chosen the ICJ as the preferred forum in order to enforce demilitarization. Unlike most economic disputes, conflicts over territorial and maritime borders are more likely to involve military force and escalate into war.[37] As Paul F. Diehl notes, "not only are territorial concerns significant in generating militarized conflict, they also play a role in the dynamics of conflict behavior between disputants."[38] Furthermore, disputed borders are potential sites of coercion, extraction, and demarcation of territory, thus increasing the stakes for settlement.[39]

The sources of tension and conflict exist in Latin America. Although the region is relatively peaceful compared to others—such as the Middle East or South Asia—border disputes have been militarized in the past, as illustrated by Cameron G. Thies in chapter 2 of this volume.[40] Territorial disputes in Latin America vary in terms of their claims and historical legacies, but they do share common features: not only do they all involve frontier disagreements, but they also reflect serious differences over how to interpret international treaties on the delimitation of borders.[41] Latin American countries typically go to a tribunal because they want someone to interpret numerous colonial documents in such a way that they support expansive claims over territory. Seen from this perspective, legalization is a way of depoliticizing and demilitarizing a conflict by making it subject to legal interpretation. But what is interesting about the Latin American cases is that efforts to legalize disputes have minimized the dangers of military escalation.

In fact, the use of legal means to de-escalate conflicts has been motivated by the desire to divert the attention of the military away from border conflicts. The end of the Cold War and the democratization of Latin America in the early 1990s provided strong incentives for governments to demilitarize border conflicts and disempower the armed forces.

Indeed, since the 1990s most Central American countries have experienced a drastic downsize of the military. The peace processes negotiated under UN auspices in El Salvador, Nicaragua, and Guatemala included conditions for downsizing and demobilizing forces. In El Salvador alone, the peace agreement imposed a 50 percent force reduction, from sixty-three thousand to just over thirty-one thousand persons. In Guatemala, the military was forced to reduce its size by 33 percent within one year and disband rural forces under military control.[42] A similar trend took place in South America, where domestic arms production and procurement were drastically reduced immediately after democratization in the late 1980s and early 1990s. In some cases, as in Argentina, military expenditures were cut by 26 percent.[43] The immediate consequences of these reductions were reflected in lower levels of readiness and operational capacity, as well as lower salaries and cuts in personnel.

But why demilitarize borders? Demilitarization was a means to reduce the threat of coups and the influence of the armed forces in domestic and foreign policy. Hence, newly and democratically elected civilians found it increasingly tempting to rely on judicial means to gradually transfer some policy decisions from military organizations to diplomatic bureaucracies where lawyers tended to predominate. This, in turn, forced a redefinition and a change in military policy. This is what Stuart Kaufman refers to as:

> a way to redefine the nature of a policy decision and force change on a subordinate organization by removing the policy decision from the organization's exclusive area of expertise . . . it allows leaders to institutionalize supervision of the policy by another organization, which enables them to monitor implementation and ensure that the change takes place.[44]

Legalization thus allowed civilian leaders to demilitarize border disputes and de-emphasize the "rally around the flag" phenomenon that often mobilizes the armed forces, as Thies discusses in chapter 2. Slowly but surely, the armed forces of Latin America were increasingly asked to reduce their physical presence in conflictive border posts. Instead of relying on military force, diplomats were more often asked to manage border policies and border dispute settlement, and this led to a de-escalation of border conflicts and spirals in the Latin American region. Indeed, according to the Stockholm Peace Research Institute (SIPRI), from the 1990s to the mid-2000s, Latin America had some of the lowest levels in the world of military expenditures as a share of the GDP, and one of the lowest rates of interstate conflict.[45] In the long run, this might have been what allowed civilian leaders to exercise more political control over the armed forces themselves during transitional periods (although notable exceptions do exist, such as in Honduras). Ultimately, judicialization was part of a domestic strategy to neutralize the armed forces by legalizing conflicts and submitting border disputes to a higher international body.

Externalities of Judicialization

What are the implications of legalizing border disputes? Not surprisingly, an attempt to settle border conflicts through judicial means affect multiple actors and arenas. As Robert Jervis informs us, foreign-policy actions have consequences, even though the effects are not always seen in the areas anticipated by policy makers.[46] In the Latin American context, the effects of legalization and judicialization have been a mixed bag of good and bad policies. The next section focuses on the unintended effects of legalizing disputes, including attention deficits and mission diversion.

Attention Deficits and Increased Illegality in Bordering Areas

Ironically, the demilitarization and legalization of border conflicts has reinforced civilian attention deficits. Today there is a widespread disinterest in defense policy and a general lack of concern for the "development of plans and processes designed to provide for the oversight, organization, training, deployment, and funding of the armed forces."[47] The incentives to fund, modernize, and equip the armed forces have been inevitably reduced by the increasing trend to legalize border disputes. If defending borders is no longer a military mission, but a legal task, then why modernize the armed forces? Hence, a measure that was designed to increase confidence building among bordering states eventually affected civil-military relations. The legalization of border disputes diminished existential threats to state survival, because the contested border was no longer threatened by the military's presence and could potentially be settled via legal means. The result was "Latin America's civilian politicians abandoned an interest in defense and instead focused on regime defense."[48] Many of these Latin American states—particularly those that invoked the powers of the ICJ—did not develop defense plans to protect and safeguard borders. Paradoxically, the states that mostly relied on the ICJ to settle border disputes (Honduras, El Salvador, and Nicaragua) had the weakest systems of civilian control and military oversight.

Simultaneously, a smaller amount of military resources was allocated to the protection of the borders, with multiple collateral effects. Unprotected borders became even more vulnerable to smuggling and illegal trafficking; organized crime settled in border territories; and illegality and black markets flourished in those very same spaces where territorial and maritime disputes once prevailed. Ironically, the legalization of border disputes implicitly created the conditions for increased illegality in bordering areas.

MISSION DIVERSION: FROM BORDER CONTROL TO LAW ENFORCEMENT

Legalization has had its most visible effect on military missions. Military missions matter because they have a greater political dimension to them, particularly since they deal with the relationship of the military with the state. Indeed, missions are specifically assigned to military forces, and while these forces may be responsible for a wide range of tasks, certain missions, individually and collectively, tend to define the military's fundamental role within a nation.[49]

Sovereignty protection and border control have gradually faded away in the military's mission repertoire, especially as border disputes have de-escalated and been settled through judicial means. Rapprochement, de-escalation, and demilitarization were indeed the intended effects of legalization. But other nonmilitary missions have gradually replaced sovereignty and border missions, so the armed forces are now actively engaged in multiple internal roles, such as policing, law enforcement, crowd control, and antinarcotics. With the exception of Argentina and Chile, in Latin America the military has become the ultimate law enforcer, with no clear external mission to perform (such as border defense).

The implications of this policy have undermined public security, defense preparedness, and even the quality of democracy. The use of military forces for law enforcement activities has contributed to the emergence of the so-called *mano dura* or iron fist approach toward policing in Central America. The mano dura approach is based on the principle that a forceful response against crime is likely to deter future criminal behavior. In Guatemala, Honduras, and El Salvador, for example, the strategy has relied heavily on military enforcement, including raids, operatives to hunt criminals, and intrusive street patrolling. In the absence of oversight, accountability, and training mechanisms, the potential for military abuses has never been properly minimized. Human rights abuses have increased in tandem with homicide rates. The irony is that even as military and border conflict between states has become unthinkable in the region, murder rates are the highest in the world. Homicides rates in Central America are higher today than they were during the civil war, when border conflicts were rife.[50]

Moreover, the use of military strategies in public security issues has weakened the military as an institution. On the one hand, antinarcotic campaigns and law enforcement operations have exposed the armed forces to the same dangers of institutional corruption that have so far tainted police forces. On the other hand, such operations undermined military professionalism and encouraged national security doctrines that have focused mostly on political order and stability at the expense of democratic civilian control. For scholars of military affairs, such as Alfred Stepan, this approach does not only affect training, professionalism, and combat readiness for conventional warfare, it also politicizes soldiers as they become increasingly concerned about internal warfare, thereby placing a premium on political stability.[51] The side consequence of the legalization strategy has thus been to obscure the distinction between police and military forces.

The Peru vs. Chile Maritime Dispute: A Case Study

On January 16, 2008, Peru instituted legal proceedings against Chile before the highest UN judicial body. According to ICJ press releases, Peru argued that its maritime border with Chile had never been delimited by agreement and thus asked the court to do so in accordance with customary international public law.[52] Although this was the first time that Peru invoked the power of the ICJ, the maritime border dispute goes back to the nineteenth century; during the War of the Pacific (1879–1883), Chile defeated Peru and Bolivia, annexing the former's coastal province of Antafogasta and the latter's provinces of Tacna, Arica, and Tarapacá.[53] Chile then promised to organize a plebiscite in Tacna and Arica to decide the future and residency of their respective populations. It failed to do this, leading to a US mediation effort in 1929 that granted Tacna to Peru and Arica to Chile. A set of treaties was signed in 1952 and 1954, delimiting the land boundary between the two South American countries.[54] However, for the Peruvian government of Alan García, who began the judicial proceedings at The Hague in 2008, the maritime boundary had never been fully defined. *The Economist* reported: "Although the coast swings abruptly north-west at the border, forming an elbow, the de facto maritime boundary ran due west close to the 181st parallel. This was the result of a 1952 treaty involving the two countries and Ecuador. From the 1980s Peru began to argue that the treaty was merely a fishing agreement that did not fix the maritime boundary."[55]

By taking the case to a judicial body, Peru was requesting the court to do three things: delineate once and for all the maritime border running equidistant between the countries' coasts; reshape the maritime boundary by starting in Punta Concordia, where the land borer hits the sea; and "confirm as Peruvian an external triangle of 29,000 square kilometers lying more than 200 miles west of Chile, but less than 200 miles from Peru's coast."[56] On January 27, 2014, six years after the proceedings began, the ICJ made its final ruling. By a majority vote of ten votes to six, the court determined a new maritime boundary at eighty miles off the coast of Arica.[57] "Beyond that, it drew a diagonal line southwest, slicing about 8,000 square miles of ocean from Chile's exclusive economic zone."[58] In so doing, Chile lost special rights to maritime resources in about 20,720 square kilometers of sea near its northern border. The new maritime borderline is favorable to Peru, which can now extend its territorial waters; although Chile retains control over its twelve-mile territorial waters where most small-scale fishing activity takes place.[59] Both countries accepted the ruling without appeals and promised to implement the court's decision.

Why did Peru and Chile choose the ICJ as the ultimate recourse? The evidence thus far suggests that Peru relied on a strategy that focused on legal authority and prestige. Lima took the case to the world's highest judicial authority in order to make it increasingly difficult for Santiago to refuse judicial settlement. Other alternatives were considered, including a regional mediation by the OAS, but Peru, like Bolivia, thought the hemispheric regional organization would not remain impartial and neutral to the conflict since its secretary general was a Chilean national. Moreover, Chile had already argued that its maritime border had been previously settled in the bilateral treaties of 1952 and 1954, so it adamantly refused any form of mediation. In this context, Lima considered that it had no option but to take the case to the highest international judicial body.[60] According to the proceedings, Peru explained that since the 1980s, it had "consistently endeavored to negotiate the various issues in dispute," but had "constantly met a refusal from Chile to enter into negotiations."[61]

In making its case to the ICJ, Peru pursued the very same legal strategy that other Latin American countries had followed when they invoked the powers of The Hague. Like Nicaragua, El Salvador, Costa Rica, and other Central American states, Lima invoked Article 21 of the American Treaty of Pacific Settlement (commonly referred to as the Pact of Bogotá) to create the basis for the ICJ's jurisdiction. According to the pact, Latin American states recognize ipso facto the authority of the court to settle disputes of judicial nature arising among them without the need of any special previous agreement.[62] Since both Chile and Peru had ratified the pact, the court could then take over the case as a "judicial dispute."[63] Hence, the maritime border conflict between Chile and Peru became "judicialized."

Santiago could have easily dismissed The Hague the way it had disregarded Peru's previous claims. Ironically, Chile somewhat reluctantly accepted the authority and jurisdiction of the court. Evidence gathered by Phillip Durán, a Chilean journalist, indicates that legal and foreign policy advisors to Chilean President Michelle Bachelet strongly suggested that she acknowledge the court's jurisdiction.[64] Indeed, the governments of Bachelet and her successor, Sebastián Piñera, strictly adhered to the ICJ's judicial proceedings. This was done in spite of many fears within the governments that the court's rulings could permanently modify Chile's national boundaries. Both the proceedings and the final rulings of the ICJ took place on the eves of presidential elections (2008 and 2013), when politicians were especially sensible to calls for nationalism and populism. Santiago reasoned that it could only reject the court's legally binding powers at the expense of its own international prestige and reputation. Ultimately, Chile was unwilling to become the first Latin American country to reject the authority of the ICJ, so it grudgingly accepted the legal challenge presented by Peru's suit.

The desire to demilitarize the maritime boundary was also present in both Chile and Peru. Although no war was fought after 1883, the unresolved boundary was the source of many militarized disputes and conflicts. One serious militarized incident occurred on April 2, 2001, when the Chilean Navy decided on its own, without previous approval from their civilian authorities and without informing Peru, to install a Quonset hut in contested waters.[65] The "hut incident" soon escalated when close to a hundred Peruvian military reserves marched at the common border to protest Chile's move. The police tried to cordon them and eventually blocked them from crossing to the Chilean side.[66] The infamous hut incident made both civilian governments realize that the military could take actions on its own using border disputes as a justification to rally around the flag. As

Durán argues, Ricardo Lagos, then President of Chile, saw the incident as a clear sign of military insubordination.[67] On the other hand, during the military escalation of 2001, Peru was attempting to impose stricter civilian control mechanisms over its military and intelligence agencies after decades of corruption, human rights abuses, and political scandals.[68]

Therefore, both countries were eager to find a means by which the maritime dispute could be de-escalated and the armed forces demobilized. In fact, judicialization provided that policy tool. Unintentionally, the ICJ proceedings enabled civilian leaders in both countries to gradually delegate maritime border issues to a small entourage of lawyers and international jurists. Both sides surrounded themselves by legal teams that included former diplomats and ambassadors to the UN (Gabriel Gaspar and Alberto van Klaveren in the Chilean camp and Allan Wagner and José Antonio García Belaúnde in the Peruvian camp); international lawyers from Europe (Allain Pallet, a French jurist was hired by Lima as coordinator of the Peruvian international team, while British lawyer Christopher Greenwood was hired by the Chilean team); and legal firms from London and Boston (Essex Court Chambers and Foley Hoag were consulted by Chile, while Eversheds was contracted by Peru).[69]

"In court we trust" was thus adopted as the unofficial motto of the bilateral relationship. The adopted strategy was known in Chile as "encapsulating" the boundary issue, whereby the maritime border dispute was temporarily frozen until the ICJ delivered its ruling.[70] This move effectively demobilized the armed forces in the conflictive border zones and allowed both neighbors to maintain fluid diplomatic ties while still fighting with each other in The Hague. There was political pressure and diplomatic tension throughout the six-year process, but bilateral conflict was legal in nature, involving diplomatic exchanges and legal threats, not armed forces and military escalation.

Paradoxically, throughout the ICJ legal proceedings, trade, business, and investment boomed without military interference or border conflict. Peru became the fourth biggest recipient of Chilean investment in the world.[71] According to *The Economist*, bilateral trade grew over US$3 billion a year. Chilean companies invested over US$13 billion in Peru, while more than one hundred and fifty thousand Peruvians moved to Chile. Both countries became members of the Pacific Alliance, a free-trading block that was founded in 2011 with Colombia and Mexico.[72]

The ICJ intervention thus contributed to demilitarization of the Chile-Peru relationship by transforming a boundary conflict issue into a strictly legal dispute.

But the move toward judicialization also furthered attention deficits in the defense sector, especially in Peru. The de-escalation of military conflict provided additional incentives to maintain military budgets at a relatively low level. According to Maiah Jaskoski, defense budgets in Peru had steadily contracted as a percentage of national spending since democratization in the late 1980s, from 14.4 percent in 1989 to 8 percent in 2006.[73] So there was already a downsizing trend in place when the ICJ proceedings began. However, between 2008 and 2013 the Peruvian economy experienced a boom, with annual growth rates in the range of 5–10 percent and inflation around 2 percent. Despite this accelerated growth, defense budgets remained stable, with minor increases. In 2008, the defense budget measured in relation to the gross domestic product (GDP) was 6.23 percent. In 2014, when the ICJ ruling was announced, the defense budget as percentage of GDP was 6.57 percent. Data from Resdal, a research group that focuses on Latin American military issues, indicate that military budgets increased only moderately in 2009 and 2010 (6.75 percent and 7.15 percent respectively as percentage of the GDP), but have since decreased.[74] For scholars such as Ciro Alegría Varona, maintaining such low levels of military spending when there was an outstanding availability of money and internal credit was problematic. Peru was due for military modernization, yet it was investing far less on defense than other countries in the region (such as neighboring Chile).[75] Within the military, this was perceived as an explicit move by politicians to neglect the military agenda, especially after border disputes with neighboring countries were legally settled.

Military acquisitions in Peru were also influenced by the move toward judicialization. Before the 2008 proceedings began at the ICJ, Peruvian politicians and defense advisors alike complained about Chile's high military expenditures and felt pressured to maintain equal levels of spending. According to Angel Páez, Santiago's purchases of 46 F-16 jets led Peru's air force to upgrade its fleet of eighteen Russian fighter-bombers.[76] However, once the proceedings began at The Hague, Lima adjusted its purchasing policies to reflect a change in priorities. In 2009, Peru was scheduled to purchase tanks, rockets, vehicles, and additional military gear from China for US$35 million. But the decision was suddenly reversed a year later when Peru acquired less sophisticated tanks from Israel. Varona notes the following:

> Instead of competing with Chile over who has the most modern tanks (tanks that cost US$10 million each and necessarily operate in groups of several), an

efficient antitank system was chosen, costing one fifth of that amount. The decision to abandon the acquisition of Chinese tanks was not due to any doubt as to weapon quality, but rather a strategic decision based on the potential scenarios in which the tanks were to be used and if such spending was actually in line with Peru's security policy.[77]

Moreover, Peru began to massively mobilize troops and resources from border management to internal security campaigns. Jaskoski argues that the focus of the armed forces on internal security missions predates the transition toward the democracy era in the 1980s and was accelerated by the threat posed by the Shining Path terrorist attacks in the 1990s. But she also suggests that the settlement of border disputes with Ecuador in 1994 prompted a change in military missions from sovereignty defense to counterinsurgency.[78] Similarly, a change in mission occurred after the maritime border dispute with Chile was forwarded to the ICJ. Troops were slowly demobilized from the Chilean border and then deployed to areas where drug trafficking was intense within Peru's territory. By 2014, the Andean country had become the world's largest producer of cocaine and the second largest cultivator of coca, after Colombia.[79] Hence, as maritime and military rivalry with Chile decreased, the threat posed by illegal narcotics substantially increased. The response to such a challenge was to make the military into the nation's prime law enforcer, delegating it with multiple public security tasks ranging from eradication and interdiction to striking organized crime in urban and rural settings.[80] In sum, the campaign against drugs became heavily militarized just as the rivalry with Chile was judicialized.

Conclusions

By configuring the analysis in the above ways, this study has been able to provide a number of theoretical and empirical insights to our understanding of border disputes. First, it has helped to explain the explosive growth of law-centered treaties and the "legalization of world politics," basically by analyzing why states have come to favor judicial forms of territorial settlement versus other methods of resolution.[81] The act of delegating authority over disputes is not only a legal one; it is also a political action of significance to countries and international institutions alike. Robert O. Keohane et al. argue the following: "The legal form does not necessarily determine political process. It is the interaction of law and politics, not the action of either alone, that generates decisions and determines their effectiveness."[82]

Second, this chapter has also explored the varying and unintended consequences of legalizing border disputes. The picture painted here is less rosy than what liberal approaches would want us to believe. Yes, militarized border conflicts are less likely in Latin America; as a result, the region does not face intense security dilemmas. But, as the Peruvian-Chile maritime case illustrates, legalizing border disputes has also generated collateral damage, such as civilians who increasingly pay less attention to border security and military issues; armed forces vested with nonmilitary missions; unprotected borders taken by organized crime (this is analyzed by Kacowicz in chapter 5); and decreased military preparedness to deal with conventional defense issues.

NOTES

1. Beth Simmons, "Capacity, Commitment, and Compliance: International Institutions and Territorial Disputes," *Journal of Conflict Resolution* 46, no. 6 (2002): 836.

2. International lawyers separate judicial settlement from arbitration; the former entails reference to established courts, while the latter requires the parties themselves to set up the machinery used to manage the dispute. I use both terms interchangeably since they both require submission to a binding agreement. See J. G. Merrills, *International Dispute Settlement* (New York, NY: Oxford University Press, 2005), 91.

3. For a list of these, see "International Disputes," CIA World Factbook 2008, https://www.cia.gov/library/publications/the-world-factbook/fields/2070.html.

4. See Carlos Escudé and Andrés Fontana, "Argentina's Security Policies: The Rationale and Regional Context," in *International Security and Democracy: Latin America and the Caribbean in the Post-Cold War Era*, ed. Jorge I. Domínguez (Pittsburgh, PA: Pittsburgh University Press, 1998), 52–79; Domínguez, "Security, Peace, and Democracy in Latin America and the Caribbean: Challenges for the Post–Cold War Era," in *International Security and Democracy*, ed. Domínguez, 15; and Kristina Mani, *Democratization and Military Transformation in Argentina and Chile: Rethinking Rivalry* (Boulder, CO: Lynne Rienner, 2011).

5. Page V. Fortna, "Interstate Peacekeeping: Causal Mechanisms and Empirical Effects," *World Politics* 56, no. 4 (2004): 487.

6. See, for example, Monica Herz and João Pontes Nogueira, *Ecuador vs. Peru: Peacemaking amid Rivalry* (Boulder, CO: International Peace Academy and Lynne Rienner, 2002); and David Mares and David Scott Palmer, *Power, Institutions, and Leadership in War and Peace* (Austin, TX: University of Texas Press, 2012).

7. See "Belize and Guatemala Dispute," Organization of American States, accessed April 8, 2015, http://www.oas.org/sap/peacefund/belizeandguatemala/.

8. The other cases brought to the Fund for Peace involve the implementation of a demarcating boundary established by the ICJ between El Salvador and Honduras, and negotiations to improve relations between Honduras and Nicaragua (who have also taken their cases to The Hague). No new cases have been referred to the fund since 2003. For

cases being analyzed by the fund, see "The OAS Peace Fund," Organization of American States, accessed April 8, 2015, http://www.oas.org/sap/peacefund/peacefund/.

9. See Larry Rohter, "Venezuelan Is Rekindling Land Dispute with Guyana," *New York Times*, September 17, 2000, http://www.nytimes.com/2000/09/17/world/venezuelan -is-rekindling-land-dispute-with-guyana.html; and Andrés Serbín, "Las relaciones entre Venezuela y Guyana y la disputa del territorio Esequibo: un paso adelante, dos atrás?" *Pensamiento Propio* 18, no. 8 (2003): 145–70.

10. See Yoshifumi Tanaka, "The Guyana/Suriname Arbitration: A Commentary," *Hague Justice Journal* 2, no. 3 (2007): 28–33.

11. "Land, Island and Maritime Frontier Dispute (El Salvador/Honduras: Nicaragua Intervening)," ICJ Ruling, December 11, 1986, International Court of Justice, http://www .icj-cij.org/docket/index.php?p1=3&p2=3&code=sh&case=75&k=oe&p3=0.

12. For a full description of the case, going back to the case presented in 1986, see "Application for Revision of the Judgment of 11 September 1992 in the Case concerning the *Land, Island and Maritime Frontier Dispute (El Salvador/Honduras: Nicaragua intervening)* (El Salvador v. Honduras)," September 10, 2002, International Court of Justice, http:// www.icj-cij.org/docket/index.php?p1=3&p2=3&code=esh&case=127&k=2e&p3=0.

13. The ICJ found that Honduras had sovereignty over Bobel Cay, Savanna Cay, Port Royal Cay, and South Cay. At the same time, it delineated a single maritime boundary in accordance with Nicaragua's preferences, at a point with the coordinates 15°00′52″ N and 83°05′58″ W; that is 2° coordinates less than what Honduras had originally claimed. See International Court of Justice, "The Court Finds that Honduras has Sovereignty over Bobel Cay, Savanna Cay, Port Royal Cay and Draws a Single Maritime Boundary between Nicaragua and Honduras," press release August 10, 2007, 23, http://www.icj -cij.org/docket/index.php?p1=3&p2=3&k=14&case=120&code=nh&p3=6.

14. For a full list of cases taken by the court see "List of Cases Referred to the Court since 1946 by Date of Introduction," International Court of Justice, accessed April 8, 2015, http://www.icj-cij.org/docket/index.php?p1=3&p2=2. See also Verónica Smink, "¿Hasta dónde puede reclamarse lo perdido en una guerra?" BBC Mundo, April 4, 2013, http:// www.bbc.co.uk/mundo/noticias/2013/04/130327_bolivia_mar_la_haya_vs.shtml.

15. Andrew Moravcsik, "Taking Preferences Seriously: A Liberal Theory of International Politics," *International Organization* 51, no. 4 (1997): 513–53.

16. Emilia Powell and Sara Mitchell, "The International Court of Justice and the World's Three Legal Systems," *Journal of Politics* 69, no. 2 (2007): 397–415. See also Sara McLaughlin Mitchell and Emilia Justyna Powell, *Domestic Law Goes Global: Legal Traditions and International Courts* (New York, NY: Cambridge University Press, 2011).

17. Beth Simmons, "See You in 'Court?' The Appeal to Quasi-Judicial Legal Processes in the Settlement of Territorial Disputes," in *A Road Map to War: Territorial Dimensions of International Conflict*, ed. Paul F. Diehl (Nashville, TN: Vanderbilt University Press, 1999), 205–37. Simmons seems to have overlooked other ICJ rulings regarding Eastern and Central European territorial and maritime settlements following the dissolution of the Soviet Union. Some of these cases may be too recent to have been included in her study. Latin America nevertheless has the highest propensity to use judicial settlements

18. The ICJ also analyzes nonterritorial disputes, such as the Ecuador-Colombia dispute on aerial spraying and United States–Mexico issues regarding consular rights for illegal immigrants.

19. See Amitav Acharya and Alastair Iain Johnston, eds., *Crafting Cooperation: Regional International Institutions in Comparative Perspective* (New York, NY: Cambridge University Press, 2007), 13.

20. Ian Hurd, *After Anarchy: Legitimacy and Power in the United Nations Security Council* (Princeton, NJ: Princeton University Press, 2007), 6.

21. Ibid.

22. Acharya and Johnston, *Crafting Cooperation*, 19.

23. See David R. Mares, "Regional Conflict Management in Latin America: Power Complemented by Diplomacy," in *Regional Orders: Building Security in a New World*, ed. David A. Lake and Patrick M. Morgan (University Park, PA: Pennsylvania State University Press, 1997), 198.

24. Personal interview with a legal advisor and lawyer, Washington, DC, October 14, 2008.

25. Merrills, *International Dispute Settlement*, 91.

26. Simmons, "Capacity, Commitment, and Compliance," 834.

27. See, for example, Beth Simmons, *Territorial Disputes and Their Resolution: The Case of Ecuador and Peru*, Peaceworks 27 (Washington, DC: US Institute of Peace, 1999); Simmons, "See You in 'Court' "; and Paul R. Hensel and Sara McLaughlin Mitchell, "International Institutions and Compliance with Agreements," *American Journal of Political Science* 51, no. 4 (2007): 721–37.

28. See Arie M. Kacowicz, *The Impact of Norms in International Society: The Latin American Experience, 1881–2001* (Notre Dame, IN: Notre Dame University Press, 2005).

29. Jorge I. Domínguez, David Mares, Manuel Orozco, David Scott Palmer, Francisco Rojas Aravena, and Adrés Serbin, *Boundary Disputes in Latin America*, Peaceworks 50 (Washington, DC: US Institute of Peace, 2002), 23.

30. Kacowicz, *Impact of Norms*.

31. See Martha Finnemore and Katherine Sikkink, "International Norm Dynamics and Political Change," *International Organization* 52, no. 4 (autumn 1998): 887–917.

32. *Uti possidetis juris* is a Latin term that translates as: "As you possess, so you may possess." It is the principle that post-independence boundaries should match those of the colonial period.

33. See A. O. Cukwurah, *The Settlement of Boundary Disputes in International Law* (Manchester, UK: University of Manchester Press, 1967), 112–16, 190–99; Peter Lyon "Regional Organizations and Frontier Disputes," in *The International Regulation of Frontier Disputes*, ed. Evan Luard (London, UK: Thames and Hudson, 1970), 122–23; Domínguez et al., *Boundary Disputes in Latin America*, 22; and Mares and Palmer, *Power, Institutions, and Leadership*.

34. Kalevi J. Holsti, *The State, War, and the State of War* (New York, NY: Cambridge University Press, 1996), 170.

35. Argentina, Brazil, and Mexico have appointed some of their own jurists to serve as chief justices in the ICJ. Mexico, for example, has rarely participated in the UN Security Council as a nonpermanent member, following a noninterventionist and mostly paci-

Similar to the case of 1979, common interests between the two countries contributed to the peaceful resolution of their dispute, including realist and geopolitical considerations. For Brazil, the territory had geopolitical implications in terms of maintaining land communication between the state of Rio Grande do Sul and the rest of the country. For Argentina, confronted at that time with much more serious territorial disputes with Chile, there was an inherent benefit in improving its relations with its large neighbor, Brazil. Moreover, the resolution of the dispute in 1895 paved the way to improve the common political and economic interests of the two parties, in a strikingly similar context to that of the dispute over the Itaipú Dam, almost a century later.

Between 1895 and 1979, a century of traditional competition took place between the two countries over regional hegemony in South America. This was exacerbated by geopolitical doctrines that amplified frustration in Argentina and the desire for power in Brazil, the latter of which developed in economic terms vis-à-vis its neighbors throughout the twentieth century. Against this background, the positive changes that have characterized the Brazilian-Argentine relationship since 1979 are remarkable.[18]

In the late 1970s, Brazil initiated a policy of "Latin-Americanization" toward its Spanish-speaking neighbors with a goal of building better relations with the rest of South America. Domestically, the ascendancy of moderate military officers in Brazil and the launching of economic and political liberalization contributed to a general climate of openness toward its neighbors. From the Argentine standpoint, also under a military dictatorship at that time, the ruling military junta became quite aware of its power inferiority vis-à-vis Brazil in economic and conventional military terms. This excluded, perhaps, the specific area of nuclear development, in which Brazil was finally catching up to Argentina's lead, making an escalating nuclear arms race a real possibility. Moreover, the mounting tensions with Great Britain over the South Atlantic Falklands / Malvinas Islands and the deteriorating relations with Chile following the 1977 British arbitration that awarded Chile the Beagle Channel Islands, both prompted the Argentines to seek an accommodation with Brazil against the prospect of an imminent war with Chile, in a similar vein to the peaceful resolution of the Misiones dispute back in 1895.

These converging motivations between Argentina and Brazil, together with Paraguay's interest in new sources of power and development, led to the resolution of a thirteen-year-old dispute over the hydropower generation of energy along the Paraná River in 1979 with the building of the Itaipú Dam. Constructed on the border between Brazil and Paraguay, the Itaipú Dam has allowed nations to exploit the originally disputed territory to their common advantage. The 1979 Tripartite Agreement between Brazil, Paraguay, and Argentina established river height levels and how much they could change as a result of the several hydroelectric projects planned and undertaken by the three countries.

The most important outcome of the tripartite agreement was to put in motion a process of rapprochement that included economic and military cooperation, especially regarding the nuclear issue. In 1980, Argentina and Brazil further expanded and improved their bilateral relations by exchanging presidential visits and a package of ten cooperation agreements, including joint arms production and nuclear cooperation (joint research and the transfer of some nuclear materials). Given the historic competition between the two countries and prestige attached to nuclear development, the bilateral nuclear rapprochement reached in 1980 was a watershed, especially considering the importance of rivalry in state development as noted by Cameron G. Thies in chapter 2 of this volume.

After democratization took place in the mid-1980s, Argentina and Brazil launched a bilateral integration program (ABEIP) in 1986, which upgraded bilateral relations in the direction of establishing stable peace. The convergence of national interests between the two countries in 1985–1990 led to their integration in the economic sphere, first at the bilateral level (1986–1989) and later through the incorporation of the two smaller buffer states of Paraguay and Uruguay, which have both been members of Mercosur since 1991.

Unlike the case of the border flows between the United States and its northern and southern neighbors (see chapter 7 by Adam Isacson in this volume), the tri-border movements in the Southern Cone are relatively recent. The TBA first began to develop as an important economic region in the early 1970s, especially with the agreement to build the Itaipú Dam between Paraguay and Brazil in 1973. This brought an economic boom to the area. Before 1961, there were only sixty thousand inhabitants in the region. The population of Foz do Iguaçu grew from thirty thousand in 1970 to one hundred and fifty thousand in 1985, when Argentina and Brazil were connected by a bridge. The importance of the TBA as a trade region was drastically increased with the signing of Mercosur in 1991. The goal of Mercosur was to promote regional trade, taking advantage of the energy produced at Itaipú, the world's largest hydroelectric plant, and the tourist potential of the Iguazú Falls.[19] The importance of Itaipú is paramount to both Paraguay and Brazil: it provides about 90 percent of the electricity of Paraguay, and about 30 percent of that of Brazil.[20]

Who Are the Actors? Criminal and Terrorist Activities in the TBA

Various black market criminal activities take place in the TBA, especially in Ciudad del Este, Paraguay. They include identification and document fraud, counterfeiting and smuggling of consumer products, drug trafficking, arms trading, human trafficking and sexual exploitation, money laundering, and terrorist financing. The amount of criminal activity has ranked Ciudad del Este third, behind Hong Kong and Miami, in the volume of cash transactions. Thus, according to Interpol, Ciudad del Este had produced US$5 billion to US$12 billion per year in money laundering as of 2012.[21] A substantial range of international criminal organizations are presently engaged in illicit business transactions in the TBA. Organized crime groups include the Yakuza from Japan, Nigerian con artists, and a variety of criminal groups from Brazil, China, Colombia, Cote d'Ivoire, Ghana, France (Corsica), Lebanon, Peru, Russia (Chechnya), and Ukraine.[22]

On several occasions there have been accusations and sustained arguments about the existence of Islamic fundamentalist terrorist organizations in the TBA. Those accusations grew out of suspicions that a considerable and prosperous Muslim and Arab community and a lack of serious control by the governments in the TBA made possible the illegal trafficking and money laundering that could support terrorism. In short, the area has repeatedly been scrutinized for providing funding and logistics to Hezbollah (Lebanon), Gamaa Al-Islamya (Egypt), Hamas (Palestinians), and Al Qaeda.[23]

In the last two decades, the TBA has reportedly served as an operational and logistical center for international terrorist groups such as Hezbollah, alongside the transnational criminal organizations that have traditionally been the focus of security concerns. Hezbollah operatives and supporters are especially present in Ciudad del Este, and are related to criminal activities such as drug smuggling, piracy, and money laundering. This criminal-terrorist nexus is a very controversial topic for the TBA countries, which formally deny the presence of terrorist cells in the region. Still, international organizations such as Interpol have specifically linked organized crime groups and the thriving black market in the TBA to terrorist groups. In 2007 the United States formally declared that tens of millions of dollars were laundered in the TBA and disbursed to terrorist organizations. Moreover, a 2005 Paraguayan intelligence report corroborated that about US$20 million was collected every year to finance the activities of Hezbollah and Hamas.[24] Two decades ago, the operational planning of terrorist attacks perpetrated in

Argentina in 1992 and 1994 were traced across the border to Ciudad del Este, Paraguay. This city provided a safe haven for terrorist groups such as Hezbollah, which was held responsible, along with Iran, for the attacks in Buenos Aires.[25]

In addition to supporting Islamic terrorist groups, the TBA provides a haven that is geographically, socially, economically, and politically conducive to organized crime. The corrupt officials who accept bribes and payoffs create a symbiotic relationship that thrives on drug and arms trafficking, money laundering, and other lucrative criminal activities.[26]

In the case of the TBA region, one might conclude that the necessary conditions for creating a safe haven of crime and terrorism are all in place. First, the particular geography of the border region makes it very difficult to monitor. Second, the resources to enforce central authority and coordinate activities to adequately govern and protect the relevant countries are very limited, especially in the case of Paraguay. Third, all three countries rank toward the bottom of Transparency International's Corruption Perception Index. Lax immigration controls and corrupt officials at the common borders have also facilitated the relatively free movement for criminal organizations. Finally, poverty is a widespread phenomenon among the three countries.[27]

Explanations for the Development of the TBA as a Dynamic Criminal/Terrorist Safe Haven

In the remaining sections of this chapter I develop several themes and specific explanations that explain why the TBA has become a criminal/terrorist hub in the Southern Cone. First, I consider the economic rationale against the background of globalization, and especially of regionalization. Second, I assess the paradox of regional peace in the context of new, nonstate security threats. Third, I consider the relevance of different identities and cultures at the national, subnational, and regional levels. In this sense, we should take account of alternative narratives that frame the TBA alternatively as a "criminal" or as a "terrorist" issue. Finally, I refer to the different state reactions to these criminal/terrorist challenges.

The Economic Rationale against the Background of Regionalization

In the taxonomy of various problematic border regions in the Americas, the TBA falls under the rubric of the implication of expanded economic activity in the problems of border management. Specifically, the establishment of Mercosur and the expansion of transnational economic exchanges have led to concomitant increases in licit trade and illicit trafficking. There is clear evidence that the cross-border flow of goods and people in the TBA have increased substantially as a result of regional integration since the mid-1980s. In 2002 the Mercosur countries signed an agreement making it easier for their citizens to travel and obtain resident visas. The agreement also allowed inspection-free transportation of commercial containers. Today there is a very high volume of traffic within the TBA, especially across the border between Brazil and Paraguay. Every day about forty thousand people go unchecked as they cross the bridge between Ciudad del Este and Foz do Iguaçu, along with more than two thousand vehicles, including many trucks laden with freight containers.

The theme of regional integration implemented by Mercosur has become a focal point for understanding life in the borderland, especially in the economic sphere; though the integration remains essentially at the rhetorical rather than practical level when it comes to its broader political and security dimensions. The image and metaphor of regional integration is present, particularly in reference to Mercosur, but concrete cross-border governmental initiatives related to regional integration remain scarce at the local level. Regional integration is depicted as a norm rather than a reality by governmental authorities—a norm with little practical relevance to the daily lives of people in the TBA.[28]

The criminal/terrorist activity has become possible in the TBA because of unintended effects of the Mercosur agreement. Such open borders make the TBA region enticing for criminals and terrorists, turning an already difficult law-enforcement situation even worse. The conjunction of regionalization in the form of Mercosur and of globalization through transnational economic flows makes the TBA particularly vulnerable to illicit operations (on the role of smuggling in the TBA see chapter 10 by Aguiar in this volume).

The roots of the criminal/terrorist problem follow an economic logic. While Brazil is the largest Latin American economy and seventh in the global ranking, Paraguay, at the other extreme, is one of Latin America's most corrupt and poorest countries. Political and economic instability have made Paraguay reluctant to challenge the existing situation because it relies heavily on the informal economy in Ciudad del Este. As a poor and landlocked country, Paraguay opened itself to the opportunities of foreign markets after the creation of Mercosur in 1991. Argentina, meanwhile, had experienced a catastrophic economic crisis in the early 2000s. Thus, huge disparities in incomes and prices among the three countries, combined with several import tariffs (despite Mercosur), contributed to the creation of a smuggler's paradise (as discussed in greater detail in chapter 10). In sum, the TBA is a transnational economic space, where the movements of people and goods reflect the asymmetric power among the three countries.[29]

THE PARADOX OF REGIONAL PEACE AMID NEW SECURITY THREATS

Among the South American international disputes of the twentieth century, the Argentine-Brazilian rivalry until 1979 was the longest and most deeply rooted, and the one most influenced by geopolitical doctrines. It had important reverberations in the domestic and international politics of the region as a whole, and had a direct impact upon the three buffer states of the Southern Cone—Uruguay, Paraguay, and Bolivia—in particular. From the second half of the nineteenth century to the late 1970s, the relationship between the region's two major powers was a complex mixture of conflict and cooperation; this was a function of disagreements about their territorial borders (until 1895) and their competing hegemonic ambitions in South America (until 1979).[30]

Before 1979, Argentina regarded Brazil as an expansionary military, economic, and demographic power that threatened areas to its south, west, and southwest. Conversely, the Brazilians regarded their smaller neighbor with suspicion and uneasiness, fearing the kind of volatility and aggressiveness that Argentina has most recently demonstrated in its futile invasion of the Falklands/Malvinas in April 1982. At the same time, the Argentine-Brazilian rivalry never escalated into militarized crises such as those between Argentina and Chile; moreover, their enduring rivalry, unlike that between Peru and Ecuador, did not include opposing claims to a disputed territory since the resolution of the Misiones dispute in 1895.

With the signing of the Tri-Partite Agreement regarding Itaipú in October 1979, Argentina and Brazil have moved along the continuum from a situation of negative peace (absence of war) through a stage of stabilization and rapprochement in their relations (1979–1990), toward consolidation of their stable peace (1991–1999), and then up to the point of forming a loose pluralistic security community. The existence of the security community in the Southern Cone, epitomized by Mercosur, implies that traditional concerns of international security, such as former geopolitical interstate "hypotheses of conflict" have become irrelevant in the contemporary relations involving Argentina, Brazil, and Paraguay. Overall, the countries of the Southern Cone have managed to develop a promising framework of security cooperation that has eliminated the traditional interstate security dilemma through transparency and confidence-building measures.

At the same time, and paradoxically, peaceful borders in the region have become open and loose, demilitarized, and "civilianized" (falling under police and civilian control). An unintended consequence of the outbreak of regional peace is that terrorism and transnational criminal activities have thrived and pose new challenges to the region's security and prospects of cooperation. This has occurred precisely because of the very vulnerability and looseness of these borders.[31]

The security problem created by the actual evaporation of the borders extends well beyond the TBA. As Pion-Berlin aptly describes, in an irony that echoes the NAFTA case-study of North America, Mercosur's success in breaking down economic barriers among neighboring states and in notably increasing the cross-border flows of people and goods led to the proliferation of illicit transborder activities as well. Yet, unlike the NAFTA case (analyzed in chapter 7 by Isacson), these flows have taken place without a concomitant increase in security and border controls, creating a reputation of anarchy and violence with negative economic and political consequences.[32]

There is a conceptual gap in international security (and in international relations in general) in the way we refer to these new security threats. There is a tendency in some countries, including the United States, to still think in terms of state threats, whereas these new threats (criminal and terrorist activities) are inherently asymmetrical and come from nonstate, transnational actors. Hence, the recourse to traditional military power and to norms of international law might be irrelevant.[33]

Interestingly, for domestic political reasons, the governments of the TBA prefer to address these new security challenges and threats by framing them in nonmilitary terms, unlike the obvious preference of the United States to lead the global "war against terrorism" by militarizing criminal issues in Latin America, such as narcoterrorism. The constitutions of several Latin American countries prohibit the use of military forces for internal security (see chapter 3 in this volume by Arturo C. Sotomayor). Furthermore, memories of the harsh military dictatorships of the 1970s and early 1980s further inhibit the civilian governments from expanding the military's role in coping with security problems that are framed as internal (only criminal), rather than international security. As a consequence, there is a logical reluctance to "securitizing" or "militarizing" the TBA security challenges. Thus, in the context of the Triple Frontier, responsibilities for security have fallen into the hands of the ministers of interior and justice, rather than those of defense or war. Rather than the armed forces, it is the police, border patrols, immigration officials, civilian courts, and intelligence agencies under their jurisdiction that play a central role.

In this context, there are two diametrically opposed security visions and clashing narratives regarding the TBA. The first contends that there are Islamic fundamentalist terrorist groups in the TBA. The second contends that the possible "terrorist threats" in the area are an invention of the United States in order to gain strategic control over the region. In my own assessment, there is enough factual evidence to corroborate the first version.

According to the first narrative, the US version, a senior Hezbollah operative, Mughniyeh, became established in 1991 in cooperation with Iran terrorist cells in Foz do Iguaçu and Ciudad del Este. Several analysts confirm that the TBA is a terrorist center for the recruiting of funds, arms and drug traffic, smuggling, and money laundering, including about US$10 billion to US$12 billion that were transferred in the region, mostly for the benefit of Hezbollah.[34]

According to the second narrative, the anti-US version, shared by some Latin American opinion leaders in the region, the United States attempts to control the economic resources of South America, first and foremost the water reserves of the Guaraní Aquifer, through the militarization of the region. The argument about the presence of terrorist groups in the TBA is a political pretext for the United States to enhance its presence in the Triple Frontier. This conspiracy theory, stemming from US foreign policy, is based on two assumptions: the image of Arabs and Muslims as terrorists, and the representation of South America as a "lawless or unlawful land." In this vein, all the agreements among the states in the region on the subject of antiterrorism take aim at the social mobilization of grassroots groups and social movements, such as peasant organizations in Brazil and Paraguay, within the TBA.[35]

The Response of the National Governments

It is obvious that the response attributed to the three national governments in the TBA is crucial in explaining the dynamic evolution of the region. In this sense, it is important to consider the historical and political realities in Brazil, Argentina, and Paraguay in order to understand their ambiguous positions regarding the criminal and terrorist activities in the TBA.

For example, in Paraguay under General Stroessner's thirty-four-year dictatorship, money laundering and counterfeiting were actually encouraged by the government. All three countries suffer from a high level of corruption in their societies, obviously facilitating the commission of crimes. According to the 2003

Index of the Perception of Corruption, Paraguay ranked 129th out of 133 countries, with a score of 1.6 out of 10 (1 being most corrupt). Brazil placed 54th, with a score of 3.9, whereas Argentina was in the 92nd position, with a score of only 2.5. Hence, the region is largely ungoverned due to weak, inadequate, or ignored laws.[36]

The governments in the region are preoccupied with the attention attracted by terrorism, to the extent that they prefer not to frame the TBA as prone to terrorist activities; otherwise the issue would dominate their bilateral relations with the United States. In addition, there is also a fear of retaliation by some of the terrorist organizations, and reticence in all the Latin American countries to recognizing terrorist organizations like Hezbollah.

Yet, at least at the formal level, the TBA governments have been involved in some efforts to stop the use of the region by criminal and terrorist groups. In 1996, Brazil, Paraguay, and Argentina established the "Tripartite Command of the Tri-Border"; this led to a security agreement in 1998 with the goal of controlling and fighting organized crime. However, the institutional problems of corruption, underfunding, poor training, and inadequate laws have hindered law enforcement in the area. After 9/11, the United States has been putting pressure on local governments, leading to the creation of a "Group of 3 + 1" in the TBA to improve the "war against terrorism."[37] Let us examine in further detail the different responses of the three governments to the rise in illicit activities in the Tri-Border region.

The Argentine Response

Puerto Iguazú in Argentina sustains relative advantages regarding security control, due to its relatively high level of development and small population. Regarding money flows, Argentina has established the Trade Transparency Unit to examine trade data on capital flows for any fraud or illicit behavior. Moreover, in 2009 the Argentine government approved a law prohibiting any forms of human trafficking. Argentina has had the most active intelligence-gathering presence in the area to combat terrorist activity.[38]

In May 2003, Argentine prosecutors linked Ciudad del Este and Foz do Iguaçu to the AMIA bombings of 1994 and issued arrest warrants for two Lebanese citizens in Ciudad del Este. Investigation of this attack has continued for two decades, but Argentine special prosecutor Alberto Nisman generated new controversy in May 2013 when he released a report accusing Iran of continuing to engage in covert activities in Latin America, including the TBA, to prepare for further terrorist attacks. Not only was this report controversial for its accusations, but also because it ran counter to the Argentine administration's policy of rapprochement with Iran.[39]

The Brazilian Response

In the interpretation of Brazilian Ambassador to the United States Rubens Barbosa, the TBA should not be considered the "front line" of the global war on terror. Ambassador Barbosa even reinforced the Argentine claim that there was no hardcore proof of terrorist activity in the area.[40] Thus, Brazil continues to deny that terrorism financing occurs in the area, positing a "lack of evidence" to warrant significant policy change, as suggested by the WikiLeak cables.[41] Yet, in tandem with the increasing importance of Brazil as an emerging global power, the country has started to improve its efforts to fight crime in the TBA by regulating smuggling (Sacoleiro Law of 2009) and by increasing its police presence around the southwestern borders, including the TBA.[42]

The Paraguayan Response

There is a strong asymmetrical relationship between Paraguay and Brazil, which has affected the responses of both countries. While the Brazilian officials and politicians consider the Paraguayan State as weak, corrupt, and inefficient, the Paraguayan officials and politicians feel denigrated by Brazil. From Paraguay, Brazil is perceived as a neighbor with strong economic power and infrastructure, and a political decisiveness that has an overwhelming impact upon the TBA. Conversely, from Brazil, Paraguay is perceived as a neighbor with an administration that is not really interested in efficiently managing its resources, and with a population accustomed to informality and disorder.[43]

As a matter of fact, Paraguay's lenient laws corroborate the claim that Ciudad del Este, as the TBA criminal hotspot, is relatively devoid of government control. Specifically, Paraguay has weak regulation of its financial sector, and tax laws are easily ignored in Ciudad del Este. Apart from a debilitated financial sector, Paraguay maintains a poor regulation system on underground markets. At the same time, Paraguay has implemented some procedures to enhance its counterterrorist apparatus. Yet, those efforts have been hampered by Paraguay's porous borders and level of corruption. In 2009, it revised its penal code to bolster penalties against trafficking crimes and reintroduced its customs office at the bridge connecting to Brazil.[44]

Conclusion

Globalization and regionalization have transformed international relations, making many of the traditional norms and concerns with territorial border disputes and international security no longer relevant; instead, new security threats across borders must be dealt with, including transnational illicit flows of goods and persons, as well as criminal and terrorist activities. This does not necessarily mean that territory in general, and borders in particular, have vanished from our attention. Rather, borders now fulfill new and different functions, especially against the background of border fixity and the proliferation of regional integration.

The TBA in the Southern Cone of South America is a peculiar case where there is a convergence of regional integration (Mercosur), regional peace, and illicit activities that pose new security threats. These threats are not only to the immediate region or to South America as a whole, but even to other countries around the world. Its high levels of crime and the opportunistic endeavors of transnational criminal organizations and global terrorist networks threaten the authority and sovereignty of Paraguay, Brazil, Argentina, and beyond.

The outbreak of regional peace has contributed to the loosening of the international borders in the TBA region. In this sense, the TBA's combination of vast ungoverned areas, poverty, illicit activities, disenfranchised groups, ill-equipped public security agents, and fragile democracies have together led to the proliferation of illicit activities.

In theoretical terms, confronting a collective problem requires improved cooperation among the three TBA countries. In 1996, the three countries established a "Tripartite Command of the Tri-Border" as a multiagency, tri-nation police endeavor. There is also some evidence that cooperative and individual national efforts of the Argentine, Brazilian, and Paraguayan authorities to fight illicit activities by organized crime and terrorist groups in the TBA have constrained these activities since 2001, but by no means eliminated them. These efforts have been hindered by endemic corruption, poor pay, a lack of logistical support, human rights abuses, and weak anti-money laundering laws. Therefore, the TBA countries would and could benefit from the implementation of high-intensity crime policies, anticorruption measures, and stronger financial regulations, alongside greater attention to border control and immigration among the three border cities.[45]

NOTES

1. I would like to thank Galia Press-Barnathan, Anne Clunan, Daniel Wajner, and the editors of this volume for their comments and suggestions, as well as Special Prosecutor Dr. Alberto Nisman, of the Public Ministry in Buenos Aires, Argentina.

2. See also Peter Andreas, *Smuggler Nation: How Illicit Trade Made America* (Oxford, UK: Oxford University Press, 2013).

3. William W. Mendel, "Paraguay's Ciudad del Este and the New Centers of Gravity," *Military Review* 82, no. 2 (March–April 2002): 1; see also Blanca Madani, "Hezbollah's Global Finance Network: The Triple Frontier," *Middle East Intelligence Bulletin* 4, no.1 (January 2002): 1–5; Ana R. Sverdlick, "Terrorists and Organized Crime Entrepreneurs in the 'Triple Frontier' among Argentina, Brazil, and Paraguay," *Trends in Organized Crime* 9, no. 2 (winter 2005): 84–93; and Heather A. Golding, "Terrorism and the Triple Frontier," *Woodrow Wilson Update on the Americas* no. 4 (April 2002): 1–4.

4. Cristina C. Brafman Kittner, "The Role of Safe Havens in Islamist Terrorism," *Terrorism and Political Violence* 19 (2007): 320.

5. Thomaz G. Costa and Gastón H. Schulmeister, "The Puzzle of the Iguazu Tri-Border Area: Many Questions and Few Answers Regarding Organized Crime and Terrorism Links," *Global Crime* 8, no. 1 (2007): 26–39.

6. David Newman, "The Lines that Continue to Separate Us: Borders in our 'Borderless World'," *Progress in Human Geography* 30, no. 2 (2006): 143, 147; and Gerald Blake, "State Limits in the Early 21st Century: Observations on Form and Function," *Geopolitics* 5, no.1 (2007): 11–12.

7. Thomas Risse, ed., *Governance without a State? Politics and Policies in Areas of Limited Statehood* (New York, NY: Columbia University Press, 2011).

8. Kittner, "Role of Safe Havens," 308.

9. Beth A. Simmons, "Trade and Territorial Conflict in Latin America: International Borders as Institutions," in *Territoriality and Conflict in an Era of Globalization*, ed. Miles Kahler and Barbara D. Walter (Cambridge, UK: Cambridge University Press, 2006), 252; and Miles Kahler, "Territoriality and Conflict in an Era of Globalization," in Kahler and Walter, *Territoriality and Conflict*, 1–21.

10. Blake, "State Limits," 2; and Newman, "Borders in our 'Borderless World,'" 143.

11. Tim Hall, "Geographies of the Illicit: Globalization and Organized Crime," *Progress in Human Geography* 37, no. 3 (2012): 1–20.

12. Arie M. Kacowicz, "Regionalization, Globalization, and Nationalism: Convergent, Divergent, or Overlapping?" *Alternatives* 24, no. 4 (November 1999): 527–56.

13. Blake, "State Limits," 14–15; and Ramiro Anzit Guerrero, *Triple Frontera: ¿Terrorismo o criminalidad?* (Buenos Aires, Argentina: Seguridad y Defensa, 2006), 13–14.

14. Christine Folch, "Trouble on the Triple Frontier," *Foreign Affairs*, 6 (Sept. 6, 2012), accessed December 24, 2013, http://www.foreignaffairs.com/articles/138096/christine-folch/trouble-on-the-triple-frontier.

15. See Fernando Rabossi, "¿Cómo pensamos la Triple Frontera?" in *La Triple Frontera: Dinámicas culturales y procesos transnacionales*, ed. Verónica Giménez Béliveau and Silvia Montenegro (Buenos Aires, Argentina: Espacio Editorial, 2010), 22–23.

16. See Philip K. Abbot," Terrorist Threats in the Tri-Border Area: Myth or Reality?" *Military Review* (September–October 2004): 51; Kittner, "Role of Safe Havens," 315.

17. Gordon Ireland, *Boundaries, Possessions, and Conflicts in South America* (Cambridge, MA: Harvard University Press, 1938), 16; and Arie Kacowicz, *The Impact of Norms in International Society: The Latin American Experience, 1881–2001* (South Bend, IN: University of Notre Dame Press, 2005), 78–81.

18. Gian Luca Gardini, "Making Sense of Rapprochement between Argentina and Brazil, 1979–1982," *Revista Europea de Estudios Latinoamericanos y del Caribe*, no. 80 (April 2006): 57–71; Arie M. Kacowicz, "Stable Peace in South America: The ABC Triangle, 1979–1999," in *Stable Peace among Nations*, ed. Arie M. Kacowicz, Yaacov Bar-Siman-Tov, Ole Elgstrom, and Magnus Jerneck (Lanham, MD: Rowman and Littlefield, 2000), 200–219.

19. Felipe Umaña, *Threat Convergence: Revisiting the Crime-Terrorism Nexus in the Tri-Border Area* (Washington, DC: Fund for Peace, 2012), 3.

20. Guerrero, *Triple Frontera*, 26.

21. Umaña, *Threat Convergence*, 3; and Folch, "Trouble on the Triple Frontier."

22. Umaña, *Threat Convergence*, 9.

23. Guerrero, *Triple Frontera*, 47.

24. Joshua L. Gleiss and Benedetta Berti, *Hezbollah and Hamas: A Comparative Study* (Baltimore, MD: Johns Hopkins University Press, 2012), 70–74; and Umaña, *Threat Convergence*, 10.

25. David Pion-Berlin, "Sub-Regional Cooperation, Hemispheric Threat: Security in the Southern Cone," in *Regionalism and Governance in the Americas: Continental Drift*, ed. Louise Fawcett and Monica Serrano (New York, NY: Palgrave-Macmillan, 2005), 217.

26. Rex Hudson, "Terrorist and Organized Crime Groups in the Tri-Border Area of South America" (Washington, DC: Congressional Research Service, US Library of Congress, 2010), 3; and Sverdlick, "Terrorists and Organized Crime," 87.

27. Kittner, "Role of Safe Havens," 315–18; see also Pion-Berlin, "Security in the Southern Cone," 211–27.

28. Verónica Giménez Béliveau, "Movilidades y escalas de la acción política: Políticos y funcionarios piensan el Mercosur desde la frontera," in Giménez Béliveau and Montenegro, *La Triple Frontera*, 47–73.

29. Verónica Giménez Béliveau and Silvia Montenegro, "Introducción," in Giménez Béliveau and Montenegro, *La Triple Frontera*, 15.

30. Kacowicz, "Stable Peace," 202; and Jack Child, *Geopolitics and Conflict within South America: Quarrels among Neighbors* (New York, NY: Praeger, 1985), 99–100.

31. Pion-Berlin, "Security in the Southern Cone," 214–16.

32. Ibid., 217.

33. Mariano César Bartolomé, "La Triple Frontera: Principal foco de inseguridad en el Cono Sur Americano," *Military Review* 82, no. 4 (July–August 2002): 73.

34. Guerrero, *Triple Frontera*, 59–70.

35. Ibid., 79–93; and John Tofik Karam, "Atravesando las Américas: La 'guerra contra el terror,' los árabes y las movilizaciones transfronterizas en Foz do Iguacu y Ciudad del Este," in Giménez Béliveau and Montenegro, *La Triple Frontera*, 119.

36. Sverdlick, "Terrorists and Organized Crime," 90; and Golding, "Terrorism and the Triple Frontier," 4.

37. Guerrero, *Triple Frontera*, 66 and 99.

38. Umaña, *Threat Convergence*, 12; and Guerrero, *Triple Frontera*, 40.

39. Simon Romero, "Prosecutor in Argentina sees Iranian Plot in Latin America," *New York Times*, May 29, 2013, http://www.nytimes.com/2013/05/30/world/americas/prose cutor-in-argentina-says-iran-plotted-with-hezbollah-in-latin-america.html?smid=pl -share.

40. Costa and Schulmeister, "Puzzle of the Iguazu," 26–39.

41. Golding, "Terrorism and the Triple Frontier," 2; "US Embassy Cables: Brazil 'cov- ered up existence of terrorist suspects,'" *Guardian*, December 5, 2010, http://www.the guardian.com/world/us-embassy-cables-documents/228192.

42. Umaña, *Threat Convergence*, 13.

43. Giménez Béliveau, "Movilidades y escalas," 65–69.

44. Umaña, *Threat Convergence*, 15.

45. Umaña, *Threat Convergence*, 18; Hudson, "Terrorists and Organized Crime," 3–4; and Golding, "Terrorism and the Triple Frontier," 3.

Chapter Six

Rivalry, Trade, and Restraint on the Colombia-Venezuela Border

Harold A. Trinkunas

L atin American states have a long history of rivalry centered on disputes over territorial boundaries.[1] There is practically no state in the region that lacks such a dispute, and these have persisted in many cases since the nineteenth century, as illustrated by Cameron G. Thies (see chapter 2, in this volume). States have regularly militarized these disputes, but have also pursued international arbitration and judicialization of border disputes, as discussed by Kristina Mani (chapter 4) and Arturo C. Sotomayor (chapter 3).[2] Even as the region has become less prone to war over time, the rivalries persist.[3] As Thies observes, border rivalries can be used instrumentally by state elites to consolidate national identity and increase state resource extraction from their populations—essentially a substitute protection racket in Charles Tilly's bellicist tradition.[4]

However, not all states in the region have maintained their historic rivalries. Argentina-Chile and Peru-Ecuador bilateral relationships were once characterized by longstanding border disputes and conflicts, but more recently have been settled in favor of deepened economic ties.[5] In the 1990s, there was also hope that the Venezuela-Colombia relationship would follow the same pattern of attenuating interstate rivalry. Venezuela and Colombia have a history of tensions that dates back to their mutual independence from Gran Colombia in 1830. The 2,200-kilometer land border was the subject of dispute throughout most of their first centuries of existence as states, and the maritime border in the Gulf of Venezuela continues to be disputed today. The borderlands themselves are highly complex, containing both largely unpopulated regions of jungle, mountains, and deserts, but also one of South America's most populated border regions, the Cúcuta–San Cristóbal region with over 1.5 million residents.[6]

Venezuela and Colombia have experienced a remarkable upsurge of binational trade since 1990, which initially gave rise to the hope that their rivalry could be contained and reduced. The coincidence of neoliberal reform agendas in the two states during the early 1990s produced an opening of the border to economic activity, a reduction in tariffs, and an array of binational institutions to manage border tensions; this is similar to Arie M. Kacowicz's depiction of the Tri-Border Area in chapter 5. The result was a nearly 1,000 percent increase in bilateral trade flows between 1990 and 2008.[7]

The question this chapter considers is what led states to choose to reduce border rivalry and promote economic interdependence in the 1990s. Economic interdependence has long been theorized to reduce conflict between states, yet the fundamental mechanisms for how interdependence reduces conflict are still debated. There is support for the argument that both rivalry and interdependence produce benefits for states, yet interdependence appears to provide greater benefits to states in terms of access to material resources.[8] This in turn leads to a second question concerning why interdependence and cross-border trade deepened even during periods of rivalry. The case of Colombia and Venezuela is particularly useful for examining this question because we see variation in the degree of rivalry and the degree of interdependence across time. In fact, high levels of mutual hostility appear to coexist side by side at certain times with high levels of cross-border trade along the Colombian-Venezuelan border, which demonstrates that rivalry and interdependence can coexist under certain circumstances.

We have to look at two levels of analysis to explain variation in the degrees of interstate rivalry and economic interdependence across the Colombia-Venezuela border. On the one hand, in the 1990s, the structural and institutional shifts in the international system do not directly explain why these two states would be willing to engage in mutual economic opening. Rather, the election of neoliberal domestic political coalitions in Colombia and Venezuela during this period produced an opportunity to move rapidly toward mutual economic openness. On the other hand, international factors do help to explain the return of rivalry between the two states when we see a new partnership between the United States and Colombia, Venezuela's growing perception of the United States as a threat, and increasing rivalry between Colombia and Venezuela driven in part by this shift.

The election of President Hugo Chávez in Venezuela in 1999 and President Álvaro Uribe in 2003 in Colombia marked the beginning of a period of acute rivalry between the two states. However, what is paradoxical is that rivalry coincided with a dramatic expansion of trade between the countries. Each became more economically dependent on the other even as each perceived the other as a greater threat, which resulted in sanctions and militarization of their bilateral relationship. Here again, the domestic political economy in each country explains the expansion of economic interdependence in spite of threat perceptions. In Colombia, the coalition supporting President Uribe included significant elements of the business community that benefited from exports to Venezuela. In Venezuela, a massive increase in domestic consumption—fueled by booming oil revenues—created a demand for Colombian products. Moreover, President Chávez benefited politically since satisfying domestic demand for products with imports from Colombia deprived his domestic opposition in the manufacturing and agricultural sectors of income and business opportunities; that deprivation meant that his opponents had fewer funds with which to actively oppose him.

This chapter will first briefly consider the relationship between economic interdependence and interstate conflict, examining both international and domestic explanations. It will subsequently analyze the history of Colombian and Venezuelan conflict over their mutual border, establishing that there is a long term norm of rivalry between the states. The chapter will then examine the unusual period of liberalized economic exchange and reduction in conflict along the border during the 1990s. The chapter will conclude by analyzing the strategic implication for both states of greater economic interdependence during the 2000s, when political relations returned to their rivalrous norm while economic trade greatly expanded.

Economic Interdependence and Conflict

The debate over whether economic interdependence reduces or exacerbates conflict between states continues unabated. Scholars in the liberal tradition of international relations theory argue that economic interdependence among states reduces conflict by, among other arguments, raising the opportunity cost of war and otherwise altering incentive structures so as to increase the attractiveness of peace.[9] Realists have traditionally countered that interdependence increases the vulnerability of states and thus produces insecurity, leading to greater probability of conflict.[10] Other authors point out that while there is a statistically significant relationship between economic interdependence and reduced conflict, the actual mechanism by which this works needs to be more fully explained.[11] The question has been studied using a wide range of approaches, and while there is evidence that economic interdependence reduces the likelihood of war, this research agenda continues to engage numerous scholars and produce new, contradictory findings.[12]

In the Latin American region, we see relatively few wars, but persistent rivalry, which is defined as dyads with repeated instances of militarization of disputes across time. The inter-American system is made up of states that accept the norms associated with international law and territorial integrity, which in the Latin American case has been embodied in the legal doctrine of *uti possidetis juris*, the principle that post-independence boundaries should match those of the colonial period.[13] Nevertheless, rivalry persists because almost every state in the region has border disputes. Hence, states continue to engage in militarization over borders to try to achieve their foreign policy objectives, and these disputes persist over time.[14]

The question then becomes: By what mechanism does economic interdependence constrain rivalry or conflict? This question has already prompted a wide-ranging discussion among scholars, but it is basically framed around debates over domestic constituency preferences and how they shape or are shaped by institutions. In the realm of foreign policy decisions, the role of domestic institutions and constituency preferences becomes even more salient. Robert O. Keohane and Helen V. Milner argue that the preferences of domestic actors shape preferences over international policy and craft institutions that support these policies, although they leave some room for institutions to affect domestic preferences.[15] Thomas Risse-Kappe emphasizes that the combination of social structures, political institutions, and policy networks influence the formulation of international policies.[16] Robert Putnam proposes two-level games as a way of understanding how domestic politics influence foreign policy, but also how international politics affect and constrain domestic decision making.[17]

In Latin America, strong presidential systems prevail, and many presidents face relatively weak counterbalancing institutions, particularly in the area of foreign policy. This is true both in Colombia and Venezuela, where presidents have a wide latitude to determine foreign policy.[18] This should lead us to expect that domestic actor preferences should have greater explanatory power than domestic institutional arrangements. Mani, in chapter 4 of this volume, notes the importance of political parties and military actors in overcoming the Chile-Argentina rivalry. Looking at Latin America in general, David Mares argues that domestic constituencies matter for decisions about foreign policy. However, he makes a rational-choice argument that state leaders make cost-benefit decisions to escalate or de-escalate interstate rivalries, and one of the elements they consider is constituent preferences and costs. They weigh these as they consider a particular political-military strategy to achieve foreign policy objectives, as well as the strategic balance vis-á-vis their neighbors and the characteristics of the force they have available.[19] So Mares would see the decision to choose rivalry, particularly militarization of interstate disputes, or to settle disputes and deepen interdependence, as a rational decision made by state leaders balancing domestic and international costs and benefits.[20] An alternative explanation considers domestic political coalitions and their preferences for extracting resources from the international system or the domestic economy. Etel Solingen has argued that coalitions have an overall approach to governing that can be either internationalist or nationalist. Economic interdependence is only one aspect of an overall strategy pursued by internationalist coalitions to attract support and extract benefits from the international system. To achieve this, they will seek to reduce trade barriers, minimize conflicts, resolve border disputes, and reduce military spending. By contrast, nationalist or "backlash" coalitions will tend to adopt statist policies and barriers to trade, and are more prone to militarize disputes with neighbors.[21]

Finally, it is also possible subnational actors, particularly along the borders themselves, may influence moves toward cooperative rather than rivalrous relations between neighboring states. Alternative views are provided by scholars such as George Gavrilis, Maiah Jaskoski, and José Antonio Lucero, who examine the informal ways in which local actors evade or "unsettle" nationally imposed institutions along borders to make local gains in trade or security.[22] Nonstate actors have their own preferences for the degree of openness of borders, and their own local knowledge that helps them evade state rules and regulations. Ethnic minorities or indigenous populations may have their own preferences or conceptions of borders and statehood. Armed actors such as insurgents and bandits may try to impose their own "rules" when their presence is strong enough. In some cases, state actors may choose to cooperate across borders to manage the actions of nonstate actors, or they may choose to negotiate informal arrangements with local actors to facilitate the management of borders. These arrangements can be upset by interference from central governments, but they can also produce local conflicts along borders that can draw central governments into wider interstate conflicts. So the actions of nonstate actors on borders can cut both ways; they can either produce informal arrangements designed to pacify borders, or produce local conflicts that run counter to the interests of central governments.

Venezuelan-Colombian Border Conflict in Historical Perspective

Colombia and Venezuela have disputed their borders practically since they became independent from Gran Colombia in 1830. The separation of the two states was not militarily conflictive but left hard feelings on both sides of the border. The untimely demise of "The Liberator," Simón Bolívar, on Colombian soil has been the subject of conspiracy theories amongst his Venezuelan compatriots for two centuries, contributing to mutual suspicion. The land border was the subject of review for decades after Venezuela and Colombia requested arbitration by the Spanish monarchy in 1881. A treaty was finally signed in 1941 delimiting the land border, but Venezuelans have since come to view this arbitration award as unfair and their signature of the treaty as the product of national weakness. This has hardened feelings in Venezuela against further compromise over the still disputed maritime border in the north, even producing a civil-military crisis in otherwise democratic Venezuela in 1981.[23]

Along the perennially conflictive Venezuelan-Colombian border there are at least four distinct sectors, each with implications for mutual security and political economy. In the south, the border region runs through jungle terrain that is sparsely populated and largely uncontrolled by either state, which has made it perfect for sheltering the activities of insurgents and narcotics traffickers. In the center, the Andean mountain range divides the two states, but there is a definite center of gravity for border flows in the Cúcuta–San Cristóbal metropolitan area. Although densely populated, these border cities are remote from the heart of power in both states. San Cristóbal is cut off from the rest of Venezuela by the Andes, and Cúcuta lies on the other side of several mountain ranges that bisect Colombia on the north-south axis. In the north, the Venezuelan-Colombian border cuts through an important oil production region, the heartland of Venezuela's most historically important petroleum fields. In the far north, the two states continue to disagree over the ownership of what are little more than rocks in the middle of the Gulf of Venezuela, the site of potential new oil fields.[24]

Even though the border looms large in the strategic imagination of each state, they exercise little real control outside of the Cúcuta–San Cristóbal urban area.

The lack of state control over most of the Venezuelan-Colombia border has made it ripe for cross-border contraband, migration, and insurgency. Historically, this was not just due to narcotics production and trafficking. Cattle smuggling between the countries is a long-standing tradition. In more recent decades, the growing statism of Venezuela's political economy, particularly price controls on coffee production and subsidies for food and petroleum products, have contributed to cross-border smuggling. For example, a recent comparison of gasoline prices shows a liter costing prices comparable to those in the developed world in Colombia, and pennies in Venezuela.[25] This price imbalance has deepened during the past decade, with inhabitants of the borderlands purchasing discounted goods in Venezuela and smuggling them for resale to Colombia.

Narcotics trafficking and its relationship to insurgency produced a shift in thinking in both Colombia and Venezuela from viewing the border as a problem of demarcation between states to the site of highly remunerative but illicit economic activities that support violent nonstate actors. The mix of insurgents and drug trafficking first prompted securitization of the border during the 1980s. This followed major drug seizures that demonstrated Venezuela was becoming a transit country for cocaine and marijuana. In Colombia, Ejército de Liberación Nacional (ELN) and Fuerzas Armadas Revolucionarias de Colombia (FARC) insurgents participated in protection rackets, which in the case of the FARC brought them into close contact with the Colombian narcotics industry and helped fund their activities. The protection racket extended to the Venezuelan side of the border, where cattle ranchers were kidnapped for ransom and intimidated to ensure free passage of illicit border actors. Insurgent attacks on Venezuelan military units engaged in counternarcotic operations further sharpened the sense that the border was out of control. Growing organized crime activities and narcotics use in Venezuela were blamed in the popular press on Colombia, and these became conflated with the largely peaceful if illicit stream of Colombian economic migrants into Venezuela. These activities combined to generate a sense within Venezuela that the border violence was a Colombian problem that Venezuela was trying to combat alone.[26]

The Colombian and Venezuelan militaries have historically considered themselves peer rivals, and a great deal of their mutual hostility has focused on defending the border. During the 1980s, this sense of rivalry deepened while being shaped by two incidents. The first occurred when the 1987 incursion of the Colombian navy corvette *Caldas* into waters claimed by Venezuela reaffirmed for the Venezuelan armed forces that the border with Colombia remained a military issue; deficiencies revealed during the mobilization prompted a Venezuelan arms purchasing spree and a greater focus on the Colombian border.[27]

The second incident, the massacre of fourteen Colombians in October 1988 on the border at El Amparo, further shifted the management of the border in the direction of the military. A Venezuelan joint police-military counterinsurgency unit conducted the killings.[28] Survivors denounced the killings as an unprovoked massacre, and the Inter-American Court of Human Rights ordered the Venezuelan government to make reparations in 1996. The Venezuelan military attributed blame for the outcome to the police, and the government appeared to agree when it shifted its strategy for border control with the creation of two primarily military theaters of operation (*teatro de operaciones* or TO) on the border; these included TO-1 in Apure state and TO-2 in Táchira state. This resulted in two important Venezuelan military garrisons on the border concerned with the operations of illicit actors.[29] However, especially in TO-1, the Venezuelan military lacked counterparts on the Colombian side with which they could collaborate to control the border, so the sense of Colombia as hostile territory deepened.

Economic Liberalization and the Expansion of Colombian-Venezuelan Licit Trade

In parallel with militarization of the border, Colombia and Venezuela engaged in an unprecedented experiment in fostering free trade during the 1990s. Traditionally, Colombia has had more limited state control that allowed more latitude to private actors. Venezuela, on the other hand, had developed a much more statist economy as a result of the windfall of oil revenue, particularly during the energy crises of the 1970s. In what is now a familiar story, government expenditures based on boom time estimates quickly outstripped revenues during the decline in oil prices of the 1980s. This was compounded by the Latin American debt crisis of the 1980s, when rising interest rates in the United States drove governments across the region to nearly default on their international debt.

In 1989, a new Venezuelan government was prepared to gamble on neoliberal economic reforms, and in the area of international trade, it found like-minded partners in Colombia and Mexico. Known as the G-3, this group of states agreed to establish a common tariff, liberalize trade, reduce barriers, and otherwise promote cross-border economic integration. The Colombia-Venezuela part of the G-3 was the most dynamic. Colombia traded an increasing percentage of its manufactured goods in return for Venezuelan petroleum and agricultural products. As a reflection of their desire to protect the new trade agreement from traditional border disputes, President Carlos Andrés Pérez of Venezuela and Colombian President Virgilio Barco created the Comisión de Integración y Asuntos Fronterizos in 1990 to resolve border issues at the highest levels.[30]

Although the neoliberal experiment came to a grinding halt in Venezuela in 1993 with the impeachment of President Carlos Andrés Pérez, the liberalization of Colombian-Venezuelan trade continued apace. Realizing that border friction could affect trade, the two countries created the COMBIFRON (Comisión Militar Binacional de Fronteras) in 1994, which acted as a civil-military talking shop and shock absorber for addressing the political consequences of ongoing violence and illicit activities at the border.

Trade liberalized apace during the 1990s and 2000s, growing from a combined amount of US$570 million in 1990 to over US$7 billion in 2008. During the 1990s, Colombia established itself as the most important South American trading partner for Venezuela, and bilateral trade grew to US$2.5 billion in 2000. Moreover, rapid growth in oil prices after 2000 led to the growth in imports to Venezuela by nearly 300 percent to over US$48 billion by 2008, most of it driven by consumption spending. It also led to the growth in Colombian exports to Venezuela to over US$5 billion (of US$7 billion total), and cattle and textile exports from Colombia were the bulk of the trade. Free trade greatly benefited the Colombian side of the equation in terms of exports, but given Venezuela's increasingly state-led economy during the 2000s, this also proved beneficial to the Chávez administration.[31]

Tension and Cooperation at the Border during the Uribe and Chávez Administrations

The tension between security interests and economic interests at the border came to a head during the Uribe (2003–2010) and Chávez (1999–2013) administrations due to profound disagreements between the two leaders on ideology, foreign policy, and domestic policy. Chávez advocated for a leftist populist model of politics at home and an anti-US foreign policy abroad. Uribe, on the other hand, was elected on a platform of taking the war to leftist insurgents at home with the help of extensive US military and security assistance; he also advocated for free trade, particularly with the United States. The two presidents could not have had more fundamentally opposed programs.

Following his election in 1998, President Chávez pursued an increasingly radical agenda at home and abroad. In domestic politics, he came to pursue what he called "twenty-first-century socialism," a policy of increasing state ownership of the means of production. Abroad, he identified the United States as the main threat to his Bolivarian Revolution, and he advocated for a multipolar world where US power was constrained. In Latin America, he supported diplomatically, politically, and materially the election of like-minded leftist political leaders.[32] He justified massive arms purchases, mostly from Russia, on the basis of an existential threat from the United States. In Colombia, he sympathized with the FARC, and according to some sources, this sympathy translated into economic and military support, with Venezuela becoming a "rear area" for the FARC leadership.[33] As early as 2000, Chávez declared Venezuela's neutrality in the conflict between the state and the FARC in Colombia, and in 2008, he advocated for international recognition of the FARC as a cobelligerent with the Colombian state. He also greatly criticized Colombia's elites, calling them a "rancid oligarchy," and he attacked Uribe's closeness to the United States, denouncing the establishment of US military forward operating locations. Chávez also withdrew Venezuela from membership in the Andean Community (a preferential trade treaty) after Colombia and the United States negotiated a free trade deal.

Álvaro Uribe was elected on a domestic platform of winning the war against Colombia's insurgency. He pursued a policy of greater closeness to the United States for the purposes of building up Colombia's military and economy. His counterinsurgency plan, known as the "Democratic Security," was designed to reestablish state presence in the 50 percent of Colombian territory where the state was absent and armed nonstate actors were present. It was also focused on taking the war to the FARC and ELN insurgents and demobilizing other violent nonstate actors, such as right-wing paramilitary forces. With a great deal of assistance from the United States, Colombia's military built up its capabilities during this period, increasing mobility and improving its use of intelligence. In politics, Uribe was considerably more conservative than his Venezuelan counterpart, pushing back against Chávez's agenda for a Latin American political bloc free from US influence.[34]

Colombian-Venezuelan diplomatic relations soured even as cross-border trade boomed. The countries downgraded their diplomatic relations at least once per year between 2005 and 2010, often in relation to the Colombian government's efforts against the FARC insurgency. The most serious moment occurred on March 1, 2008, when Colombian aircraft attacked an insurgent encampment of the FARC located within the border territory of Ecuador, killing senior FARC leaders. Colombian military and police forces helicoptered into Ecuadorian territory to complete the attack and gather intelligence information. President Uribe of Colombia only notified his Ecuadorean counterpart Rafael Correa after the raid had been completed, provoking outrage in Ecuador over the violation of its sovereignty and leading to a break in diplomatic relations. Venezuelan President Chávez, politically aligned with Rafael Correa, reacted by ordering a military mobilization to the Colombia-Venezuela border and breaking diplomatic relations with Colombia. To the relief of many in the region, a meeting of Latin American presidents in Santo Domingo under the auspices of the Group of Rio produced a handshake between Presidents Uribe and Chávez and the de-escalation of military tensions at the border eight days later.[35]

Although the crisis was resolved, repercussions from the attack continued. In 2009, Venezuela froze its trade with Colombia after President Uribe accused Chávez of supplying the FARC with weapons on the basis of those found during the 2008 attack in Ecuador; those weapons had been first sold to Venezuela from Sweden during the 1990s. This trade freeze led to a sharp drop in Colombian exports to Venezuela to less than US$1.5 billion, and Venezuela froze US$600 million in loan payments to Colombian businesses.[36] This in turn led to considerable disruption in Venezuelan trade in food and basic consumer goods, especially since these now had to travel through the highly congested Venezuelan ports rather than over the land border with Colombia.[37]

While from the 1990s to the present we have seen positive economic relations despite international tensions over border security questions—the central focus and puzzle in this chapter—for a brief moment economic relations did decline in the late 2000s. It was only with the election of Colombian President Juan Manuel Santos in 2011 that relations became less conflictive. President Santos, who had been a hard-line minister of defense under Uribe, completely reversed the course of Colombian-Venezuelan relations upon taking office. Trade resumed to levels approaching those that preceded the Venezuelan embargo, and President Chávez assumed a more cooperative stance vis-à-vis Colombia and the control of border violence. President Santos also pursued a negotiated peace with FARC insurgents, even seeking the assistance of Cuba and Venezuela in producing an agreement.[38] The two countries have renegotiated a trade integration agreement after a meeting between Presidents Santos and Chávez in November 2011, leading to the possibility that tariffs will be reduced to zero on over 3,800 tradable goods.[39]

From Interdependence to Rivalry (and Back Again?)

Security concerns along the binational border are constant in Venezuela-Colombia relations, and the border lies at the root of their mutual rivalry. The border crosses difficult terrain and, with the exception of Venezuela's Táchira state, is an obstacle to easy travel or trade. The armed forces of each state, based on their doctrines and war plans, consider the other their most likely adversary in an interstate dispute (although President Chávez believed that the United States was a more likely threat).[40] Armed nonstate actors on both sides of the border who periodically engage in combat with security forces, provide a number of pretexts for escalation. As already mentioned, a rivalrous relationship has existed between the two states since their independence from Gran Colombia, and this rivalry occasionally flares into militarization, although never war.

Given this record, it was the shift toward economic interdependence and more open borders during the 1990s that is anomalous and requires explanation. Although this was a momentous period in international relations due to the collapse of the Soviet Union, there were no specific changes in the subregional balance of power between Colombia and Venezuela during the 1990s that would lead us to expect both countries felt less vulnerable and more amenable to interdependent economic relations. The militarization of the binational maritime border dispute in 1987 would suggest the opposite—that both countries had reasons to continue in a state of mutual suspicion. In fact, in 1988 and 1989, Venezuela increased military acquisitions. There were also no major changes in the international institutions or alliance structures that both countries were part of that would lead us to expect they would feel more secure and able to pursue interdependence. This suggests that we should look to changes in the domestic politics of each country for an explanation for the improved interdependence.

There are two domestic political explanations for growing interdependence; one is based on domestic realpolitik and the other on the ideology of governing coalitions. Mares would argue that the decision to choose cooperation over rivalry in the early 1990s was a response to the relative costs of the two when considered in balance with the other relevant factors, such as the strategic balance and constituency costs. In both countries, by the late 1980s and early 1990s, traditional economic models were no longer working, particularly in Venezuela. In essence, liberalization of trade with Colombia was part of an overall Venezuelan strategy to break from its statist developmental model, and Colombia offered a market for products that was close at hand, with conditions that were more favorable for

Venezuelan producers than the possible alternatives. Moreover, continued militarization, and in particular the arms acquisitions program Venezuela pursued after the 1987 border incident with Colombia, was simply economically untenable. Existing signed contracts with international suppliers were a heavy burden on the Venezuelan defense budget at a time when the currency had devaluated and inflation jumped in response to the liberalization program.[41]

From the Colombian perspective, economic liberalization was already on the agenda as part of the political program of the outgoing Barco administration in 1989 and of the incoming César Gaviria administration, elected in 1990. These liberalization plans were part of an overall reform effort that was aimed at addressing major domestic social conflict and that included drafting a new constitution. Greater integration with Venezuela was consistent with this reform program. Most Colombian interest groups favored international trade liberalization, with the exception of the weak labor movement. While the manufacturing and agricultural production sectors were opposed to trade liberalization in general, they actually benefited in particular from improved access to the Venezuelan market where they were more competitive.[42] On the other hand, the alternative strategy for addressing border issues—continued militarization—had already proven to not accomplish Colombia's goals, as during the 1987 border crisis with Venezuela. In the context of the serious domestic social crisis faced by the Gaviria administration due to conflict with major drug trafficking cartels, continued confrontation with Venezuela was a needless distraction.

Solingen's insights into the interaction effects of internationalist coalitions in domestic politics would also predict economic liberalization between the two countries.[43] In the early 1990s, internationalist domestic coalitions came to power in both Venezuela and Colombia, and under these conditions, governments in both states would be expected to emphasize trade and economic interdependence, de-emphasize military spending, and minimize sources of conflict. The reduction of tariffs and other measures to liberalize mutual trade were legislated and put into place in both countries during this period. In addition, the 1990s were a period of reduced military spending in both states. The creation of bilateral institutions, such as the COMBIFRON, by Colombia and Venezuela suggests that both governments sought mechanisms to reduce conflict so as to avoid derailing mutual benefits from trade. These are all consistent with the argument that internationalist coalitions will engage in a range of signals and policies that are designed to minimize the likelihood of conflict and maximize economic engagement with the international system.

The period of the Chávez administration in Venezuela (1999–2013) and the Uribe administration in Colombia (2003–2010) was marked by high levels of political tension and conflict between the two states, yet it was also marked by a boom in cross-border trade, briefly interrupted at the peak moment of tensions. Changes in the international system during this period would help to explain the increasing level of rivalry that we observe. One consequence of the terrorist attacks on the United States on September 11, 2001, was the development of a deeper security partnership between the United States and Colombia. Following these terrorist attacks, most restrictions on Colombian use of US-provided military equipment—initially targeted for counternarcotics operations—were removed. In fact, US support to the Colombian armed forces, already higher as a result of Plan Colombia instituted in the late 1990s, increased during the George W. Bush administration. This caused consternation to President Chávez and in the Venezuelan armed forces.

Paradoxically, even as rivalry returned, both states experienced a rapid increase in economic interdependence. This is not consistent with either liberal or realist expectations of the effects of shifts in the balance of power or alliances in the international systems; nor is increased rivalry an expectation of a period of growing economic interdependence. To explain the simultaneous increases in rivalry and interdependence, we need to again turn to a domestic politics explanation. Essentially, the institutions put in place during the 1990s between Venezuelan and Colombia favored bilateral free trade, and while they were not heavily used during the years that followed, these agreements lay the groundwork for an expansion of Colombian exports to Venezuela. What drove the increase in interdependence was the boom in consumer consumption in Venezuela as a consequence of high levels of oil income and aggressive efforts by the Venezuelan government to distribute this income and support consumption. Colombia was simply a readily available source of important consumer goods, particularly food and textiles, which could be imported under favorable conditions due to the reforms undertaken in the early 1990s.

From a domestic politics perspective, it makes sense that both leaders would allow economic interdependence to increase in spite of their rivalrous behavior. There are important domestic constituencies in Colombia that profit greatly from cross-border trade in licit and illicit products. The Colombian business community was a key element of the coalition for both the Uribe and Santos administrations in Colombia during the 2000s. Sustaining increased trade with Venezuela was an important payoff to a domestic constituent. Moreover, Venezuela's economic strategy under Chávez undermined domestic sources of production in preference for imports paid for with oil revenues. Colombian exporters stood ready to fill the gap, aided by the preexisting institutions that favored liberalized binational trade. In this way, Hugo Chávez could fulfill his promises of increased consumption opportunities for his supporters without benefiting his political adversaries in the Venezuelan business community and middle class.

Economic interdependence is somewhat asymmetrical in that the Colombia-Venezuela trade balance favors Colombia. Venezuela needs Colombia's electricity, natural gas, food, and goods, especially in the more remote border areas. However, Colombia's exports to Venezuela are an order of magnitude greater than those flowing in the other direction, which makes the Colombian business community particularly vulnerable to threats of border closure. Nevertheless, the asymmetry in trade between the two countries proved to be a weaker lever than Hugo Chávez had hoped. He attempted to use the asymmetric nature of the economic relationship with Colombia to his advantage during moments of acute rivalry, such as the Colombian attack on the FARC encampment in Ecuador in 2008 and the conflict over US basing rights in Colombia in 2010, but was less successful than he had hoped. Chávez found that following the 2010 freeze of economic relations, Colombia was able to divert some exports once destined for Venezuela to new markets, so the blow was not as telling on his adversary as he had hoped. In contrast, Venezuela had to seek alternatives for its imports from other suppliers, mainly Argentina, that were more costly and placed further stress on its overloaded maritime ports. So the outcome was suboptimal for both sides economically and did not appear to confer overwhelming advantage to Venezuela. The speed with which both trade and negotiations on an even more liberalized trade regime resumed in 2011 indicates that the Venezuelan and Colombian governments both had a preference and an expectation that mutual economic liberalization and trade were a preferable outcome.[44]

The ideological rift between internationalist and backlash coalitions fits the atmospherics of the Chávez-Uribe relationship, but does not provide much additional explanatory power over rational choice explanations. Hugo Chávez came to power in 1999, and he represented a classic backlash coalition of elements in the state and society that feared the effects of globalization and liberalization and favored state entrepreneurship and expanded military spending.[45] We see this in Venezuela's domestic policies that favored a growing state role in society through military civic action programs, the social welfare *misiones*, and greatly expanded military spending.[46] We also see this in Venezuela's international politics, which favored regional ties to other states controlled by backlash coalitions, including Nicaragua, Cuba, Ecuador, and Argentina. On the other hand, Colombia's administration under Álvaro Uribe more closely resembled an internationalist coalition in that it privileged exports and favored free trade with the United States, although it did not follow a pure internationalist strategy because it also expanded military spending to combat domestic insurgents. Colombia also tied its foreign policy closely to the United States, which also favored internationalist coalitions in the region, strengthening the case for thinking of the Uribe, and later Santos, administrations as basically internationalist in character.

The combination of backlash and internationalist coalitions produced a zone of restrained conflict between Venezuela and Colombia. In a zone of restrained conflict, the opportunity for conflict remains but is constrained by the gains already made from trade. Both internationalist and backlash coalitions have incentives to strengthen like-minded political allies across the region, much as occurred in the case of Venezuela (successfully) and Colombia (less so). This scenario produces restraint because there are gains from trade that governing coalitions need to weigh against the costs of conflict. It is more difficult to interpret the Venezuelan and Colombian governments' decisions to allow economic interdependence to strengthen after 2010, even after outbursts of highly rivalrous behavior, including military mobilization and economic sanctions.[47]

Ultimately, explanations centered on rational choice and domestic political economy are sufficient to explain the course of Venezuelan-Colombian rivalry and interdependence. However, it is worth noting that even local border and non-state actors contribute toward a preference for higher levels of cross-border trade and more border openness throughout this period. Colombian narcotics traffickers use Venezuela as an important transshipment route for their products toward the United States and Europe.[48] There are also important levels of gasoline smuggling from Venezuela, where it is highly subsidized, to Colombia, where consumers pay market prices. This is an activity in which numerous local actors are complicit, including local military garrisons and border community inhabitants. Venezuela's subsidies for a wide range of consumer products contribute to smuggling of other items, such as coffee, cooking oil, and food staples, on a smaller scale. As Venezuela entered a severe economic crisis in 2013, the new Nicolás Maduro administration made recurrent attempts to cut down on smuggling by periodically closing the Colombia-Venezuela border and introducing rationing in border communities.

The large volume of cross-border trade produces a constituency of licit and illicit actors that favor open over closed borders, normal diplomatic relations over no relations, and lower levels of militarization over higher levels. High volumes of trade benefit legal businesses and provide cover for illicit trafficking and smuggling. Given the volume of money that is laundered from illicit to licit businesses in Colombia, it is reasonable to believe (although extraordinarily difficult, if not impossible, to prove) that an underground illicit constituency also favors an internationalist strategy and has a number of mechanisms with which to influence legitimate politics in Colombia in favor of open borders. On the Venezuela side of the border, Javier Corrales and Carlos Romero suggest that the armed forces, an important member of Chávez's coalition, may have favored continuing bilateral trade during the 2000s.[49] In addition, the militarization of border security in the 1980s on the Venezuelan side put important military garrisons in charge of controlling border flows. Given the statist and increasingly authoritarian nature of the Venezuelan regime, the armed forces became important actors in providing governance. As a result of the combination of a boom in economic interdependence between Venezuela and Colombia and the progressive militarization of controls on the Venezuelan side of the border, Corrales and Romero argue that military officials have become much more involved in extracting rents from licit and illicit cross-border trade. This trade therefore is an important part of the political economy of Venezuelan civil-military relations. Yet the bottom line is that the kinds of effects that border actors might have on decisions regarding rivalry or interdependence along the Colombian-Venezuela border tend to favor openness and trade rather than hard boundaries and conflict.

Conclusions

Colombia and Venezuela have a long history of rivalry, yet the growth in economic interdependence that began in the 1990s and accelerated in the 2000s requires explanation. What is even more puzzling is that both interdependence and rivalry increased apace during the 2000s, contra the predictions of classic theories of international relations. Therefore, this chapter has examined explanations based on domestic politics to explain growing interdependence.

The election of two liberalizing administrations in Venezuela and Colombia in 1988 and 1990 set the stage for greater interdependence between the two states. Both had protected markets and domestic actors that would be hurt by greater competition unless the opportunity existed to participate in a binational free trade area. Institutions associated with bilateral economic and border relations developed during the early 1990s, and even though liberalization programs were not pursued for very long in either case, they persisted beyond the governments that created them, and then made the growth of mutual trade in the 2000s possible.

Rivalry returned in the 2000s, in part as a consequence of the growing closeness between the Uribe and Bush administrations, and their increasing distance from the Chávez administration. In this context, decisions to engage in self-help by improving military capabilities and seeking new allies fit standard accounts of how states balance potential adversaries. What does not fit is the increasing trade between the two rivals. Here, domestic politics comes to the forefront. In Colombia, important domestic coalition members in the Uribe administration benefited greatly from trade with Venezuela and preferred to avoid conflict. In Venezuela, trade with Colombia allowed the Chávez administration to satisfy growing domestic consumption without benefiting its domestic adversaries.

While rivalry and economic interdependence would appear to be mutually exclusive, their coexistence makes sense in the context of how Presidents Uribe and Chávez managed border relations and state-to-state relations. Both sides experienced costs from allowing rivalry to become too great, either in the form of militarization or economic sanctions. Instead, the Santos and Chávez administrations moved decisively toward liberalizing mutual trade, while the Santos administration pursued peace talks with the FARC insurgents—to whom Chávez and Maduro were and are ideologically sympathetic—and a shift back to less rivalrous relations then took place.

The two countries are more or less constantly at risk for conflict in the security domain due to the large number of armed illicit actors operating along the border, and a history of mutual suspicion and hostility over border issues. This is a recipe for complex binational relations that require a great deal of high-level management to resolve; Santos and Chávez appeared willing to pursue this, particularly through negotiating a peace settlement with the FARC, a major violent nonstate actor with a significant border presence. The relations of a post-Chávez Venezuela toward Colombia remain complicated. There have been episodes that appear rivalrous, as with the Venezuelan government's strident protests of an opposition leader's meeting with Colombian President Santos.[50] And yet, as Venezuela's economic crisis grew worse in 2013, the Santos administration threw President Maduro a lifeline, agreeing to finance (through Colombian government agencies) the export of over US$600 million in food and other consumer goods to Venezuela.[51] Because of the mutual economic dependence the states have developed, both sides have tools short of war with which to influence each other and they both have an interest in the persistence of trade, which will continue to weigh on impulses to remilitarize relations between the states.

NOTES

1. Diehl and Goertz define rivalry by the regular militarization of an interstate relationship over time; Paul Francis Diehl and Gary Goertz, *War and Peace in International Rivalry* (Ann Arbor, MI: University of Michigan Press, 2001).

2. See also Jorge I. Domínguez, "Boundary Disputes in Latin America," *Peaceworks* 50 (Washington, DC: US Institute of Peace, 2009); and Arturo C. Sotomayor, "Foros a la carta o difusión de políticas," *Pensamiento Propio* 14, no. 29 (January–June 2009): 127–52.

3. David Mares, *Latin America and the Illusion of Peace*, Adelphi Series 52, no. 429 (London, UK: International Institute for Strategic Studies, May 2012).

4. Cameron G. Thies, "War, Rivalry, and State Building in Latin America," *American Journal of Political Science* 49, no. 3 (2005): 451–65.

5. Mares, *Latin America*, 181.

6. Lucrecia M. Morales and Juan C. Morales, "Vecindad, integración y desarollo: Referencia a la frontera Colombo-Venezolana al 2006," *Aldea Mundo* 12, no. 24 (November 2007–April 2008): 65–78.

7. María del Pilar Esguerra Umaña, Enrique Montes Uribe, Aarón Gavarito Acosta, Carolina Pulido González, "El comercio Colombo-Venezolano: Características y evolución reciente," *Apuntes del CENES* 24, no. 49 (June 2010): 123–62.

8. Cameron G. Thies, "State Building in Latin America: How Borders Have Shaped National Identity, State Capacity and Regional Peace and Security," paper prepared for the ISA Workshop on "Hot, Cold and Cool Borders in the Americas: Politics of Cooperation and Conflict in Frontiers," San Francisco, CA, April 2, 2013.

9. For a recent paper in a series supporting the link between economic interdependence and peace, see Håvard Hegre, John R. Oneal, and Bruce Russett, "Trade Does Promote Peace: New Simultaneous Estimates of the Reciprocal Effects of Trade and Conflict," *Journal of Peace Research* 47, no. 6 (2010): 763–74.

10. Katherine Barbieri, "Economic Interdependence: A Path to Peace or a Source of Interstate Conflict?" *Journal of Peace Research* 33, no. 1 (1996): 29–49; and Philippe Martin, Thierry Mayer, and Mathias Thoenig, "Make Trade Not War?" *Review of Economic Studies* 75, no. 3 (2008): 865–900.

11. Omar M. G. Keshk, Brian M. Pollins, and Rafael Reuveny, "Trade Still Follows the Flag: The Primacy of Politics in a Simultaneous Model of Interdependence and Armed Conflict," *Journal of Politics* 66, no. 4 (2004): 1155–79.

12. Brandon J. Kinne, "Multilateral Trade and Militarized Conflict: Centrality, Openness, and Asymmetry in the Global Trade Network," *Journal of Politics* 74, no. 1 (2012): 308–22.

13. Mark W. Zacher, "The Territorial Integrity Norm: International Boundaries and the Use of Force," *International Organization* 55, no. 2 (2001): 215–50.

14. Domínguez, "Boundary Disputes."

15. Helen V. Milner and Robert O. Keohane, "Internationalization and Domestic Politics: An Introduction," in *Internationalization and Domestic Politics*, ed. Robert O. Keohane and Helen V. Milner (Cambridge, UK: Cambridge University Press, 1996), 3–24.

16. Thomas Risse-Kappe, "Public Opinion, Domestic Structure, and Foreign Policy in Liberal Democracies," *World Politics* 43, no. 4 (July 1991): 479–512.

17. Robert D. Putnam, "Diplomacy and Domestic Politics: The Logic of Two-Level Games," *International Organization* 42, no. 3 (1988): 427–60.

18. Elsa Cardozo da Silva and Richard S. Hillman, "Venezuela: Petroleum, Democratization and International Affairs," and Arlene B. Tickner, "Colombia: US Subordinate, Autonomous Actor or Something In Between?" both in *Latin American and Caribbean Foreign Policy*, ed. Frank O. Mora and Jeanne K. Hey (New York, NY: Rowman and Littlefield, 2003).

19. David Mares, "Illusion of Peace," 65–66; and Mares, *Violent Peace: Militarized Interstate Bargaining in Latin America* (New York, NY: Columbia University Press, 2001).

20. David R. Mares, "The Challenge of Promoting Cooperation While Defending Sovereignty," in *Routledge Handbook of Latin American Politics*, ed. Peter Kingstone and Deborah J. Yashar (New York, NY: Routledge, 2013), 348–63.

21. Etel Solingen, "Mapping Internationalization: Domestic and Regional Impacts," *International Studies Quarterly* 45, no. 4 (2001): 517–55.

22. George Gavrilis, *The Dynamics of Interstate Boundaries* (Cambridge, UK: Cambridge University Press, 2008); Maiah Jaskoski, "Militaries and Borders: The Ecuadorian Case," paper presented at workshop on "Borders and Borderlands in the Americas," Stanford University, Palo Alto, CA, June 18–19, 2012; and José Antonio Lucero, "States and Identities in the Amazonian/Andean Borderlands," paper presented at workshop on "Borders and Borderlands in the Americas," Stanford University, Palo Alto, CA, June 18–19, 2012.

23. John D. Martz, "National Security and Politics: The Colombian-Venezuelan Border," *Journal of Interamerican Studies and World Affairs* 30, no. 4 (winter 1988): 119–20.

24. Morales and Morales, "Vecindad, integración y desarollo."

25. "Pick Your Poison," *The Economist* 403, no. 8782, April 28, 2012, 42, http://www.economist.com/node/21553509.

26. Martz, "Colombian-Venezuelan Border," 127–33.

27. Ibid., 117–38.

28. Amnesty International, "Venezuela: El Amparo Massacre," Index number: AMR 53/05/93, April 1993, https://www.amnesty.org/en/documents/amr53/005/1993/en/.

29. Harold A. Trinkunas, *Crafting Civilian Control of the Military in Venezuela: A Comparative Perspective* (Chapel Hill, NC: The University of North Carolina Press, 2005).

30. María Teresa Belandra, "Venezuela y Colombia. Avances y retrocesos en su relación. Impacto en América Latina," *Mundo Nuevo* 2, no. 7 (2011): 79–100.

31. Esguerra Umaña, Montes Uribe, Gavarito Acosta, and Pulido González, "El comercio Colombo-Venezolano."

32. Harold A. Trinkunas, "The Logic of Venezuelan Foreign Policy during the Chávez Period," in *Venezuela's Petro Diplomacy: Hugo Chávez's Foreign Policy*, ed. Ralph Clem and Anthony Maingot (Gainesville, FL: The University Press of Florida, 2011), 16–31.

33. *The FARC Files: Venezuela, Ecuador and the Secret Archive of "Raúl Reyes"* (London, UK: International Institute for Strategic Studies, 2011).

34. Peter DeShazo, Tanya Primiani, and Phil McLean, *Back from the Brink: Evaluating Colombia's Progress 1999–2007* (Washington, DC: Center for Strategic and International Studies, November 2007).

35. Mares, "Illusion of Peace," 94–107; and Belandra, "Venezuela y Colombia," 79–100.

36. "Politics vs. Trade," *The Economist*, 10 September 2009, http://www.economist .com/node/14416724; and Mark Weisbrot and Jake Johnston, *The Gains from Trade: South American Economic Integration and the Resolution of Conflict* (Washington, DC: Center for Economic Policy and Research, November 2010).

37. "Canceling Christmas," *The Economist*, 1 December 2012, http://www.economist .com/news/americas/21567381-inefficiency-promoting-autarky-perhaps-design-cancelling -christmas.

38. Kyle Johnson and Michael Jonsson, "Colombia: Ending the Forever War?" *Survival* 55, no.1 (2013): 87–102.

39. Robert Valencia, "State of Affairs: The Nascent Venezuelan-Colombian Rela-tions," Council on Hemispheric Affairs, 11 July 2011, http://www.coha.org/state-of-affairs -the-nascent-colombian-venezuelan-relations/.

40. Omar Piña, "Plan Colombia: How US Military Assistance Affects Regional Bal-ances of Power," master's thesis, Naval Postgraduate School, June 2004.

41. Trinkunas, *Crafting Civilian Control*, 170–79.

42. Sebastián Edwards and Roberto Steiner, "On the Crisis Hypothesis of Economic Reform, Colombia 1989–91," *Cuadernos de Economía* 37, no. 112 (2000): 445–93.

43. Solingen, "Mapping Internationalization," 522–25.

44. Weisbrot and Johnston, "Gains from Trade," 6–7.

45. Solingen, "Mapping Internationalization," 526.

46. Javier Corrales and Michael Penfold, *Dragon in the Tropics: Hugo Chávez and the Political Economy of Revolution in Venezuela* (Washington, DC: Brookings Institution Press, 2011).

47. Corrales and Penfold, *Dragon in the Tropics*.

48. John Otis, *The FARC and Colombia's Illegal Drug Trade* (Washington, DC: The Wil-son Center, November 2014); and "Smuggling in Venezuela: The Wild Frontier," *Econo-mist* (UK), August 16, 2014, http://www.economist.com/news/americas/21612186-border -colombia-closed-crackdown-contraband-wild-frontier.

49. Javier Corrales and Carlos Romero, *Relations between the United States and Vene-zuela, 2001–2009: A Bridge in Need of Repairs* (New York, NY: Routledge, 2010).

50. "La relación de Venezuela y Colombia, en vilo por la visita de Capriles," Reuters España, May 31, 2013, http://es.reuters.com/article/topNews/idESMAE94T00H20130530.

51. Mery Mogollon and Chris Kraul, "Venezuelan Food Supply Getting Huge Boost with Colombian Exports," *Los Angeles Times*, September 13, 2013, http://www.latimes.com /world/la-fg-venezuela-woes-20130914,0,2812220.story.

Northbound "Threats" at the United States–Mexico Border

What Is Crossing Today, and Why?

Adam Isacson

The past twenty years have witnessed a historic buildup of the US government's security force presence along the common border with Mexico. The result has been the construction of a complicated, expensive arrangement of law enforcement, military, and intelligence agencies with overlapping responsibilities and inadequate coordination.

The buildup sought to address four types of perceived "threats" crossing the border from Mexico. These were (1) terrorism, (2) "spillover violence," (3) undocumented migrants, and (4) illegal drugs. In the past decade, the border has seen no incidences of terrorist activity, a remarkable lack of spillover violence, a sharp drop in migration, but a sharp increase in drug seizures.

The United States–Mexico border, then, is quite secure. The trends in the four types of threat phenomena, however, tell us that the US border buildup—while a key factor—gets only some of the credit. It likely has no more explanatory weight than variables inside Mexico, including relative economic growth, demographic changes, and organized crime control of border territories.

Because the recent border security "success" owes so much to reasons other than public policy, there is little sense in US political debates that the border security problem has been definitively "solved," or that current government efforts are enough to prevent a recurrence of insecurity.

Border alarmism grew louder as migration from Central America appeared to increase sharply since 2012, especially with an unprecedented 2014 surge of families and unaccompanied children. Whether the surge was a "threat" depended on what side one took in the US political debate, which grew more polarized during the 2014 US legislative election campaign. Some political actors, including many congressional candidates who successfully employed the issue in their campaigns, portrayed the wave of Central American families as evidence of a deterioration of border security.

Others, including prominent Democratic Party leaders and border-area representatives, regarded it as a humanitarian crisis—even a refugee crisis—requiring a compassionate response. They noted that the Central American arrivals were actively seeking out, not avoiding, US authorities, and that the "surge" was occurring only in one of the Border Patrol's nine sectors, while migration continued its steady decline in the other eight, and apprehensions of Mexican citizens continued their historic decline.

Nonetheless, a consensus view in US domestic politics continues to hold that the border with Mexico remains a source of real or potential economic, criminal, and national security threats. This consensus is shared nearly everywhere except in border communities themselves, where objection to the buildup is strong and—except for the most remote zones—threat perceptions are low. However, these communities' views are routinely overruled, as evidenced by the 2013 debate in the US Senate over immigration reform. A broad majority that included some of the most liberal members but ignored many border-zone legislators' outcries, approved a dramatic, new border-security escalation; the escalation was added to entice reluctant conservatives to support the larger reform bill.

Perceptions have not caught up to reality, and events in 2014—both the Central American unaccompanied children crisis and the Barack Obama administration's November executive order easing deportation standards—widened the gap. Despite the evidence indicating sharp changes in northbound threats, strong support for a security buildup continues to guide US policy making with regard to its southern border. That is, the buildup is designed principally to confront threats of the past.

Milestones Along the Way to a Tougher Border

Since the 1980s, a long series of economic, political, and security events has encouraged a steady toughening of Washington's approach (table 7.1). Some of these events increased migration. Some caused the United States to clamp down further on a border that, until then, had been lightly guarded and not viewed as a zone of great security concern. In 1993, 3,444 Border Patrol agents were assigned

Table 7.1   Milestones that hardened US border policy and legislation

Milestones in the United States	Milestones in Mexico
1980s • Simpson-Mazzoli "amnesty" immigration reform	• Debt crisis and economic "lost decade" • To the south, civil wars in Central America • 1985 Mexico City earthquake • 1986 kidnapping and homicide of Kiki Camarena • 1989 arrest of Arellano Félix
1990s • Peak of the "war on drugs" (crack epidemic) • Military given a counterdrug role at the border • Border Patrol operations "Gatekeeper" and "Hold the Line" • North American Free Trade Agreement • Border Patrol doubles 1993–1998	• North American Free Trade Agreement • Peso crisis • To the south, Hurricane Mitch in Central America • 1994 assassination of Luis Donaldo Colosio • Zedillo electoral reforms opening up electoral competition and undermining PRI hegemony
2000s • September 11, 2001, attacks • Department of Homeland Security created • Secure Fence Act of 2006 • Border Patrol doubles 2004–2010 • Financial collapse 2008 • Rise of the "Tea Party"	• 2000 Election of opposition party candidate • Worsening drug and organized-crime violence • 2006 War on Drugs launched by Felipe Calderón
2010s • SB1070 and peak deportations • Immigration reform debate • Unaccompanied minors crisis	• 2012 election of Enrique Peña Nieto

to the 1,969-mile United States–Mexico border. In 2012 there were 18,412.[1] And some events brought border security and migration to the forefront of the US political debate, usually for a short period and in a distorted and sensationalistic way.

As of the mid-2010s, a new and different milestone has emerged. The importance of the Latino voting bloc, which voted overwhelmingly for Obama and Democratic Party candidates in 2012, placed immigration reform at the center of the United States' legislative agenda for the first time in decades. The bill that passed the US Senate, but failed in the harder-line House, would have created a "path to citizenship" for millions of currently undocumented migrants in the United States. In order to placate so-called immigration hawks in the Senate, however, this bill also proposed to add tens of billions of dollars in new funding to tighten border security even further.

This new border security funding would have come without the US government having performed any real assessment of the effectiveness and necessity of the byzantine border-security edifice that has grown over the past twenty years. Such an assessment is an increasingly urgent step, and this chapter contributes to the need to reevaluate whether US border policies match the actual threats present. Carrying out this analysis requires that we ask what border threats we are guarding against, whether the tools we have are adequate to defend against them, and if not, how resources can be better employed. This chapter focuses on policy analysis, beginning with an evaluation of the key bureaucratic actors in the US government who implement border policies. It then examines the perceptions and misperceptions regarding the threats faced by the United States on its border with Mexico. The chapter concludes by suggesting that our policies are designed to address threats that are based on misperceptions of border realities, and are thus largely ineffective.

The Buildup

The analysis begins by looking at the border buildup itself. Understanding the buildup requires looking at the work of numerous agencies with border security responsibilities, all with independent budgets, intelligence capabilities, and strategies, and often overlapping mandates. None is guided by a single "Southwest Border Security Strategy." Though the White House produces a periodic Southwest Border Counternarcotics Strategy, and the Border Patrol revises its own strategy document every several years, there is no interagency plan laying out all law enforcement and security challenges at the border, much less contemplating coordinated responses to them. An in-depth exploration of these agencies is beyond the scope of this paper; what follows is a brief summary.

DEPARTMENT OF HOMELAND SECURITY

The George W. Bush Administration created the Department of Homeland Security in the wake of the attacks on September 11, 2001. This department has the largest border security role, and its law enforcement agencies with border responsibilities include Immigration and Customs Enforcement (ICE) and Customs and Border Protection (CBP). The CBP in turn includes the Border Patrol, air and marine units, and an Office of Field Operations running forty-five official land crossings, or ports of entry, along the length of the United States–Mexico border.

It is this latter office—Field Operations—that has grown the least of all Homeland Security components during the buildup years. The majority of drugs, and a significant number of migrants, pass northward through the ports of entry. Most arms and bulk cash shipments for the cartels pass southward through the ports of entry. Yet these facilities remain badly understaffed, as evidenced by the hourslong wait times that are routine for vehicles and pedestrians seeking to enter the United States from Mexico.

With 5,500 CBP officers interviewing would-be crossers and inspecting vehicles and cargo, the Office of Field Operations has grown by only 15 percent since 2005, a period in which the Border Patrol—which is responsible for guarding the border between ports of entry—has doubled.[2] (A 2014 budget increase will fund two thousand new CBP officers, though it is not yet clear how many will be sent to the United States–Mexico border.) The lag in growth at the ports of entry owes heavily to a perception in Washington and border-state capitals that threats are concentrated in the areas between ports of entry. This perception is not based on any empirical analyses.

It has, however, led to a dramatic expansion in the Border Patrol, which is responsible for securing the spaces between official ports of entry and within one hundred miles of the border. Founded in 1925, it is empowered to patrol, detain and search, gather intelligence, and maintain border fencing. The agency grew fivefold between 1993 and 2009, and doubled between 2004 and 2010 alone.[3] The Border Patrol's budget multiplied more than sixfold during the entire period, from US$565 million in 1993 to US$3.55 billion in 2011.[4]

The Border Patrol is responsible for maintaining the border fence, which thirty years ago was sparse, primitive, and constructed of landing-mat paneling and barbed wire, if it existed at all. Today, especially since passage of the Secure Fence Act of 2006, it is a real barrier covering at least 649 miles of the 1,969-mile common border, often with a 14-foot wall.[5] Much of it comes with constantly monitored cameras, stadium-style lighting, and sensors. Recent construction has cost roughly US$3.9 million per mile.[6] The fence is highest, newest, and most layered near more densely populated areas. In the vast majority of the 1,254 miles where the border follows the Rio Grande between Texas and Mexico, no fencing exists at all. To build it along the entire Texas-Mexico border would "take 10 to 15 years and US$30 billion," Texas Governor Rick Perry has said.[7]

The CBP Office of Air and Marine (OAM) maintains fleets of over 290 aircraft and 250 vessels at 80 locations, only a fraction of them near the Mexico border.

This aircraft fleet, the largest of any domestic US law-enforcement agency, is headquartered in El Paso. Since October 2005, OAM has managed an Unmanned Aerial System "drones" program, using ten unarmed Predator B aircraft to patrol all US borders and coasts, with an eventual goal of increasing them to twenty-four.[8] Operating at a cost of about US$12,255 per flight hour, the drones' performance on the border, meanwhile, has been modest in terms of drugs seized or migrants detected: "CBP has invested significant funds in a program that has not achieved the expected results, and it cannot demonstrate how much the program has improved border security," reads a strongly critical December 2014 report from the Department of Homeland Security's Inspector-General.[9]

Elsewhere in the Homeland Security Department is Immigration and Customs Enforcement (ICE), which calls itself "the second largest investigative agency in the federal government" after the FBI. With more than twenty thousand employees worldwide, ICE is charged with enforcing federal border control, customs, trade, and immigration laws. Its rapidly growing Homeland Security Investigations (HSI) Directorate has made ICE an important domestic intelligence agency, though it is not considered part of the US intelligence community, and thus not subject to policy direction from the director of National Intelligence or oversight by the congressional intelligence committees. Immigration and Customs Enforcement manages nine border enforcement security task forces (BEST Teams) near the southwest border and one in Mexico City, and all include personnel from several US government agencies. According to an ICE "fact sheet," BEST teams pool information and coordinate activities between United States and (some) Mexican authorities.[10]

DEPARTMENT OF JUSTICE

The Department of Justice (DOJ) includes two very active agencies with border-security responsibilities. Because the agencies work closely with federal prosecutors, they have to be kept in the DOJ and not moved to Homeland Security. Both the Drug Enforcement Administration (DEA) and the Federal Bureau of Investigation (FBI) have grown in the post–September 11 period. Because of the border's importance for drug trafficking, DEA maintains a strong presence of agents seeking to interdict drugs or weaken drug-trafficking organizations. Its intelligence-gathering capacity is centered at its El Paso Intelligence Center (EPIC), a secretive facility that has sprawled under the border buildup. Between 2007 and 2009, its staff grew by 22 percent to 343 people, and its budget leapt by

46 percent, from US$13.4 million to US$19.6 million.[11] The other main Department of Justice agency with a presence on the border is the FBI, which maintains seven field intelligence groups at field offices near the border.

DEPARTMENT OF DEFENSE

The Department of Defense has been involved in border security since the late 1980s, when the armed forces were given the leading role in international drug interdiction. This includes military involvement in law enforcement on US territory within twenty-five miles of the border. This has been controversial in the United States, where the military has been prohibited from playing a police role, except for temporary emergencies, since the 1878 passage of the Posse Comitatus Act.

The US military's involvement in border security has grown during the post–September 11, 2001, period, but in part because of these concerns, it has not grown as quickly as that of civilian agencies. The Defense Department's role has been most visible through the support role that active-duty military personnel play in the Northern Command's El Paso–based Joint Task Force North (JTF-N), and in Operations "Jump Start" and "Phalanx," the National Guard deployments that Presidents Bush and Obama ordered to the border in 2006 and 2010. Today, the National Guard maintains a reduced (about three hundred people) presence, with an additional one thousand deployed with Texas state government funding between the summer of 2014 and spring of 2015.

STATES

Some states have built up their own border security programs, often with federal funding. In Texas, Governor Perry, who has been in office since before the attacks on September 11, 2001, established "Operation Border Star" within the Texas State Department of Public Safety (DPS); the Texas DPS includes the state criminal investigative body, the Texas Rangers. Independent investigations of "Border Star" have found that these programs depend heavily both on federal funding—over US$161 million in 2011 alone—and on private contractors to whom many basic duties have been outsourced.[12] Arizona has a smaller program in which the state government has assigned one hundred and forty members of the Arizona National Guard to a Joint Counter-Narcoterrorism Task Force (JCNTF), which monitors the border zone, principally through air surveillance.

THE MÉRIDA INITIATIVE

The State and Defense Departments have accompanied the buildup on the US side with a sharp increase in assistance to Mexico under a framework called the Mérida Initiative. Since 2008, Mexico has received US$2.8 billion in aid from Washington, of which US$1.8 billion have gone to the country's security forces.[13] Most of this aid has been focused on Mexico's entire geography, not just the border regions. However, a significant amount has paid for scanning and other detection equipment at border crossings (including crossings at Mexico's southern border with Guatemala and Belize). At least US$90 million has supported Mexico's National Migration Institute, the government agency that staffs ports of entry and detains and deports undocumented migrants within Mexico. Starting in 2014, the US government, having identified "$86.6 million in validated requirements," accelerated deliveries of assistance to help Mexico confront Central American migration at its southern border with Guatemala and Belize.[14]

A TANGLED WEB

Attempting to map this welter of agencies, many of which have doubled or expanded even further in personnel and budget in the past decade, is difficult. All have their own intelligence-gathering capabilities, all have their own sophisticated equipment, and none is guided by a government-wide strategy document that applies to all and apportions resources. Information often goes unshared. Databases, equipment, and cultures are often incompatible. There is recognition that a problem exists, as evidenced by a profusion of task forces, coordination centers, fusion centers, and liaison offices designed to improve interagency coordination. But efforts are frequently duplicated, results are not publicly evaluated or in many cases well measured, and cost inefficiencies often go unidentified, with some agencies finding themselves greatly overburdened while others enjoy excess capacity.

Four Threats

A buildup this formidable, with so little evaluation of results, could only happen in response to an urgent sense of threat emanating from the border. A review of the past decades' "milestones," and of US officials' public statements and agency documents, reveals four distinct types of threats that are employed to justify, and build support for, tighter and more expensive border security. These are terrorism, "spillover" violence, drug trafficking, and undocumented migration. Of these four, three have declined or failed to materialize, while one has increased.

TERRORISM

Though the September 11, 2001, attackers came to the United States by air with visas, the scenario of terrorists intending to do harm on US soil arriving via the United States–Mexico border continues to be the principal stated justification for viewing the border as a scene of potential national security threats. "The priority mission of the Border Patrol is preventing terrorists and terrorists' weapons, including weapons of mass destruction, from entering the United States."[15] Politicians commonly raise the specter of cross-border extremist terrorism, as Senator Charles Schumer (D–New York), chairman of the Judiciary Subcommittee on Immigration, Refugees and Border Security, did during the 2002 debate over the Homeland Security Act: "If, God forbid, a terrorist group should get hold of such a nuclear weapon . . . that weapon could be smuggled into this country, say, on one of the large containers that are unloaded from our ships or brought through the borders—Canadian and Mexican—on trucks, with virtually no detection."[16] The nightmare scenario of extremist terrorists crossing the border illegally demands vigilance and is impossible to dismiss, both in intelligence terms and political calculations. It has justified a good deal of the additional funding and activity that the United States has dedicated to border security since 2001.

To date, though, it has not materialized. The State Department's August 2012 *Country Reports on Terrorism* was unequivocal: "No known international terrorist organization had an operational presence in Mexico and no terrorist group targeted U.S. citizens in or from Mexican territory."[17] An *Arizona Daily Star* investigation of records obtained from CBP found that, between 2005 and 2010, the agency apprehended 2,039 migrants from countries considered to be of "special interest" for terrorism. Of these, none represented "a credible terrorist threat."[18] While Republican members of the House of Representatives issued a 2012 report citing three cases of people tied to Islamic extremists seeking to cross the border, none of the examples cited any involvement in a terrorist conspiracy.[19] Cross-border terrorism, thankfully, remains an entirely hypothetical scenario.

"SPILLOVER" VIOLENCE

In recent years, as Mexico, particularly its border regions, has faced spiraling organized crime-related violence, a threat frequently cited to justify securitization is "spillover." The term refers to the likelihood that Mexico's organized criminal groups and gangs are increasing their activity on the US side of the border and putting US communities at risk. "Spillover" has crept into official rhetoric, especially at the state and opposition-politics level, as a chief argument for further increasing US investment in border security, including greater use of military capabilities at the border.

"Conditions within these border communities along both sides of the Texas-Mexico border are tantamount to living in a war zone in which civil authorities, law enforcement agencies as well as citizens are under attack around the clock," reads a September 2011 report by two retired generals commissioned by the Texas Department of Agriculture.[20] In a June 2010 interview with Fox News, Arizona Governor Jan Brewer declared: "We cannot afford all this illegal immigration and everything that comes with it, everything from the crime and to [sic] the drugs and the kidnappings and the extortion and the beheadings and the fact that people can't feel safe in their community. It's wrong! It's wrong!"[21]

Faced with no evidence of any beheadings, Governor Brewer later partially retracted her statement. In fact, one of the most remarkable and least-reported phenomena along the border has been the surprising *lack* of spillover of Mexico's horrific violence.

Politicians who sound alarms about spillover generally cite a small number of high-profile incidents, as well as anecdotal concerns voiced by ranchers in remote rural zones where the number of border crossers passing through their lands is fewer but seen as "more menacing." The data, however, show communities on the US side experiencing their lowest violent crime rates in decades. Taken together, the ten US cities over 100,000 in population and within 100 miles of the Mexico border had a rate of 3.6 homicides per 100,000 people in 2010, lower than the US national average (4.8) and one-twenty-seventh of the shockingly high average of Mexico's border cities over 100,000 in population (96).[22] That year, Ciudad Juárez, Mexico, was considered perhaps the most violent city in the world; just across the narrow Rio Grande River, El Paso, Texas, had the distinction of enjoying the lowest homicide rate of any US city that is over 500,000 population. The ten counties that make up Arizona's southern half experienced an 18 percent drop in homicides between 2002 and 2011.[23] Of the 32 Texas cities with more than 100,000 in population in 2011, none of the four border cities was among the top ten most violent.[24] According to FBI data, border counties experienced 118 fewer violent crimes per 100,000 inhabitants than the country as a whole in 2011.[25]

The US border-security buildup may explain some of the lack of spillover. An even greater cause, though, may be the importance of border crossings to the drug economy. Law-enforcement officials interviewed in border areas believe that drug traffickers have deliberately chosen to "behave" in a nonviolent manner on the US side of the border in order to not provoke any closures of the ports of entry through which the majority of their drugs flow. Another likely explanation is the physical presence of drugs themselves; while shipments are staged and stored on the Mexican side of the border, inviting violent competition to control territory and valuable stockpiles, once they enter the United States the drugs spend very little time in border communities. They quickly disperse into the US interior (for a discussion of smuggling in the United States, see chapter 8 by Peter Andreas).[26]

The buildup, then, may not be the principal explanation for the remarkable lack of spillover of Mexican violence. The real reason may be less virtuous, and more closely related to a larger decoupling of drug trafficking and violence that, amid dropping crime rates, many US cities have experienced since the 1990s. While US drug law enforcement agencies report little change in the price or purity of illegal drugs sold on the street, most cities have seen violent crime drop dramatically over the past twenty years. New York and Washington, DC, for example, have experienced homicide decreases of 75 percent or more since the early 1990s.[27] A similar dynamic may be observed in Mexican border cities considered today to be under the uncontested dominion of the Sinaloa drug cartel (Tijuana, Mexicali, Nogales, Ciudad Juárez, and smaller cities along the western half of the border). In these cities, homicide rates have dropped precipitously in the past five years, though there is little evidence that the amount of drugs transiting the zone is reduced. Trafficking continues—but it is better "behaved."

DRUGS

There is no doubt that it continues. It is impossible to estimate how many drugs make it successfully over the border. However, if the Border Patrol can contend that fewer migrant apprehensions means fewer migrants are attempting to cross (discussed below), then we should conclude that increased drug seizures mean that more—or at least as many as ever—drugs are being shipped over the border.

And indeed, drug seizure statistics (except for cocaine) are up dramatically since 2005. Between that year and 2010, seizures of marijuana went up 49 percent, methamphetamine 54 percent, heroin 297 percent, and ecstasy 839 percent, even as violent crimes in the four US border states dropped during the same period.[28]

The seizure data indicates that US drug interdiction personnel have increased their effectiveness. It also indicates, though, that drug traffickers are not reducing their attempts to cross the border, and that in fact they are willingly sustaining greater losses instead of seeking alternate routes or conveyances. This leads to the conclusion that the border-security buildup of the past decades has not significantly discouraged drug trafficking.

Still, US officials continue to employ the drug threat as a principal argument for an intensified buildup. Though they rarely use this as an argument specifically to build up capacities at the ports of entry through which, according to several interviews with officials, the majority of all drugs pass.

The decline in US drug-related violence, along with slowly shifting attitudes toward drug use and addiction in the United States, has reduced the drug threat's impact as an argument for still tighter border security. In 1989 and 1990, at the height of the violent crime wave fed by crack, when a Gallup opinion poll asked US citizens what was the "most important problem facing this country" at that time, their most frequent response was "illegal drugs"; this response was from 30 percent of respondents.[29] By the early 2000s through today, though, Gallup was registering only about 0.5 percent of respondents identifying illegal drugs as the main threat facing the country, and the drug issue almost completely ceased to surface in presidential and other national electoral campaign debates.

UNCONTROLLED MIGRATION

Until relatively recently, the flow of undocumented migrants that had been a constant throughout the twentieth century had not been viewed as a national security threat. That has changed. Amid US fears of terrorism and the spillover of Mexico's "Border Wars" (the title of a reality TV show on the National Geographic cable network), all undocumented migrants are suspect. The Border Patrol's 2004 *National Border Patrol Strategy* stated this quite clearly: "Some would classify the majority of these aliens as 'economic migrants.' However, an ever-present threat exists from the potential for terrorists to employ the same smuggling and transportation networks, infrastructure, drop houses, and other support and then use these masses of illegal aliens as 'cover' for a successful cross-border penetration."[30]

Some political leaders, though, portray illegal migration as a national-security threat without any reference to terrorism. They hold a view of the migrant population as inherently disorderly and antisocial. "We had a hearing yesterday on crime in America," said Alabama Republican Senator Jeff Sessions during the

September 2006 debate over the Secure Fence Act. "We had the Director of the Bureau of Prisons. He told us that in the Federal prison penitentiaries 27 percent of the people detained are not American citizens. Can you imagine that— 27 percent? . . . So somehow we are picking up a larger number of the criminal element than we ever have."[31]

Of course, much of the animus toward migrants at the United States' southwest border stems from concerns other than national security. Economics is a major factor in this hostility. Since the 1980s, economic growth in the United States has been poorly distributed. Real wages have stagnated or even dropped for semiskilled, nonprofessional labor and for workers educated at the highschool graduate or lower levels.[32] Along with movement of manufacturing overseas, the labor of migrants—both documented and undocumented—has been widely portrayed in the media as a chief cause for downward pressure on wages.[33] By the 1990s, politicians like Ross Perot and Pat Buchanan were capitalizing on this "illegal immigrants are taking American jobs" sentiment. This has grown stronger after the historically deep recession that began in 2007, intensified after the US banking crisis of 2008, and continued in the sluggish recovery of the early 2010s.

The economic argument that fuels securitization of migration is often accompanied by a more sinister cultural sentiment: racism. "There is a dynamic that has emerged in the immigration debate in which, while it might be improper in some civilized settings to make overt racialized attacks on Mexicans and Mexican-Americans, by couching the attack as against 'undocumented immigrants,' anything goes," explains Steven Bender.[34] Alarm at a flow of nonwhite migrants, however, is usually occluded; though US political culture has grown very conservative during the past thirty years, it still punishes and marginalizes politicians and community leaders who overtly capitalize on racist sentiment among the electorate.

This alarm over undocumented migration, however, is directed at a phenomenon that is rapidly diminishing. It appears that far fewer people are attempting to enter the United States over the border from Mexico, and of those that are coming, fewer are Mexican.

While there is no way to know the number of undocumented people who attempt this crossing each year, data about those apprehended by the US Border Patrol tell us much about trends. The trend of the past few years is rather striking: 479,371 people were apprehended at the United States' southwest border in 2014, 59 percent fewer than in 2005.[35] This was 151,794 more than in 2011, the year that saw the lowest number of border-zone apprehensions since 1972, before the seeds of the border-security buildup even began to be planted.

This post-2011 increase owed entirely to a jump in migration from the economically battered, hyperviolent countries of Central America's "Northern Triangle" (Honduras, Guatemala, and El Salvador), even as the number of apprehended migrants from Mexico continued to decline (by 20 percent from 2011 to 2014). By 2014, for the first time since US authorities began keeping records, the Border Patrol apprehended more non-Mexican citizens (252,600, nearly all of them Central American) than Mexican citizens (226,771) at the border with Mexico.[36]

The Central American migration trend came to dominate US headlines for several weeks in June and July 2014, as US authorities were overwhelmed by an unprecedented wave of children and families fleeing violence in Honduras, Guatemala, and El Salvador. Between October 2013 and September 2014, the US Border Patrol apprehended a staggering 68,541 children who arrived in the United States without a parent. This was 77 percent more than a year earlier and 330 percent more than in October 2010–September 2011. Of these unaccompanied minors, 75 percent came from the three violence-torn Central American countries of El Salvador, Guatemala, and Honduras. The Border Patrol also apprehended another 68,445 members of "family units"—parents with children—mostly from these countries; this was a 361 percent increase over 2013.[37]

This sudden, often heartbreaking wave of new migration set off alarms in the United States, with politicians calling for further increases in border security spending and Texas even deploying National Guard soldiers. The 2014 crisis, however, was no indicator of a deterioration in border security—nor was it necessarily preventable.

Seventy-five percent of the Central American children and families who arrived that year did so in only one of the Border Patrol's nine sectors; this was the Rio Grande Valley, which comprises the easternmost 200 miles of the entire 1,970-mile border. (This sector is the shortest distance from Central America, and the winding, flood-prone Rio Grande makes the cost of fencing prohibitive, resulting in the longest stretch of unfenced border near a US population center.) In the other eight sectors, migrant apprehensions *declined* by 14 percent in 2014.[38]

The crisis was also short lived. Apprehensions of children and families shot upward in March 2014 and began declining in July 2014. Fifty-three percent of them took place in the four months between March and June. By September 2014, child and family apprehensions had fallen below September 2013 levels.[39]

This sharp drop was likely due to Mexico's greatly increased apprehensions and deportations of Central American citizens, and to a widely disseminated, but false, rumor—likely spread by smugglers—that until June 2014 the US government was offering special permits to allow children and families to stay.

When they arrived, most families and children did not seek to evade authorities. Hidalgo County Judge Ramón García explained what usually happened instead: "When these kids cross that river, nobody has to chase him. They chase the Border Patrol down. They look around—they're looking for that man in green that is going to take them to be processed and be giving a permiso—a permit, telling him that you can go on and be free—freely travel about our country until you're asked to appear."[40] Rio Grande Valley Border Patrol agents told the author in August 2014 of sites along the river where, every evening, smugglers on the Mexican side would send rafts full of Central American children and families across to waiting agents. The smugglers had instructed the Central Americans to surrender to the agents.

This situation—rather unique and impossible to defend against—is tragic, but difficult to portray as a "security threat" or evidence of vulnerability. It did, however, distract from the larger trend of reduced migration, both of Mexican citizens and everywhere else along the border except the southernmost tip of Texas.

This larger trend of decreasing migration is borne out by an April 2012 study by the Pew Hispanic Center, which found the number of Mexican citizens moving to the United States between 2005 and 2010 (1.4 million) equaled the number of Mexican citizens returning (or being deported) from the United States to Mexico.[41] The net migration during those six years was virtually zero, or even below zero, Pew found.

There are three principal reasons for the drop. It is difficult to weigh each of these three variables, but it is unlikely that one single variable explains most of the reduction. The border-security buildup gets some credit, but not most of the credit.

A strong factor deterring immigration is the simple fact that little employment has been available in the post-2007 United States. The recession that began in 2007 and the financial crisis that hit in 2008 caused unemployment to surge, especially in sectors that have traditionally hired much undocumented immigrant labor (e.g., construction). By 2012, though the US economy was no longer in recession, a sluggish recovery with little job creation has offered few incentives for economic migrants to brave the journey northward. Continued economic growth in 2013, however, may have increased the still-modest rate of migrant flows.

The crisis also hit Mexico quite hard in 2009, but the Mexican economy has recovered more quickly. While the US gross domestic product grew by 1.7 percent in 2011 and 2.2 percent in 2012, the corresponding increases in Mexico were 3.9 percent in both years. Even amid the current wave of violence, Mexico's border cities have seen factories and maquiladoras opening and hiring.[42] Meanwhile, Mexico's middle class has grown significantly, and family sizes—especially in rural areas—have shrunk dramatically since 1970, reducing the number of potential migrants.[43]

Those impoverished Mexicans and Central Americans who still consider migrating northward face a strong deterrent to attempting the trip: the gauntlet of predatory criminal organizations, kidnapping and extortion gangs, and associated corrupt officials through which they must run on the journey through Mexico. As organized-crime groups have become more powerful and diversified, much research has highlighted the increase in human rights violations, including extortion, kidnapping, rape, and murder suffered by Central American and other migrants passing through Mexico.[44] Mexico's national human rights ombudsman estimates that about twenty thousand migrants are abducted for ransom in Mexico each year.[45] Many are killed. In perhaps the highest-profile case, in August 2010 the bodies of seventy-two migrants from Central and South America, massacred by the Zetas criminal group, were found in San Fernando, Tamaulipas.

The increased risk of attempting the journey through Mexico no doubt deters many would-be migrants. Though residents of violent Central American cities' poorer districts, where the risk of falling victim to criminal violence is already high, may not be discouraged by the dangers of traveling northward.

The US border-security buildup is the third important factor explaining the drop in undocumented migration. More fencing and more security personnel force migrants to take dangerous routes, increase the risk of being caught, and increase the consequences once apprehended. Intensified border-control efforts since the mid-1990s have caused migration's center of gravity to shift from the San Diego and El Paso areas to the forbidding deserts of Arizona, and now increasingly to the dry scrublands of south Texas. Meanwhile, would-be migrants are further deterred by news of harsh measures like Arizona's SB 1070 law and the dark national mood toward immigrants in the United States.

It is unlikely, though, that the US and Mexican buildups are the principal reason for the drop in migration. A surprisingly large number of apprehended migrants today are not economic migrants; they are seeking to enter in order to be reunited with family members.

Between January and June 2011, US Immigration and Customs Enforcement records show the government deported 46,486 parents of US-citizen children, 22 percent of all deportations during that period.[46] A University of Arizona survey of 1,113 recent deportees in Mexico found a disturbingly high incidence of family separation: "Half [51 percent] had at least one family member who was a U.S. citizen, and nearly one in four [22 percent] had at least one child under the age of 18 who had U.S. Citizenship."[47] Reunification with these family members is a motivation that will outweigh many risks, including the likelihood of being detained again.

Note, meanwhile, that drug traffickers—who appear not to be deterred from continuing to engage in illicit trafficking—do not face the first two factors. Economic motivations do not apply because they already have a "job" of sorts. Nor does the possibility of running afoul of criminal groups affect them, since they make up criminal groups. Drug traffickers face only the deterrent of the official security buildup. Why would this factor, by itself, be such a strong deterrent to would-be migrants?

Conclusion

Following decades of milestones leading to an ever-tougher border security buildup, the United States finds itself with a sprawling security apparatus facing a much smaller population of border crossers. During 1993, the Border Patrol apprehended 327 migrants for every agent stationed along the border. By 2012, that number had dropped to 19 apprehensions per agent per year, an average of one apprehension every 19 days. The agents are backed up, meanwhile, by drones, regular military and National Guard personnel, new fencing, intelligence agents, and other assets that were not present in 1993. Yet staff at ports of entry remain overwhelmed, and interagency cooperation and strategic guidance are still weak.

Meanwhile, the border—at least on the US side—is safer and more controlled than it has been in decades. Though trafficking persists at ports of entry and in lightly populated border zones, it is almost entirely nonviolent. Migrant flows remain near all-time lows, and would be breaking records were it not for the migration of Central Americans. The threat of cross-border terrorist flows, while requiring persistent vigilance, has not materialized.

This, however, is not the perception guiding US policy making in the mid-2010s. If the language of immigration-reform legislation before Congress is any indication, most US citizens and their political leaders continue to believe that the border is insufficiently guarded and that a variety of cross-border menaces are worsening.

Border communities, and their political leaders, do their utmost to counter this narrative. Their zones are safe, they insist, adding that the most urgent needs are a greater focus on guarding ports of entry as well as an immigration policy that allows "guest workers" to come, and to leave, legally. But border communities' narratives are complicated and do not always provide support to the other agendas—from economics to drug-war concerns to racial discrimination—discussed in this chapter. As a result, border-zone voices are often drowned out, and the wide national gulf between perception and reality persists.

NOTES

1. "Border Patrol Agent Staffing by Fiscal Year," US Border Control, Customs and Border Protection, Department of Homeland Security, February 2013, https://catalog.data .gov/dataset/u-s-border-patrol-fiscal-year-staffing-statistics.

2. "Testimony of Congressman Silvestre Reyes (TX-16) Before the Committee on Appropriations, Subcommittee Homeland Security," Congressman Silvestre Reyes website, April 14, 2011, http://web.archive.org/web/20121212125201/http://reyes.house.gov/news /documentsingle.aspx?DocumentID=249470; and "Additional Actions Needed to Strengthen CBP Efforts to Mitigate Risk of Employee Corruption and Misconduct," US Government Accountability Office, December 4, 2012, http://www.gao.gov/assets/660 /650505.pdf.

3. "Border Patrol Agent Staffing," US Border Control.

4. "Enacted Border Patrol Program Budget by Fiscal Year," US Border Control, accessed May 2013, http://www.cbp.gov/sites/default/files/documents/BP%20Budget%20 History%201990-2014_0.pdf.

5. US Government Accountability Office, *DHS Progress and Challenges in Securing the U.S. Southwest and Northern Borders* (Washington, DC: GAO, March 30, 2011), 9, http://www.gao.gov/new.items/d11508t.pdf.

6. US Government Accountability Office, *Secure Border Initiative Fence Construction Costs*, GAO-09-244R (Washington: GAO, January 29, 2009), http:// www.gao.gov/new .items/d09244r.pdf.

7. Julia Preston, "Some Cheer Border Fence as Others Ponder the Cost," *New York Times*, October 19, 2011, http://www.nytimes. com/2011/10/20/us/politics/border-fence -raises-cost-questions.html.

8. US Department of Homeland Security, Office of the Inspector General, *U.S. Customs and Border Protection's Unmanned Aircraft System Program Does Not Achieve Intended Results or Recognize All Costs of Operations* (Washington, DC: DHS OIG, December 24, 2014), http://www.oig.dhs.gov/assets/Mgmt/2015/OIG_15-17_Dec14.pdf.

9. Ibid.

10. "Border Enforcement Security Task Force (BEST)," US Immigration and Customs Enforcement, accessed May 2013, http://www.ice.gov/best/.

11. US Department of Justice, Office of the Inspector General Evaluation and Inspections Division, *Review of the Drug Enforcement Administration's El Paso Intelligence Center*, I-2010-005 (Washington, DC: Department of Justice, June 2010), http://www.justice.gov /oig/reports/DEA/ a1005.pdf.

12. Texas State Auditor's Office, *State of Texas Compliance with Federal Requirements for Selected Major Programs at the Department of Public Safety and the University of Texas Medical Branch at Galveston for the Fiscal Year Ended August 31, 2011*, 12-019 (Austin, TX: Texas State Auditor's Office, February 2012), http://www.sao.state.tx.us/reports/main/12-019 .pdf; and Tom Barry, "Texas Outsourced its Own Border Security Model to Beltway Consultants," *Border Lines* (blog), March 11, 2012, http://borderlinesblog.blogspot.com/2012 /03/ret.html.

13. For the author's most current estimate of US assistance to Mexico, based on official US government documents, consult the relevant page of the CIP-LAWG-WOLA Just the Facts website, http://www.justf.org/latin-america-and-caribbean/mexico.

14. US Department of State, Bureau of International Narcotics and Law Enforcement Affairs, "INL Assistance for Mexico's Southern Border Strategy," June 18, 2014, 1, http:// www.mxusborder.org/files/140618_sborder_inl.pdf.

15. US Customs and Border Patrol website, accessed December 25, 2013, http://www .cbp.gov/xp/cgov/border_security/border_patrol/.

16. Senator Schumer, "Homeland Security Act of 2002–Motion to Proceed," *Congressional Record* 148, no. 109 (September 3, 2002), p. S8067.

17. "Country Reports on Terrorism 2012," US Department of State, July 31, 2012, http://www.state.gov/j/ct/rls/crt/2012/index.htm.

18. Brady McCombs and Tim Steller, "Border Seen as Unlikely Terrorist Crossing Point," *Arizona Daily Star*, June 7, 2011, http://azstarnet.com/news/local/border/article_ ed932aa2-9d2a-54f1-b930-85f5d4cce9a8.html.

19. Adam Isacson, "Cross-border Terrorism: Does 'Evidence to Compel' Further Action Exist?" Border Fact Check, January 17, 2013, http://borderfactcheck.tumblr.com /post/40769077146/cross-border-terrorism-does-evidence-to-compel.

20. Barry R. McCaffrey and Robert H. Scales, *Texas Border Security: A Strategic Military Assessment* (Austin, TX: Texas Department of Agriculture, September 2011), http:// www.statesman.com/multimedia/archive/01175/Texas_Border_Secur_1175852a.pdf.

21. "Gov. Jan Brewer Talks of Beheadings in the Arizona Desert," *Tampa Bay Times*, Politifact.com, September 8, 2010, http://www.politifact.com/truth-o-meter/statements /2010/sep/08/jan-brewer/gov-jan-brewer-talks-beheadings-th-arizona-desert/.

22. US Federal Bureau of Investigation, "Crime in the United States by Metropolitan Statistical Area, 2010–2011," http://www.fbi.gov/about-us/cjis/ucr/crime-in-the-u.s/2011 /crime-in-the-u.s.-2011/tables/table-6; and Molly Molloy, "The Mexican Undead: Toward a New History of the 'Drug War' Killing Fields," *Small Wars Journal* 9, no. 8 (2012).

23. "2012 Crime in Arizona Report" (Phoenix, AZ: Arizona Department of Public Safety, 2013), http://www.azdps.gov/About/Reports/docs/Crime_In_Arizona_Report _2012.pdf.

24. US Federal Bureau of Investigation, "Crime in the United States by Region, Geographic Division and State, 2010–2011," http://www.fbi.gov/about-us/cjis/ucr/crime-in-the-u.s/2011/crime-in-the-u.s.-2011/tables/table-4.

25. Ibid.

26. Jeffrey S. Passel and D'Vera Cohn, *A Portrait of Unauthorized Immigrants in the United States* (Washington, DC: Pew Hispanic Research Center, April 14, 2009), i–ii.

27. Richard A. Oppel Jr., "Steady Decline in Major Crime Baffles Experts," *New York Times*, May 23, 2011, http://www.nytimes.com/2011/05/24/us/24crime.html?_r=0; and Richard Simon, "Washington, D.C., Finishes 2012 with Fewer Than 100 Homicides," *Los Angeles Times*, January 1, 2013, http://articles.latimes.com/2013/jan/01/nation/la-na-nn-washington-dc-2012-homicides-20130101.

28. US Department of Justice, National Drug Intelligence Center, *National Drug Threat Assessment 2011* (Johnstown, PA: NDIC, August 2011), 50, http://www.justice.gov/archive/ndic/pubs44/44849/44849p.pdf; and General Accountability Office, *Southwest Border Security: Data Are Limited and Concerns Vary about Spillover Crime along the Southwest Border*, GAO-13-175 (Washington, DC, GAO, Feb 26, 2013).

29. Frank Newport, "Terrorism and Economy Seen as Top Problems Facing Country Today, but Neither Dominates," Gallup.com, March 20, 2002, http://www.gallup.com/poll/5500/terrorism-economy-seen-top-problems-facing-country-today.aspx.

30. US Customs and Border Protection, Office of Border Patrol, *National Border Patrol Strategy* (Washington, DC: CBP, September 2004), http://www.au.af.mil/au/awc/awcgate/dhs/national_bp_strategy.pdf.

31. Senator Sessions (AZ). "Secure Fence Act of 2006–Motion to Proceed." *Congressional Record* 152, no. 118 (September 20, 2006), p. S9745.

32. Lawrence Mishel and Heidi Shierholz, "The Sad But True Story of Wages in America" (Washington, DC: Issue Brief 297, Economic Policy Institute, March 15, 2011); and Steven Greenhouse and David Leonhardt, "Real Wages Fail to Match a Rise in Productivity," *New York Times*, August 28, 2006.

33. Neil Malhotra, Yotam Margalit, and Cecilia Hyunjung Mo, "Economic Explanations for Opposition to Immigration: Distinguishing between Prevalence and Conditional Impact," *American Journal of Political Science* 57, no. 2 (2013): 392.

34. Katie Ryder, "A Better Border Is Possible," Salon.com, May 26, 2012, http://www.salon.com/2012/05/26/a_better_border_is_possible/singleton/; and Steven Bender, *Run for the Border: Vice and Virtue in U.S.-Mexico Border Crossings* (New York, NY: New York University Press, 2012).

35. "Southwest Border Sectors: Total Illegal Alien Apprehensions by Fiscal Year," US Border Patrol, accessed January 2015, http://www.cbp.gov/sites/default/files/documents/BP%20Southwest%20Border%20Sector%20Apps%20FY1960%20-%20FY2014_0.pdf.

36. "U.S. Border Patrol Monthly Apprehensions from Mexico and Other Than Mexico," US Border Patrol, accessed January 2015, http://www.cbp.gov/newsroom/media-resources/stats.

37. "U.S. Border Patrol Southwest Border Family Units and UAC Apprehensions," US Border Patrol, accessed January 2015, http://www.cbp.gov/sites/default/files/documents/BP%20Southwest%20Border%20Family%20Units%20and%20UAC%20Apps%20

FY13%20-%20FY14_0.pdf; and "U.S. Border Patrol Total Monthly UAC Apprehensions by Month, by Sector," US Border Patrol, accessed January 2015, http://www.cbp.gov/sites/default/files/documents/BP%20Total%20Monthly%20UACs%20by%20Sector%2C%20FY10.-FY14.pdf.

38. "U.S. Border Patrol Fiscal Year Southwest Border Sector Apprehensions," US Border Patrol, accessed January 2015, http://www.cbp.gov/sites/default/files/documents/BP%20Southwest%20Border%20Sector%20Apps%20FY1960%20-%20FY2014_0.pdf.

39. "U.S. Border Patrol Total Monthly UAC Apprehensions," US Border Patrol.

40. Kelly McEvers, "Court System Not Equipped for Deluge of Underage Immigrants," National Public Radio, July 5, 2014, http://www.npr.org/2014/07/05/328888371/court-system-not-equipped-for-deluge-of-underage-immigrants.

41. Jeffrey Passel, D'Vera Cohn, and Ana Gonzalez-Barrera, *Net Migration from Mexico Falls to Zero—and Perhaps Less* (Washington, DC: Pew Hispanic Center, April 23, 2012), 7–8.

42. Ian Sherwood, "Ciudad Juarez: Mexico's 'Deadliest City' Sees Economic Gains," British Broadcasting Corporation, June 29, 2012, http://www.bbc.co.uk/news/world-latin-america-18637470.

43. For a good overview of economic and demographic trends, see Damien Cave, "Better Lives for Mexicans Cut Allure of Going North," *New York Times*, July 6, 2011, http://www.nytimes.com/interactive/2011/07/06/world/americas/immigration.html.

44. Adam Isacson and Maureen Meyer, *Beyond the Border Buildup* (Washington, DC: Washington Office on Latin America, April 2012), 35–36.

45. Comisión Nacional de los Derechos Humanos de México, *Informe especial sobre los casos de secuestro en contra de migrantes* (Mexico, DF: Comisión Nacional de los Derechos Humanos, June 15, 2009).

46. Daniel Gonzalez, "Stats Detail Deportation of Parents with U.S.-Born Children," *Arizona Republic*, April 4, 2012, http://www.azcentral.com/news/articles/2012/04/04/20120404deportation-stats-detail-parents-american-born-children.html.

47. Jeremy Slack, Daniel Martínez, Scott Whiteford, and Emily Pfeiffer, *In the Shadow of the Wall* (Tucson: University of Arizona, March 2013), http://las.arizona.edu/sites/las.arizona.edu/files/UA_Immigration_Report2013web.pdf.

PART III / Licit and Illicit Behavior
of Borderland Actors

Chapter Eight

Illicit Americas

Historical Dynamics of Smuggling in the United States'
Relations with Its Neighbors

Peter Andreas

The proliferation of illicit cross-border flows in the Americas—ranging from unauthorized migrant workers and psychoactive substances to arms and dirty money—is often portrayed as an alarming and unprecedented challenge to borders and government authority in the region.[1] Policing such border flows has also become an increasingly prominent (and sometimes highly divisive) issue in US relations with its neighbors, as Washington has pushed for tighter border controls and more intensive crackdowns on smuggling, a dynamic also discussed by Adam Isacson (see chapter 7 in this volume).[2]

At first glance, there is indeed much that is new and novel; this is most dramatized by the sheer magnitude of drug-related violence in recent years in countries such as Mexico and Honduras. Yet from a much broader historical perspective, illicit cross-border flows of various sorts have been a defining feature of US commercial relations with its neighbors from the very start, suggesting that there is much more continuity with the past than conventional accounts recognize.[3] Indeed, as this brief review points out, the drug story is actually a relatively late chapter—and not necessarily the most important one—in a much longer story of intense battles over smuggling in the Americas, with illicit flows moving not just south to north but also north to south. Since the drug issue receives thorough treatment by others, including Isacson in chapter 7, I devote little attention to it here.

Porous borders and weak government capacity have long defined the region, and attempts to secure borders and tighten controls have often had the perverse and unintended consequence of creating a more formidable smuggling challenge. At the same time, efforts to regulate illicit border crossings have expanded the reach of central government authority and stimulated the development of border enforcement infrastructure and capacity. Bringing this history back into contemporary policy debates can offer fresh perspectives and lessons and provide an antidote to the often shrill and hyperbolic public discourse today about "out of control" borders.

Early History: The Illicit Trade and Conflict Connection

Much is made of the connection between illicit trade and insurgency today, with labels such as "narcoinsurgents," "narcoguerillas," and "narcoterrorists" commonly used to describe the close link between Colombia's Fuerzas Armadas Revolucionarias de Colombia (FARC) and the cocaine business. Such a link no doubt contributes to the FARC's stubborn persistence (though there is considerably debate regarding the nature and extent of the link). But there is nothing fundamentally new to this story. In various ways and to varying degrees, insurgents have long relied on different sorts of illicit commerce to fund their cause. This so-called crime-conflict nexus is not a post–Cold War invention. It goes back not just decades (note the controversial links between drugs and conflict during the Cold War in places ranging from Southeast Asia to South Asia to Central America) but centuries—as evident by looking at the United States' own early history.

Nowhere is this more apparent than in the case of the American Revolution. This is not meant to suggest that the FARC are the equivalent to America's Founding Fathers, but neither should the parallels be conveniently glossed over because they are impolite. Indeed, if anything, smuggling played a far more important role in the colonial era than today, with colonial merchants leading players in a thriving Atlantic smuggling economy.[4]

Smuggling goods in violation of strict British mercantilist trade rules was the cornerstone of colonial New England trade relations with the non-British Caribbean. Illicitly imported molasses from the West Indies kept Rhode Island and Massachusetts rum distilleries running. Rum exports, in turn, were a crucial ingredient in the infamous triangle trade, in which New England rum was traded for West African slaves, who in turn were sold to Caribbean plantations in exchange for more molasses. John Adams frankly acknowledged the importance of molasses as a precursor to the American Revolution: "I know not why we should blush to confess that molasses was an essential ingredient in American independence."[5]

The increasingly militarized British policing campaign against clandestine commerce in the decade prior to the Revolution provoked mob riots, burning of customs vessels, and tar-and-feathering of customs agents and informants. Pivotal incidents and protests, such as the Boston Tea Party, were closely connected to smuggling interests.

Deploying the British Royal to do antismuggling enforcement work was a deeply unpopular move in the colonies. Benjamin Franklin was one of the harshest critics of militarized interdiction, sarcastically writing:

> Convert the brave, honest officers of your navy into pimping tide-waiters and colony officers of the customs. Let those who in the time of war fought gallantly in defense of their countrymen, in peace be taught to prey upon it. Let them learn to be corrupted by great and real smugglers; but (to show their diligence) scour with armed boats every bay, harbor, river, creek, cove, or nook throughout your colonies; stop and detain every coaster, every wood-boat, every fisherman . . . O, this will work admirably![6]

Much of course has changed since Franklin wrote those words, but his basic critique of turning the military into antismuggling law enforcers still holds true today.

Once the armed rebellion in the American colonies began, the smuggling of war supplies—especially Dutch gunpowder transshipped through the Caribbean—sustained the Revolution in the crucial first phase before the French formally intervened on the side of the American rebels.[7] Partly thanks to smuggling, a ragtag force of colonial rebels was able to take on and defeat the world's most powerful military. Smugglers put their illicit transportation methods, skills, and networks to profitable use by covertly supplying George Washington's troops with desperately needed arms and gunpowder. Motivated as much by profit as by patriotism, they also served as privateers recruited by Washington for his makeshift naval force.[8]

And this was just one of a number of major American military conflicts in which success on the battlefield was tied to entrepreneurial success in the underworld of smuggling. Smuggling and fighting in war went hand in hand throughout the nation's early history, from "trading with the enemy" in the War of 1812 to blockade running during the American Civil War.

One of the many profiteers of the American War of Independence was John Brown of Providence. He emerged from the war as probably the wealthiest man in Rhode Island and also dabbled in the slave trade even after it was banned.[9] Meanwhile, his abolitionist brother, Moses Brown, preferred to engage in the illicit acquisition of British industrial technologies. He hired Samuel Slater (who smuggled himself out of England in violation of strict emigration laws) to work on and perfect the machinery. Slater is remembered as the father of the American industrial revolution.

Smuggling proved to be equally important in the American Civil War, deeply implicating neighboring Mexico and the Bahamas in Confederate efforts to evade the Northern blockade of Southern ports. Particularly important was the smuggling of cotton out to finance the smuggling of arms and other war supplies in. Cotton had all the attributes of a highly profitable "conflict commodity"—using today's language, we could call it "blood cotton." Mexico provided a convenient backdoor for Confederate cotton, as did Nassau in the Bahamas. As has been true for other insurgencies past and present, smuggling was a crucial factor in explaining why the American Civil War lasted as long as it did. However, in contrast to the American Revolution, smuggling was ultimately not enough to fundamentally shift the military balance of power on the ground in favor of the South. The Northern blockade was highly porous (and highly profitable for blockade runners), but still effective enough to constrain the Southern war effort.[10]

Then, as now, it was often difficult to clearly differentiate between greed and grievance in motivating rebellion. But there is certainly no evidence to suggest that today's insurgents are more profit driven than some of their American predecessors: one need only look at the large and lucrative privateering business (which the British defined as piracy) during the American Revolution or the blockade-running business during the American Civil War to realize how much the profit motive can contribute to a rebel political cause. The grievances were real, but so too were the contraband fortunes made from war. In this regard, "blood diamonds" and other "conflict commodities" today are no more important than Confederate cotton was in fueling a war that cost more American lives than any other conflict in US history.

Finally, we should not forget the crucial role of the United States in illicitly supplying neighboring rebellions. One example is the Haitian Revolution in the early years of the new republic, when American merchants defied Thomas Jefferson's orders to stop supplying the island's rebellion against French rule; another is the Mexican Revolution in the early twentieth century, when arms still flowed south despite the deployment of thousands of US troops to the border to stop the flow and enforce neutrality laws.[11] The parallels to today's gunrunning across the border are striking, even if the American guns are now supplying drug traffickers rather than revolutionary bandits such as Pancho Villa.

The Early History of Human Smuggling

The smuggling of people, not just goods, has also long been a crucial illicit economic link between the United States and its neighbors—long predating today's preoccupation with the smuggling of Mexicans and other migrants across the southern border. Indeed, the United States–Mexican War can be interpreted as a war over illegal American immigration, with the famous battle of the Alamo a de facto militarized immigration control campaign. Mexico banned further American migration to Texas, but the Americans kept coming.[12]

American slavers and American built and flagged slave ships were also the leading players in the transatlantic slave trade despite an 1808 federal ban on US involvement.[13] Southern US plantations continued to illicitly import slaves after the ban, but by far the most important importers were Cuba and Brazil. New York City was the world's leading center for outfitting slave ships right up until the outbreak of the American Civil War, much to the frustration of the British-led maritime campaign to suppress the trade.[14]

A very different sort of slave smuggling—the smuggling of fugitive slaves out of the United States via the so-called underground railroad—was made possible by neighboring countries (Mexico and Canada) ignoring US fugitive slave laws and successfully resisting intense US diplomatic pressure.[15] The fugitive slave issue was a major diplomatic irritant in United States–Canada and United States–Mexico relations, and was not resolved until the abolition of slavery itself.

It is also useful to remember that the first illegal migrants from Mexico that preoccupied US border enforcers were not Mexican but Chinese.[16] Indeed, the federal government did not get into the business of controlling immigration in a serious and sustained way until the efforts to prohibit Chinese immigration in the 1870s and 1880s; these efforts marked the beginning of Washington's long and tumultuous history of trying to keep out "undesirables." Before then, regulating immigration was mostly left to the states to sort out.

Starting in the 1850s, tens of thousands of Chinese laborers (many of whom left China in violation of their country's emigration laws) were welcomed in the American West as a source of cheap labor, especially for the building of the transcontinental railroad. But they were never welcomed as people. From the start, Chinese could not become citizens. So it is little surprise that when the demand for Chinese labor dried up, an anti-Chinese backlash quickly followed. And it is also no surprise that the backlash was most intense in California, home to most of the country's Chinese population. By 1870, Chinese composed some 10 percent of the state's population and about one-fourth of its workforce.

As political pressure to "do something" about the "yellow peril" intensified, Congress first passed the Page Act of 1875 (with enforcement mostly aimed at keeping out Chinese prostitutes), followed by the far more sweeping Chinese Exclusion Act of 1882. These exclusions were renewed, revised, strengthened, and extended to other Asian groups in subsequent years and decades (and were not repealed until 1943).[17]

As front door entry through San Francisco and other seaports became more heavily policed in the late nineteenth century, more and more Chinese immigrants turned to entry though the back door: America's vast and minimally policed northern and southern land borders. Canada became the favored transit country for smuggling Chinese immigrants into the United States in the late 1880s and 1890s. But as enforcement improved due to greater Canadian cooperation by the turn of the century, Chinese migrants and their smugglers increasingly turned to Mexico as the favorite gateway to the United States. Mexico was far less inclined than Canada to cooperate with the United States given the still festering wounds from having lost so much of its territory after the Mexican-American War more than half a century earlier. The US State Department tried to negotiate agreements with the Porfirio Díaz regime to curb Chinese entries, but these efforts went nowhere.

The United States–Mexico border, long an entry for smuggled goods, was now also becoming a gateway for smuggling people. As was the case in Canada, new steamship, railway, and road networks greatly aided migrant smuggling through Mexico. But unlike the Canadian case, Mexican transport companies showed little willingness to cooperate with the United States. An agent for one steamship company reportedly told US authorities that his next scheduled ship was expected to carry some three hundred Chinese passengers to the Mexican port of Guaymas in the border state of Sonora. "For all I know they may smuggle themselves into the United States and if they do I do not give a d-n, for I am doing a legitimate business."[18] Guaymas was connected by railway to the border town of Nogales.

Both the Treaty of Amity and Commerce signed by China and Mexico in 1899, and the establishment of direct steamship travel between Hong Kong and Mexico in 1902, opened the door for a surge in Chinese migration to Mexico, providing, in turn, a convenient stepping-stone for clandestine migration to the United States. In 1900 there were just a few thousand Chinese in Mexico, but less than a decade later nearly sixty thousand Chinese migrants had departed for Mexico. Some stayed, but the United States was a far more attractive destination. A banker in Guaymas told US Immigration Inspector Marcus Braun in 1906 that about twenty thousand Chinese had come to the state in recent years, but that less than four thousand remained. In his investigations, Braun witnessed Chinese arriving in Mexico, and reported, "On their arrival in Mexico, I found them to be provided with United States money, not Mexican coins; they had in their possession Chinese-English dictionaries; I found them in possession of Chinese-American newspapers and of American railroad maps."[19]

In 1907, a US government investigator observed that between twenty and fifty Chinese arrived daily in the Mexican border town of Juárez by train, but that the Chinese community in the town never grew. As he put it, "Chinamen coming to Ciudad Juarez either vanish into thin air or cross the border line."[20] Foreshadowing future developments, a January 1904 editorial in the *El Paso Herald-Post* warned: "If this Chinese immigration to Mexico continues it will be necessary to run a barb wire fence along our side of the Rio Grande."[21] The El Paso immigration inspector stated in his 1905 annual report that nearly two-thirds of the Chinese arriving in Juárez at the time were smuggled into the country in the vicinity of El Paso, and that migrant smuggling was the sole business of "perhaps one-third of the Chinese population of El Paso."[22]

With Mexico becoming the most popular back door to the United States, some smugglers relocated their operations from the United States–Canada border to the United States–Mexico border. One smuggler who made this move, Curley Roberts, reported to a potential partner: "I have just brought seven yellow boys over and got $225 for that so you can see I am doing very well here."[23] Some historians note that border smuggling operations involved cross-racial business collaborations, with white male smugglers often working with Chinese organizers and Mexicans serving as local border guides. A 1906 law enforcement report on Chinese smuggling noted, "All through northern Mexico, along the lines of the railroad, are located so-called boarding houses and restaurants, which are the rendezvous of the Chinese and their smugglers, and the small towns and villages throughout this section are filled with Chinese coolies, whose only occupation seems to be lying in wait until arrangement can be perfected for carrying them across the border."[24]

As US authorities tightened enforcement at urban entry points along the Mexico-California border, smugglers shifted to more remote sections farther east in Arizona, New Mexico, and Texas. And following the earlier pattern on the United States–Canada border, this move provided a rationale for the deployment of more agents to these border areas. In addition to the hiring of more port inspectors, a force of mounted inspectors was set up to patrol the borderline by horseback. As smugglers in later years turned to new technologies such as automobiles, officials also pushed for the use of the same technologies for border control.

With the tightening of border controls, smugglers sometimes opted to simply buy off rather than try to bypass US authorities in their efforts to move their human cargo across the line. This was the case in Nogales, Arizona, where border inspectors, including the collector of customs, reportedly charged smugglers between $50 and $200 per head until their arrest by special agents of the Treasury Department and Secret Service operatives in August 1901. Covering the case, the *Washington Post* reported, "with two or three exceptions, the whole customs and immigration administration at Nogales" was involved in the smuggling scheme.[25]

Chinese were not the only ones coming in illegally. They were simply at the top of a growing list of "undesirables." By the last decades of the nineteenth century federal law also prohibited the admission of paupers, criminals, prostitutes, "lunatics," "idiots," and contract workers in general (not just Chinese). And the list of inadmissible aliens kept growing: "those convicted of a crime of moral turpitude," polygamists, and persons with loathsome or dangerous contagious diseases were added in 1891. By 1903 there was a lengthy list of excludable illnesses, with trachoma the most common health reason given for exclusion. Anarchists were added to the exclusion list in 1903, and "imbeciles" and Japanese laborers were added in 1907. Illiterates were banned from entry in 1917. The head tax also increased sharply, from fifty cents in 1891 to four dollars in 1907 and eight dollars in 1917. Not surprisingly, as seaports became more tightly regulated and policed, immigrants who feared being placed in one of these excludable categories increasingly turned to the back door. Those groups that were disproportionally being turned away at the front door ports of entry—including Lebanese, Greeks, Italians, Slavs from the Balkans, and Jews—found Mexico to be a convenient alternative.

Chinese reportedly ran much of the smuggling business in border towns west of El Paso but relied on Mexicans to guide immigrants across the line. Also, given the importance of railways as the primary means of long-distance transport, it is little surprise that railroad workers, ranging from brakemen to dining car cooks to conductors, were found complicit in schemes to deliver smuggled migrants from the El Paso railroad terminal to interior destinations as far away as Chicago.

Since Mexicans were still of little concern to border inspectors, one deceptive ploy immigrants used to avoid being noticed was to try to appear Mexican. Almost all of the traffic back and forth through the port of entry in El Paso and in other urban areas along the border involved local residents who were typically not inspected. It was therefore not uncommon for unauthorized US-bound immigrants, ranging from Greeks to Lebanese to Chinese, to attempt the border crossing simply by blending in.

The relationship between smugglers and law enforcers along the border was not entirely adversarial. Not only was corruption sometimes part of their relationship but they also occasionally rubbed shoulders socially. For example, in his memoir, former immigration inspector Clifford Perkins notes that El Paso Deputy Sheriff Mannie Clements "had been mixed up with the smuggling of narcotics and Chinese," and also recalls drinking rice whiskey with Charlie Sam, a prominent figure in the El Paso Chinese community who was reputed to be "the brains behind the smuggling of Chinese." On another occasion, Tom Kate, dubbed the "king of smugglers" in the El Paso area, apparently threw a party for the city's attorneys and judiciary members. The list of prominent attendees included federal judicial commissioners whose workload contained cases involving Chinese-migrant smuggling and the assistant US attorney prosecuting such smuggling cases.[26]

The Mexican Revolution between 1910 and 1917, and World War I, disrupted the use of Mexico as a stepping-stone for illegal entry by non-Mexicans into the United States. But migrant smuggling through Mexico strongly rebounded when international steamship service was resumed. It then involved smuggling Europeans rather than Chinese. Mexico had become a far less hospitable environment for Chinese during the course of the Mexican Revolution, with many Chinese residents in Mexico robbed and abused as a particularly vulnerable minority population. (Many fled the chaos and violence of the revolution years by moving to the United States illegally.)

The growing influx of unauthorized Mexican workers, meanwhile, was largely tolerated, and employers informally recruited large numbers of Mexicans to work in southwest agriculture. Formal, legal entry was complicated, but crossing the border illegally was relatively simple and generally ignored. Strict controls against Mexicans crossing the border were widely perceived as neither viable nor desirable. As a substitute for European and Asian workers, Mexicans were considered an ideal labor force: flexible, compliant, temporary, and a vital source of labor for agriculture.

The Prohibition Era

The importance of smuggling for US economic relations with its neighbors received a major boost when the sale of alcohol was prohibited in America between 1920 and 1933. This was America's first true "drug war," with powerful ripple effects across the region. But unlike today's southern-focused drug war, much of the attempted control of alcohol smuggling concentrated on the northern border. The alcohol smuggling role of Canada and Canadian border towns (particularly Windsor across from Detroit) rivals the importance of Mexico and Mexican border towns today in the drug trade. But government complicity was even more blatant than it is today; Canadian distillers were given licenses to set up warehouses on the banks of the Detroit River, and Canadian customs agents would sign off on paperwork indicating the booze was not destined for the US market just across the line.[27]

Mexico also took advantage of the booming booze smuggling business, specializing in illicit tequila shipments across the border. At first, *tequileros* (smugglers on horseback) dominated the business of moving the product into Texas, but a successful US crackdown put them out of business by the late 1920s—only to be replaced by more organized, sophisticated, and violent smugglers using cars and trucks.[28] This dynamic of law enforcement "success" in putting some smugglers out of business, which then prompted the rise of smugglers more difficult to police, would play out again and again in later antidrug trafficking campaigns in Mexico and elsewhere in the region.

Finally, the Caribbean would again take advantage of geographic proximity to the United States in playing a lead role in the Prohibition-induced alcohol smuggling boom. Repeating the arms-for-cotton transshipment role it played during the American Civil War, Nassau in the Bahamas became a hub for supplying "Rum Row"—the flotilla of ships with cargoes of alcohol anchored off of the Atlantic coast just outside of US territorial waters. Small, fast boats would then dart out from the shore to load up and return while trying to evade US Coast Guard ships.[29] History would repeat itself half a century later when Colombian drug traffickers such as Carlos Lehder used the Bahamas as a convenient jumping off point for their US-bound illicit cargoes.

From Evading Tariffs to Violating Prohibitions

Some of the pioneers of illicit trade between the United States and its southern neighbors were smugglers of legal goods evading high tariffs and taxes—the classic "contrabandistas." In the twentieth century, as in the previous one, much of this contraband commerce flowed north to south, ranging from illicitly shipping Levi blue jeans to Paraguay, cigarettes to Colombia, and kitchen appliances to Mexico. Small aircraft became the preferred mode of transportation. Emptying their cargoes on the southbound trip, some of these planes began to load up with marijuana and other illegal drugs for the northbound return. This was a mostly nonviolent trade. Corruption in the form of paying off inspectors and air traffic controllers was routine.[30]

Although high taxes on particular luxury goods, most notably booze and cigarettes, continues to invite the smuggling of legal commodities today, the dramatic lowering of trade barriers through market liberalization across the region has removed much of the incentives for this type of smuggling. In this sense, globalization through trade liberalization has actually significantly decreased smuggling.[31]

But while the lowering of trade barriers as part of the broader process of economic liberalization and market reform has drastically curtailed the smuggling of legal goods, the persistence and expansion of selective trade criminalization has given life to the smuggling of all sorts of prohibited goods. Some smugglers therefore simply switched products and adapted to changing market conditions. Moreover, the rising flow of legal goods across borders provided a convenient cover to hide illegal goods in commercial cargo conveyances.[32]

The switch to illicit drugs—especially cocaine, heroin, and marijuana, but later also synthetics such as crystal meth and MDMA—is the most obvious example. This is a trade magnified in importance by its profitability. Additionally, endangered species and antiquities flow north, and small arms and dirty money flow south. The Cayman Islands and other places in the Caribbean have become major financial havens with strict bank secrecy laws, serving a diverse clientele ranging from tax-evading corporate executives to drug traffickers stashing their ill-gotten gains.[33]

FUTURE TRAJECTORIES

While the sheer magnitude of illicit border crossings is likely higher today than ever before, as a percentage of overall cross-border economic activity these flows are not necessarily more significant today than in earlier eras. Viewed from this broader historical perspective, it is clear that the limited and highly uneven capacity to police illicit cross-border flows has always been a reality for US government authorities. If anything, it should be recognized that US capacity to police its borders today is probably greater than at any other time in history. But that does not mean that border controls are terribly effective, and this is a reality that is unlikely to change anytime soon. More border agents will continue to be deployed, new detection and interdiction technologies will continue to be developed, but smugglers will also continue to go around, through, over, or under the border barriers. Policing campaigns will continue to shape the methods, organization, and location of smuggling, yet are unlikely to completely deter the trafficking.

So where is this story headed? One thing for certain is that the story does not end. Smuggling will persist, as it always has. What will vary are its location, organization, method, and content. In 1984, the *Wall Street Journal's* editorial page advocated a constitutional amendment: "There shall be open borders."[34] But until that actually happens—an unlikely prospect anytime soon—we will continue to simultaneously treat borders as both bridges and barriers, and be frustrated by the inherent awkwardness and difficulty of facilitating and enforcing at the same time.

In the case of drug trafficking, we can speculate that the violence that has overwhelmed Mexico in recent years will eventually subside but without a substantial reduction in the flow of drugs to the United States, consistent with evidence presented by Isacson in chapter 7 regarding drug trafficking and the United States–Mexico border. One possibility is a partial shift in trafficking routes back to the Caribbean, but via a growing use of submersible and semisubmersible vessels. This is an alarming development from a US national security perspective—since such delivery mechanisms can also transport other things—but it is actually a positive trend from the perspective of reducing drug corruption and limiting the collateral damage of the drug trade along trafficking routes. After all, the more removed the illegal drug trade is from legal commerce, population centers, and transportation channels, the better. Of course, if the use of submersibles and semisubmersibles, which is still at a fairly early stage, really takes off, perhaps this will provide a rationale to adapt and deploy the US navy's latest submarine detection technologies for counternarcotics purposes.

At the same time, we may see a growing domestication of the drug trade. A legalized or at least substantially decriminalized marijuana market, for example, would give domestic growers a distinct competitive advantage over foreign suppliers. Tighter border interdiction in recent decades has already served as an unintended form of marijuana protectionism; because marijuana is a bulky and smelly product, it is the easiest drug to interdict, and the vast majority of border drug busts indeed involve marijuana seizures. More effective interdiction would likely only reinforce this dynamic. Moreover, the development of new synthetics, including potentially synthetic cocaine, could reduce imports if the barriers to entry and law enforcement–induced risks were sufficiently low. Of course, we may also simply see a repetition of the methamphetamine story, in which domestic law enforcement pressure has pushed much of the production to Mexico. In that case, we would have yet another illustration of history repeating itself.

Continuity and Change

So what has really changed in this centuries-long smuggling story? Perhaps the most striking change is the enormous historical variability in what cross-border economic activities are (and are not) criminalized and prioritized by law enforcement. The single most important smuggling business today—drug trafficking—involves commodities that were not even illegal a century and more ago. And the backbone of much smuggling in earlier historical eras—the smuggling of legal goods to evade tariffs and taxes—is now more of a sideshow in the world of smuggling.

Much smuggling today involves violating prohibitions designed to eradicate rather than regulate the targeted activity. These prohibitions typically involve moral condemnation; criminalization designates particular behavior as inherently "evil" and "bad." It is not about generating revenue for state coffers or protecting domestic industries, but rather about signaling moral disapproval and protecting dominant societal values. In this sense, smuggling today, even while thriving, is considered much more taboo than in earlier centuries. And no country in the world today is more aggressive in promoting and exporting its favored prohibitions than the United States, with its Latin American neighbors receiving a disproportionate amount of the attention. At the same time, the United States is highly selective in its moral condemnation—for example, targeting the drugs flowing north while virtually ignoring the weapons flowing south that arm the drug traffickers.

It is also reasonable to conclude that certain forms of smuggling today involve more violence than in the past. This is particularly evident in the case of the international drug trade, where the firepower wielded by some trafficking organizations presents a formidable threat to state authority, as was the case in Colombia in recent decades, and Mexico and some Central American countries today. Part of this is due to the unusually high financial stakes and high risks of the drug trade, an increasingly militarized war on drugs that rewards the most ruthless traffickers, and the availability of high-powered weaponry (much of which originates in the United States and is smuggled to drug exporting and transit countries such as Mexico).

But this claim of change regarding the violent nature of smuggling should not be misunderstood or overstated. After all, no modern drug trafficking organization can come close to rivaling the power and reach of the British East India Company, which enjoyed a virtual monopoly on smuggling opium into China in its heyday. And indeed, when China finally balked at such smuggling and tried to crack down, the result was the Opium Wars of the mid-nineteenth century in which the Chinese opium market was kept open through the barrel of a gun. Similarly, while much is made today of the smuggling of "conflict commodities" and arms trafficking in sustaining many contemporary wars, it would be hard to argue that any conflict commodity today has been more important than the role of smuggled cotton in helping to perpetuate the American Civil War, or the role of arms trafficking in helping George Washington's troops defeat the world's leading military power.

Moreover, the many who today focus mainly on those illicit trades most closely associated with high violence (the drug trade and sex trafficking) too often overlook the substantial diversity of illicit trade and its mostly nonviolent nature. This includes, for example, the smuggling of endangered species (though this, too, is violence if one counts the substantial brutality inflicted on the animals being smuggled), art, and antiquities; money laundering (though some of these funds come from violent trades such as drugs); and intellectual property theft.

And even within the drug trade there is considerable variation in the levels and types of violence that is too often overlooked. Cocaine and heroin, for example, are much more closely associated with violence than marijuana and hallucinogens such as LSD and MDMA. There is a clear selection bias in media coverage and policy attention that privileges the most violent illicit trades, which in turn misleadingly suggests that illicit trades are inherently violent. For the most part, smugglers are sneaky rather than violent and predatory. They typically wish to evade and buy off the state rather than bully it. And while business disputes are sometimes resolved through violence or threats of violence because there are no legal protections—meaning some illicit actors resort to killing rather than suing each other—there may nevertheless be other forms of informal and largely nonviolent dispute resolution mechanisms.[35]

The revolutions in transportation and communication associated with globalization are also arguably a major source of change for both licit and illicit trade. As President Barack Obama put it in July 2011, "During the past fifteen years, technological innovation and globalization have proven to be an overwhelming force for good. However, transnational criminal organizations have taken advantage of our increasingly interconnected world to expand their illicit enterprises."[36] True enough. The Internet has even given rise to a new form of smuggling—"cybersmuggling"—of commodities that range from pirated software and industrial secrets to Hollywood films and child pornography. But in some respects this is simply a new medium rather than an entirely new type of crime.

Furthermore, as transformative as new technologies have been in shaping both licit and illicit business transactions, it would be difficult to argue that these new technologies have had a more profound impact than the rise of transoceanic commerce, the development of the telegraph, the proliferation of train travel, and the invention of the automobile. Those technologies arose long before globalization became a buzzword. In other words, new technologies do matter, often profoundly, but this is also an old story that dates back not just years, but centuries.

Law enforcement authorities have long grumbled about how new technologies advantage criminals. But less noticed is that law enforcement has also been a major beneficiary of technological change; consider, for example, how much the invention of photography and fingerprinting enhanced criminal investigations and the development of government-issued identification documents. The invention of the telephone aided not only criminals but also police, and included the use of wiretapping as a crucial tool in undercover investigations.

And new technologies today continue to be exploited by government authorities, as evident in the creation of more tamper-resistant travel documents and "smart" IDs with biometric identifiers; the creation of more expansive and sophisticated databases for "data mining"; and the proliferation of high tech cargo tracking, monitoring, and inspection devices. Technology has also enabled governments to usually stay one step ahead of currency counterfeiters. Currency counterfeiting remains a serious problem today, but pales in comparison to the much more rampant counterfeiting during much of the nineteenth century.

Final Thoughts

There never was a golden age of secure borders. To suggest otherwise is pure mythology, a false nostalgia for a past that never existed. Moreover, too often conveniently forgotten is that the magnitude of today's border smuggling challenge is partly self-created; pressure on Colombian drug trafficking routes through the Caribbean and South Florida in the 1980s pushed the illicit trade westward to the United States–Mexico border. This shift is much to the delight of Mexican traffickers who today are Mexico's most serious security challenge. Similarly, enforcement crackdowns on illegal migration at urban ports of entry along the southwest border in the 1990s pushed migrants to rely much more on the services of professional people smugglers to navigate the border crossing, thereby creating a much more profitable and sophisticated transnational crime problem.

As has always been the case, there are inherent limits to how much border enforcers can deter, detect, and interdict illicit economic activities, especially while maintaining an open society and keeping borders open for legal trade and travel. In the case of the United States, for example, an average of nearly a million people; more than sixty thousand truck, rail, and sea containers; and about a quarter-million privately owned vehicles legally entered the country *every day* in 2010. That same year, more than $2 trillion in legal imports crossed out borders. Facilitating this enormous volume of licit border crossings while attempting to enforce laws against illicit crossings is and will remain an inherently cumbersome and frustrating task.

But this situation need not lead to more collective hyperventilating about broken borders and transnational crime threats. The sky is not falling. Of course, border crossings can and should be more effectively and efficiently regulated—which is needed not only to discourage unwanted crossings but also to facilitate legitimate trade and travel. But drawing more attention to these enormous challenges should not require resorting to shrill calls to "regain control" when borders were never actually under control in the first place.

NOTES

1. Official estimates of the size and magnitude of such illicit flows in the Americas and elsewhere are "guesstimates," at best. For a more detailed and critical discussion, see Peter Andreas and Kelly M. Greenhill, eds., *Sex, Drugs, and Body Counts: The Politics of Numbers in Global Crime and Conflict* (Ithaca, NY: Cornell University Press, 2010).

2. This contrasts sharply with the otherwise strong push to liberalize markets and promote free trade in the region in recent decades—which can also produce tensions and contradictions. For early accounts in the case of the drug trade, see Peter Andreas, "Free Market Reform and Drug Market Prohibition: US Policies at Cross-Purposes in Latin America," *Third World Quarterly* 16, no. 1 (1995): 75–88; and Peter Andreas and Coletta

Youngers, "U.S. Drug Policy and the Andean Cocaine Industry," *World Policy Journal* 6, no. 3 (1989): 529–62.

3. For a more detailed account, see Peter Andreas, *Smuggler Nation: How Illicit Trade Made America* (New York, NY: Oxford University Press, 2013).

4. For a more detailed account, see Andreas, *Smuggler Nation*, chs. 1–3.

5. John Adams to William Tudor, August 11, 1818, in John Adams, *The Works of John Adams, Second President of the United States: With a Life of the Author, Notes and Illustrations, by his Grandson Charles Francis Adams*, ed. Charles Francis Adams, 10 vols. (Boston, MA: Little, Brown, 1856), Vol. 10, 345.

6. *The Political Thoughts of Benjamin Franklin*, ed. Ralph L. Ketcham (1965; reprint Indianapolis, IN: Bobbs-Merrill, 2003), 262.

7. See Andreas, *Smuggler Nation*, ch. 3.

8. Robert H. Patton, *Patriot Pirates: The Privateer War for Freedom and Fortune in the American Revolution* (New York, NY: Pantheon, 2008).

9. See, for example, Charles Rappleye, *Sons of Providence: The Brown Brothers, the Slave Trade, and the American Revolution* (New York, NY: Simon and Schuster, 2006).

10. On the dynamics of blockade running, see Stephen R. Wise, *Lifeline of the Confederacy: Blockade Running during the Civil War* (Columbia, SC: University of South Carolina Press, 1988).

11. On illicit supplies to the Haitian rebels, see Donald R. Hickey, "America's Response to the Slave Revolt in Haiti, 1791–1806," *Journal of the Early Republic* 2, no. 4 (winter 1982): 361–79. On the smuggling of US arms into Mexico during the Mexican Revolution, see Charles H. Harris and Louis R. Sadler, *The Border and the Revolution: Clandestine Activities of the Mexican Revolution, 1910–1920* (Silver City, NM: High Lonesome, 1988). On the particular importance of El Paso, Texas, see Harris and Sadler's *The Secret War in El Paso: Mexican Revolutionary Intrigue, 1906–1920* (Albuquerque, NM: University of New Mexico Press, 2009).

12. See Peter Andreas, *Border Games: Policing the U.S.-Mexico Divide* (Ithaca, NY: Cornell University Press, 2000).

13. For a comprehensive review of state and federal antislave trade laws, see W.E.B. Dubois, *The Suppression of the African Slave Trade to the United States of America 1638–1870* (1898; repr., New York, NY: Russell & Russell, 1965, first published 1898).

14. See Ann Farrow, Joel Lang, and Jennifer Frank, *Complicity: How the North Promoted, Prolonged, and Profited from Slavery* (New York, NY: Ballentine, 2006); and Warren S. Howard, *American Slavers and the Federal Law, 1837–1862* (Berkeley, CA: University of California Press, 1963).

15. See Ronnie C. Tyler, "Fugitive Slaves in Mexico," *Journal of Negro History* 57, no. 1 (January 1972): 1–12; and Ethan A. Nadelmann, *Cops across Borders* (University Park, PA: Pennsylvania State University Press, 1993), 36.

16. See especially Patrick Ettinger, *Imaginary Lines: Border Enforcement and the Origins of Undocumented Immigration, 1882–1930* (Austin, TX: University of Texas Press, 2009).

17. See Erika Lee, *At America's Gates: Chinese Immigration during the Exclusion Era, 1882–1943* (Chapel Hill, NC: University of North Carolina Press, 2003).

18. Quoted in Lee, *At America's Gates*, 181.

19. Quoted in Ettinger, *Imaginary Lines*, 100.

20. Quoted in Lee, *At America's Gates*, 159.

21. Quoted in Ettinger, *Imaginary Lines*, 93.

22. Quoted in James Bronson Reynolds, "Enforcement of the Chinese Exclusion Law," *Annals of the American Academy of Political Science* 34, no. 2 (1909): 368.

23. Quoted in Lee, *At America's Gates*, 159.

24. Quoted in Ettinger, *Imaginary Lines*, 60.

25. "Bribes from Chinese," *Washington Post*, August 25, 1901.

26. The information in this paragraph is drawn from Clifford Perkins, *Border Patrol: With the U.S. Immigration Service on the Mexican Boundary, 1910–54* (El Paso, TX: Texas Western Press, 1978).

27. There is a substantial literature on the Prohibition era. See, for example, Daniel Okrent, *Last Call: The Rise and Fall of Prohibition* (New York, NY: Scribner, 2010); and John Kobler, *Ardent Spirits: The Rise and Fall of Prohibition* (1973; repr, New York, NY: Da Capo, 1993). On the dynamics of smuggling across the United States–Canada border, see Andreas, *Smuggler Nation*, 243–48.

28. See George T. Diaz, "Twilight of the Tequileros: Prohibition-Era Smuggling in the South Texas Borderlands, 1919–1933," in *Smugglers, Brothels, and Twine: Historical Perspectives on Contraband and Vice in North America's Borderlands*, ed. Elaine Carey and Andrae M. Marak (Tucson, AZ: University of Arizona Press, 2011).

29. See, for example, Robert Carse, *Rum Row: The Liquor Fleet that Fueled the Roaring Twenties* (1928; repr., Mystic, CT: Flat Hammock Press, 2007); Harold Waters, *Smugglers of Spirits: Prohibition and the Coast Guard Patrol* (New York, NY: Hastings House, 1971); and Everett S. Allen, *The Black Ships: Rumrunners of Prohibition* (Boston, MA: Little, Brown, 1979).

30. Evert Clark and Nicholas Horrock, *Contrabandista!* (New York, NY: Praeger, 1973).

31. This is an obvious but often forgotten point. For a discussion, see Peter Andreas, "Illicit Globalization: Myths, Misconceptions, and Historical Lessons," *Political Science Quarterly* 126, no. 3 (fall 2011): 403–25.

32. For a more detailed discussion of how economic liberalization interacts with and shapes illicit cross-border flows, see Peter Andreas, "Transnational Crime and Economic Liberalization," in *Transnational Organized Crime and International Security*, ed. Mats Berdal and Mónica Serrano (Boulder, CO: Lynne Rienner, 2002).

33. For a useful recent examination of money laundering and anti-money laundering initiatives, see J. C. Sharman, *The Money Laundry: Regulating Criminal Finance in the Global Economy* (Ithaca, NY: Cornell University Press, 2011).

34. "In Praise of Huddled Masses," *Wall Street Journal*, July 3, 1984.

35. On the relationship between violence and illicit markets, see the special issue of *Crime, Law & Social Change*, September 2009 (guest edited by Peter Andreas and Joel Wallman, and sponsored by the Harry Frank Guggenheim Foundation).

36. Daily Comp. Pres. Docs., 2011 DCPD No. 201100523, introductory statement.

Chapter Nine

The Colombian FARC in Northern Ecuador

Borderline and Borderland Dynamics

Maiah Jaskoski

The Colombia-Ecuador border has received a great deal of attention from scholars and the international policy community due to the entrenched presence of Colombian insurgents in northern Ecuador.[1] The borderline, which has been uncontested since the early twentieth century,[2] has seen little presence by either the Colombian or Ecuadorian state in recent decades. Instead, the Fuerzas Armadas Revolucionarias de Colombia (FARC), currently Latin America's largest, most powerful guerrilla movement, have physically delineated the borderline. In doing so, the group has helped safeguard northern Ecuador as a respite zone. That is, the very insurgents that rely on free passage to neighboring borderlands for rest, training, and supplies, most directly enforce the borderline. This finding runs counter to the views that such a guerrilla movement would want an ill-defined border, and that only states define borders.

Here, the Ecuadorian state's role in marking the border has been indirect. The FARC have enforced the international border largely in response to Ecuadorian state actions. As the chapter will show, Ecuador's government consistently has taken the position that FARC combatants—or for that matter, members of any armed Colombian group—are not to cross into or operate in Ecuador in any capacity, and there has been an increased army presence in the north to implement that policy. However, serious inadequacies in the capacity of the army have meant that it has not assertively fortified the borderline. In reaction to this increased but limited state effort, the FARC have pursued various tactics that have helped to both physically delineate the border and safeguard their access to the north. When the guerrillas first moved south in the 1980s, they contributed to demarcating the borderline through combat against the Ecuadorian armed forces. Since the 1990s, having become reliant on Ecuador's borderlands for rest and training, the FARC have helped define the borderline by behaving differently in Colombia, where they are engaged in warfare, than in Ecuador's borderlands, where they are not. The insurgents have also enforced the border by exercising coercion and economic influence within Ecuadorian border communities and by actively maintaining peaceful relations with the Ecuadorian army.

Insurgents, Borders, and Weak States

Analyses of Colombia's internal conflict have observed the FARC's reliance on territory across Colombia's international borders for respite and training, especially during Plan Colombia, a major counterinsurgency and antinarcotics effort that started in 2000 and was funded by the United States and Colombia. Experts have emphasized how territory in Ecuador and Venezuela has been particularly attractive to the FARC, as those "live" borderlands are home to sizable populations and economic activity. In contrast, the guerrilla group has not moved with much force into Peru's sparsely populated borderlands, or into neighboring Brazilian territory, which lacks significant populations while enjoying considerable state presence.[3]

These studies of spillover from the Colombian conflict leave out how international borders matter to the FARC. Specifically, a crucial piece of the story is that in order for neighboring borderlands to serve as a source of support, the actual borderline must be easily crossable—that is, it must not be heavily guarded by state actors—and yet must also carry real meaning, in that it needs to separate conflict zones from resting spaces. This dynamic involving insurgents and borders has been observed by research on conflict in Africa, where fixed borderlines delineate peaceful zones for insurgents to rest and resupply; these are areas that are accessible when the state is absent from the border.[4]

To understand how borderlines remain in place despite a lack of such physical state presence, we can turn to research on state building in the developing world. In *Blood and Debt*, Miguel Centeno argues that unlike in Europe, where wars contributed to strong states and state-defended international borders, most Latin American countries lacked the national unity and administrative capacity to benefit from wars in these ways (see also chapter 2 in this volume). That is, international warfare has done little to redraw or physically mark the boundaries left by colonial powers.[5] Similar to the Latin American reality, international boundaries in Africa have persisted and have been respected despite the lack of state capacity to defend them. Jeffrey Herbst has highlighted the power of unfortified international borderlines in Africa as institutions. In a context of economic crisis, weak societal cohesion, and challenging geography, leaders at the helm of weak states that lack physical control over territory nonetheless have extended national government authority: "African boundaries have perhaps been the critical foundation upon which leaders have built their states," serving, for example, as a basis for defining currencies and citizenship.[6]

Consistent with Centeno and Herbst, the present analysis finds that the Colombia-Ecuador borderline has not experienced strong state presence and yet still has carried important meaning. However, in contrast to these other analyses, this chapter takes a local perspective on border making. In doing so, it reveals two shortcomings to stories of borders that rest on a strong state–weak state dichotomy. First, in practice, the Colombia-Ecuador border has been enforced most powerfully not by the state, but by the guerrillas that rely on routine border crossings. Second, the insurgents who are physically delineating the borderline have not operated in a setting of state absence. Instead, their behavior has been a response to the Ecuadorian state, which has been active in the north to an intermediate degree. Others, too, have observed that a weak but not absent state apparatus in a given region can help an insurgency thrive. Ken Menkhaus and Jacob N. Shapiro note this for other countries: "In weak states, groups like Al-Qa'ida found a target-rich environment where they were protected from Western counterterrorism efforts and yet were not significantly interdicted by the state's corrupt law enforcement and intelligence apparatus. Meanwhile, in failed states like Somalia, Al-Qa'ida suffered from logistical constraints, a hostile set of local political actors, and relatively unrestricted Western counterterrorism efforts."[7]

Similarly, this chapter focuses on how the FARC grew in strength in Ecuador's borderlands and on the Colombia-Ecuador borderline because of limited state capacity. Yet in contrast to Menkhaus and Shapiro's findings, there is a dynamic relationship between FARC power and the Ecuadorian state. In response to a feeble Ecuadorian army in the north, the FARC have competed with the state to control the borderline and thus achieve access to Ecuador's borderlands. Because of weak state capacity, the insurgents have "won," successfully achieving control of the border.

FARC Dominance in Southern Colombia

Crucial to the FARC's role on the borderline and in northern Ecuador is the insurgency's entrenchment in southern Colombia. The country's internal conflict in recent decades has involved the leftist FARC and Ejército de Liberación Nacional (ELN) insurgencies, illegal right-wing paramilitary groups with ties to the Colombian military, and the military itself.[8] Beginning in the mid-1980s, the FARC spread into Colombia's southern coca-producing department of Putumayo, which borders the northeastern Ecuadorian jungle province of Sucumbíos.[9] The FARC became so dominant in southern Colombia that the Andrés Pastrana administration (1998–2002) yielded to the guerrilla group an expanse of territory the size of Switzerland. The FARC ran this region, known as "el despeje," like a government, collecting taxes and organizing markets, from November 1998 until the collapse of peace talks between the government and the FARC in February 2002.[10] That breakdown marked a shift in Colombian policy away from negotiating with the FARC. Central to President Álvaro Uribe's (2002–2010) hardline policies was Plan Colombia, intensified by the 2004 US-backed Plan Patriota, a military offensive on insurgents in the south.[11] The power of the FARC and the ELN was greatly reduced under Uribe. Nonetheless, the groups still survive, and the FARC have remained embedded in the south and southwest.[12] The ELN and paramilitaries have also operated in parts of the south.

For purposes of this analysis of the FARC's border role, the lack of Colombian state presence at the border is as important as FARC power in southern Colombia. The Colombian military's counterinsurgency strategy in the south has been to attack the FARC in border zones from bases located inland from the border; as of the mid-2000s, the armed forces did not have established posts along the international border.[13]

Border Delineation by Military Force: FARC Attacks on Ecuador's Army, 1980s–1990s

The FARC first took part in physically demarcating the international borderline when they violently responded to Ecuadorian state presence on the border in the 1980s and 1990s, staging military attacks on army border patrols and posts. Lacking the capacity to take on a northern front, Ecuador's army retreated, granting the FARC control of the borderline and access to the northern borderlands.

In 1986 and 1987, after having established themselves in Putumayo, the FARC carried out a string of attacks on several Ecuadorian army posts in Sucumbíos—

including the Coembí, El Conejo, and Santa Rosa detachments—and ambushed Ecuadorian army border patrols, as described by a former Ecuadorian army helicopter pilot who worked in the north during the attacks. Ecuadorian army leaders reacted by removing all posts from Sucumbíos's international border.[14]

The FARC staged their last military assault on Ecuadorian state security forces in 1993. Late that year, the Ecuadorian army and police conducted two antinarcotics river operations on the border, supported by the US Drug Enforcement Administration. Between two hundred and three hundred FARC members ambushed the second operation, killing eleven Ecuadorian security personnel—seven from the police, and four from the army.[15] The army withdrew immediately; when members of Ecuador's national police went to Sucumbíos to investigate the killings, they sought assistance from an army unit in the north. The unit refused to accompany the police for the stated reason that the area was now FARC territory.[16] Following the ambush, the army halted assertive river patrols, and there were no more FARC attacks on the army.

The Ecuadorian army's timidity toward the FARC on the borderline during the 1980s and early 1990s can be explained by its limited capacity to take on the guerrillas as an enemy. The army was intensely focused on defending the country's southern border against Peru's armed forces, amid a longstanding border dispute; after their defeat by the Peruvian military in 1981, the Ecuadorian armed forces had embarked on a period of training and equipment acquisitions to prepare for future confrontations against their rival.[17] Confronting a second, northern front against an armed insurgency would have been too much for the Ecuadorian army. Indeed, according to an Ecuadorian journalist and the former army helicopter pilot, the decision to close the Sucumbíos border detachments was linked directly to the army's prioritization of southern border defense. In the early and mid-1990s, the Peru-Ecuador conflict escalated. Starting in 1991 the Ecuadorian military sent troops to the disputed territory, which in 1994 led the Peruvian military to patrol the zone.[18] The outcome of these actions was the 1995 Cenepa War between the two countries.

The Ecuadorian army's weakness kept it from aggressively guarding the border against the FARC, despite government and military concern about the guerrillas. The Ecuadorian state was not eager to hand control of the border over to the FARC. In the early 1990s, for example, the central government did send more military personnel to the north when "guerrilla activities seemed on the rise."[19] For its part, the Ecuadorian army took seriously the attacks on army detachments in the mid-1980s; army personnel who survived the ambushes received medals.[20]

The FARC's Reliance on Ecuadorian Borderlands
since the 1990s

In the 1990s the FARC's relationship to northern Ecuador changed. The expanding insurgency came to depend on Ecuador's three northern border provinces—Sucumbíos, Carchi in the northern highlands, and the coastal, jungle province of Esmeraldas—as areas in which to recuperate, resupply, and train. The importance of the provinces to the guerrillas grew during the heightened combat resulting from Plan Colombia and Plan Patriota.[21] This section describes the different legal and illegal facets of FARC presence in the north beginning in the 1990s. Subsequent sections discuss Ecuadorian state policy toward the insurgents during this period and how they have reacted to that policy to ensure their ongoing access to the north.

The FARC's Illicit Activities

Perhaps the most stunning aspect of illegal FARC behavior in northern Ecuador is that armed, uniformed guerrillas have operated training and resting posts in Ecuador. Based on information provided in 2003 by detained members of the FARC, Ecuador's military intelligence agency reported that there were approximately one hundred such installations in Sucumbíos alone.[22] The FARC camp in northern Ecuador most known internationally was located in the area of Angostura, Sucumbíos, nearly two kilometers from the Colombian border. The camp received substantial attention after a 2008 Colombian military operation crossed into Ecuador and destroyed the post, killing twenty-five individuals, including FARC combatants.[23]

Camps facilitate border crossings by guerrillas engaged in combat. In August 2001, one base in Ecuador measuring roughly eighty square meters was large enough for two hundred insurgents. It included trenches, nets over the trees for camouflage, and an underground tunnel that opened into the San Miguel River— which marks the international borderline—to allow insurgents to escape from Colombia to Ecuador.[24] The FARC have actually planned and initiated some of their attacks in Colombia from these posts in Ecuador, as was the case in June 2005, when they killed nineteen Colombian army personnel in a confrontation just across the border from Carchi.[25]

Although the 1993 ambush of the Ecuadorian river patrol was the FARC's last organized military attack in Ecuador, they have continued to engage in other types of violence in the northern part of the country. Some such acts have targeted paramilitaries, who have been active in the north, as well. For example, in August 2000, Colombian paramilitaries carried out an unsuccessful extortion attempt in Nueva Loja, the capital of Sucumbíos, seeking to "shake down" their victim for collaborating with the FARC. Soon after the event, the FARC killed two accomplices of those paramilitaries.[26] Other FARC violence has been directed at civilians. In August 2000, the FARC killed three Ecuadorian merchants over a business dispute on a road leading to Nueva Loja.[27] In a highly publicized case, individuals believed to be members of the FARC kidnapped ten oil workers in northern Ecuador in October 2000 and transported them to Colombia for ransom.[28]

Notably, the spillover of violence and crime from southern Colombia into northern Ecuador has involved acts committed by Colombian and Ecuadorian civilians, and not just members of illegal armed groups. Often it has been difficult to know whether insurgents or civilians have been responsible for violent acts, but the general impression of security experts, human rights observers, and public officials is that the FARC—as well as paramilitaries—have the resources to hire Colombian and Ecuadorian civilians to carry out their "dirty work" in Ecuador.

The cocaine trade looms large because it is critical for funding the paramilitaries and the FARC.[29] Northern Ecuador contributes considerably to the cocaine trade by producing and moving chemical precursors used to process cocaine, including petroleum ether, a byproduct of the oil refining process. As of 2004, smugglers stole approximately fourteen thousand gallons of this "white gas" (*gasa blanca*) daily from the state oil company's (Petroecuador) refinery in Sucumbíos.[30] Coca leaves, cocaine, and "base" and "paste" created in the cocaine-production process, have been transported across the north to be exported via ports along Colombia and Ecuador's Pacific coasts. According to Ecuadorian antinarcotics officials, northern Ecuador has been attractive for transporting all of these goods, because by circumventing Colombian territory, drug traffickers have avoided paying the FARC taxes.[31]

Weapons transfers in the region also support the FARC. Based on captures between 1998 and August 2000, Colombian police intelligence identified Ecuador as the principal provider of munitions to Colombian insurgents, and second to Venezuela as a weapons provider.[32]

Violence in northern Ecuadorian towns and cities, such as San Lorenzo in Esmeraldas and Nueva Loja in Sucumbíos, has included targeted killings and gang violence associated with paybacks by paramilitaries and the FARC for drug and arms deals gone bad, as well as violence caused by dissident factions of, or deserters from, Colombia's illegal armed groups.[33] In Sucumbíos, annual homicides increased fourfold between the intervals of 1993–1999 and 2000–2005.[34] In the first half of 2002, assassins connected to Colombian illegal armed groups killed more than one hundred people in Nueva Loja, and in mid-2002, the FARC maintained a list of three hundred people in the area targeted for execution.[35] Extortion has been common in Carchi, where refusal to hand over demanded amounts has led to kidnappings, beatings, and deaths.[36]

The FARC in the Legal Economy

Added to the FARC's illicit activities, the guerrillas also participate in the legal economy in the north. In 2000, business leaders in the north estimated that as much as 80 percent of commerce in some northern cities was based on business with the FARC.[37] It would be difficult to overstate the importance of FARC investment for Sucumbíos, in particular. A 2001 survey in Sucumbíos found that 70 percent of respondents engaged in direct or indirect commercial relations with the insurgency.[38]

Members of Colombian illegal armed groups, including FARC guerrillas, cross to Ecuador dressed as civilians to frequent northern hospitals, restaurants, hotels, and other establishments unavailable to them in war-stricken southern Colombia.[39] Nueva Loja has been home to an unusually high number of health clinics, which have treated Colombians suffering from war wounds on a regular basis.[40] Colombian insurgents have even created their own medical facilities in the north.[41]

A final legal activity in Ecuador's northern provinces that is linked to Colombia's conflict is the purchase of various items such as cooking gas, which is subsidized in Ecuador, as well as food, medicine, and other necessities. These goods have helped to supply insurgents in addition to civilian communities in Colombia.[42]

Border Delineation through Nonmilitary Means: The FARC since the 1990s

Since the 1990s, at the same time that the FARC have still relied on regular passage to the northern borderlands, they have also needed the international border to carry real meaning. That is, the borderline has had to separate their combat zones in Colombia from their resting spaces in Ecuador. The insurgency has taken three types of actions that have helped to physically define the borderline and maintain the borderlands as a peaceful refuge. These include (1) altering its behavior when crossing into Ecuador, specifically refraining from staging military attacks; (2) establishing and maintaining economic and coercive power in communities on the borderline; and (3) communicating with the Ecuadorian army to prevent the breakout of conflict between the two organizations.

The Context: Ongoing Limited Ecuadorian State Presence

These actions, which are discussed in more detail below, can be understood as responses to weakly implemented Ecuadorian government policy. On the one hand, the government seeks to block insurgents from entering or operating in Ecuador in any capacity. On the other hand, however, this policy is poorly administered due to limited state capacity.

The Ecuadorian government has been cognizant of the multifaceted security challenges raised by Colombia's conflict, and national policy has been to stop illegal activities in the north. From the administration of Gustavo Noboa (2000–2003) through that of Rafael Correa (2007–present), the government has sought to increase security in the north, including defense of the border against armed guerrillas.[43]

More military personnel, particularly within the army, have been assigned to the region for the border effort.[44] With US financial support, Ecuadorian state efforts in the north increased under Plan Colombia in the form of police and military operations to impede drug and weapons trafficking, contraband, and illegal migration.[45] The government has also opposed the participation of unarmed members of the FARC in legal commercial activities in the north.[46] Importantly, while the Ecuadorian government has taken a consistent stance of defending national sovereignty from encroachment by Colombian guerrillas, it has also wanted to avoid being pulled into the Colombian conflict, and has therefore refused to engage in coordinated counterinsurgency operations involving the Ecuadorian and Colombian militaries, despite US and Colombian pressures to do so.[47]

With a mandate to block the entry of the FARC into Ecuador and to control guerrilla activities in the north, the Ecuadorian army has in fact done little in either regard. Army patrols have been few and cautious.[48] As in the 1980s and early 1990s, the reason for this border neglect was weak army capacity. However, in contrast to the earlier period (when the army oriented its resources to defend the southern border against the Peruvian armed forces), in the 1990s army resources were stretched thin in a different way. As analyzed in detail elsewhere, after peace was established between Ecuador and Peru in 1998, the Ecuadorian army, now without its traditional southern border mission, underwent a crisis, reaching out aggressively to institutionalize its responsibilities in policing missions. When Plan Colombia subsequently brought state and popular attention to the northern border, Ecuadorian army leaders wanted to avoid entering into a conflict with the FARC that could make the army unavailable for its policing duties.[49]

AVOIDANCE OF COMBAT IN NORTHERN ECUADOR

In a context of increased, yet still limited state efforts to defend the border from guerrilla crossings, perhaps the simplest way the FARC have helped enforce the borderline has been by behaving differently on each side. They carefully respect the international borderline by not engaging in combat against Ecuadorian state actors or Ecuadorian communities, lest that combat would trigger a response from the state and compromise their resting space in the country's borderlands.[50]

COMPETITION WITH THE ECUADORIAN ARMY ON THE BORDERLINE

A second way the FARC have physically helped delineate the border since the 1990s has been by achieving and maintaining territorial control along some stretches of the Ecuadorian side of the borderline, in competition with the Ecuadorian state. This discussion refers to Ecuadorian border communities, as they are located on the Ecuadorian side of the borderline. Yet it is noteworthy that many of those communities are in some ways as much Colombian as Ecuadorian, due to the close friendship and familial ties among the two nationalities on the border.[51] In some border towns in Ecuador, Colombians make up the majority of the population, such as in General Farfán, an Ecuadorian town due north of Nueva Loja, where 60 percent of the residents are Colombian.[52]

As one indicator of FARC power at locations along the border in Sucumbíos, the FARC have implemented curfews, preventing transit after six in the evening in towns including General Farfán, Pacayacu, Santa Elena, and Santa Rosa.[53] In such spaces, the FARC generally have not harmed people, and on occasions they have helped solve problems of crime or controversy in the community, according to a senior army officer and a Catholic Church representative with extensive experience working directly on the border.[54] The FARC have also exercised economic influence along the borderline. On the San Miguel River, members of the FARC's Front 48 (based in Putumayo) regularly purchased food, cigars, and drinks in border towns.[55] An estimated four thousand peasants from Sucumbíos have crossed to Colombia each year to farm in coca fields.[56]

The FARC's success in controlling stretches of Ecuador's borderline is perhaps most evident when contrasting their power in such communities to the much weaker influence of the Ecuadorian state, especially that of the army. In 2005 I asked forty-one Ecuadorian army officers about the relationships between Ecuadorian border communities and Colombian insurgents.[57] Of those officers, twenty-seven explained collaboration between communities and the FARC by pointing to communities' economic incentives and/or their fear of the guerrillas.

Not only did officers worry that Ecuadorian communities supported the FARC, but they considered this support directly indicative of the FARC's power relative to that of the army; thirty-five of the forty-one officers who discussed relations between Ecuadorian border communities and Colombian insurgents perceived that border community support for insurgents and for the army was zero-sum—that more community support for the insurgents constituted less support for the army, and vice-versa. Officers' main concern about this trade-off was intelligence. For them, close ties between communities and insurgents meant members of these communities served or could serve as informants for the insurgents and not for army personnel.

Many officers said that, because the FARC were able to meet communities' material needs and the state was not, Ecuadorians on the border collaborated with the insurgents. A special forces officer described this dynamic as follows:

> When you go to patrol on the border, and you enter in the populations, they are really reserved. You can't trust them or their information . . . we don't have resources—for instance our doctor only attends two or three kids when we go through a town, or we bring notebooks with the national hymn . . . it is not enough to win their trust . . . Guerrillas, on the other hand, have helped them build houses . . . They do big projects, because they are right there, across the border.

The FARC are not the only insurgent group with a normalized presence on, and even control of, sections of the borderline. As of the early 2000s, the ELN had visited Carchi's northern border with regularity, including the town of El Chical, as told by Ecuadorian police and army officers. According to a senior army officer, when the army began patrolling Esmeraldas's border with Colombia in 2000, army personnel learned that the ELN had established itself in towns on the Esmeraldas border inland from the coast. The Colombian illegal armed groups that have most frequented the coastal Esmeraldas border have been paramilitaries. In a 2002 case along the Mataje River—which runs along the northern border of Esmeraldas—paramilitaries upheld their own harsh version of the law when they killed pirates who had kept the townspeople from their livelihood of fishing. The residents of the nearby town of Palma Real were grateful for this service. In recounting the events, an academic who had conducted research in the town noted that its fishermen had already approached the local Ecuadorian navy unit for help, to no avail.

Because of the power of the ELN and paramilitaries on the borderline, the Ecuadorian state has not been the FARC's only competitor there. At times, northern border communities have been directly caught between warring groups. For example, in 2004 paramilitaries threatened to attack the Sucumbíos border town of Corazón Orense for collaborating with the FARC.[58] In July 2005, a similar dynamic led paramilitaries to cross into Ecuador and kill eight peasants in El Azul, on the San Miguel River.[59]

COMMUNICATION WITH THE ECUADORIAN ARMY

In a context in which the Ecuadorian army has been reluctant to engage in combat against the FARC, another measure the guerrillas have employed that has helped delineate the international boundary and secure their continued access to northern Ecuador has been to coordinate with the Ecuadorian armed forces directly. Again we see how weak, but not absent, Ecuadorian state presence has caused the FARC to take actions to define the border—in this case by interacting with the key state authority in Ecuador's borderlands to establish what FARC activities are acceptable in northern Ecuador.

As discussed by army officers interviewed, the long peace between the Ecuadorian military and the FARC that began after the 1993 river ambush was based on the following understanding between the two organizations: as long as armed FARC members did not cross into Ecuador or attack Ecuadorian military personnel, the Ecuadorian army would not pursue them. During interviews, army officers generally described an unofficial modus operandi. For example, a retired officer noted the following: "the guerrillas don't cause problems for the Ecuadorian army, for the Ecuadorian people, and pass very friendly, no? To have fun, to make purchases, but not to cause problems here." Yet there have also been formal agreements between the FARC and the military since the Putumayo attack. These agreements are documented in reports of the Ecuadorian military intelligence agency accessed by an Ecuadorian journalist who was interviewed for this study. According to a retired army officer, in 2001 there was another pact between the FARC and the intelligence agency in which each side agreed not to attack the other.

Added to such high-level truces, local FARC actions to keep the peace have been common. One important moment in the development of local relations between the two sides began in the mid-1990s, when, as discussed above, the Ecuadorian army did not have the capacity to devote significant forces to the north. At that time, army detachments began selling provisions to the FARC, according to army officers and Ecuadorian journalists. At first, commanders sold food, clothing, and other basic goods,[60] and then later, weapons, drugs, and uniforms. These practices continued through the 1990s.[61]

The sales by Ecuadorian army personnel of weapons and munitions to the FARC continued through the 2000s. Though some transactions have involved high-ranking officers and evolved into public scandals, sales to the FARC in the field have been steady and have frequently gone unnoticed.[62] According to an officer interviewed, it was relatively simple for Ecuadorian officers and soldiers stationed in the north to sell ammunition to the FARC; for army accounting purposes, army personnel would falsely report sold materials as having been used up during army training exercises.

Local communications between FARC and Ecuadorian army personnel have gone beyond economic exchanges. In the words of a journalist who specializes in the FARC's presence in northern Ecuador, in the early 1990s amid the material exchanges between the Ecuadorian army and the FARC, the latter came to serve as a kind of "extension" of the Ecuadorian military by helping to prevent incursions by the Peruvian armed forces into the northeastern corner of Ecuador, where Colombia, Peru, and Ecuador meet. More recently, FARC personnel have sought out leaders of Ecuadorian army detachments to reassure them that the guerrillas do not want conflict with the Ecuadorian state. Meetings have been held between local commanders of the two groups, in the river running between the two countries. According to officers interviewed, the FARC always initiated these meetings, sending messengers to invite the Ecuadorian officers to talk. During the brief meetings, FARC commanders have reassured the officers that they want no conflict with Ecuador or with its army. These meetings have been tense. One officer recounted his own experience of meeting in the middle of the river with a FARC commander. The remaining combatants in the FARC unit were lined up along the northern river bank, their weapons in firing position, aimed south. Directly across from them, on the southern bank, the Ecuadorian army soldiers were identically positioned, facing north.[63]

Conclusion

To summarize, the very insurgency that relies on access to neighboring border-lands for its war back home has enforced the international borderline, and it has done so as a response to a limited degree of state presence. The FARC's on-the-ground delineation of the Colombia-Ecuador border has been functional in part; by merely using northern Ecuador for rest, training, and resupplying, the insurgency has given new meaning to the borderline as separating the FARC's war zone from its resting space. Yet in other ways the guerrillas have much more proactively guaranteed their ability to move easily between the two countries. They gained control of the borderline first by attacking Ecuadorian state security forces in the 1980s and early 1990s. Then, starting later in the 1990s, they controlled border populations by becoming the legitimate provider of order and economic benefits, and also interacted directly with Ecuadorian military personnel to convince them of their peaceful intentions in the country.

While this chapter has focused primarily on actions by insurgents, it also tells us about the implications of a state actor—the army—that seeks to remain neutral with respect to a neighboring internal conflict, particularly when that state entity is weak. In this situation, the state can hand the borderline over to the insurgents; in making the borderlands inviting to unarmed insurgents, the state creates an incentive for them to cross the border and control the borderline in order to do so. When the insurgents already enjoy territorial control on their own side of the border, gaining power of the borderline is relatively straightforward, because it involves extending their reach only a short distance. At the same time, by emphasizing the largely economic logic of FARC presence in the northern borderlands—involving exchanges between the FARC and the army and local communities—we can conclude that the insurgency's territorial control is likely to remain along the borderline, without spreading into the neighboring country's borderlands.

NOTES

1. I am grateful to Peter Andreas, Anne Clunan, Ben Lessing, and David Pion-Berlin for their feedback on earlier versions of this chapter.

2. David R. Mares, *Violent Peace: Militarized Interstate Bargaining in Latin America* (New York, NY: Columbia University Press), 163, 253, n. 11.

3. On the implications of Plan Colombia for Colombia's neighbors, see Richard Millett, *Colombia's Conflicts: The Spillover Effects of a Wider War* (Carlisle, PA: Strategic Studies Institute, US Army War College, 2002), 21–22; Carlos Basombrío, "El Plan Colombia y el Perú: Una primera aproximación a sus efectos en la política, el narcotráfico y la seguridad," in *Turbulencia en los Andes y Plan Colombia*, ed. César Montúfar and Teresa Whitfield (Quito, Ecuador: Centro Andino de Estudios Internacionales, Universidad Andina Simón Bolívar Ecuador, 2003), 180; International Crisis Group (ICG), *Colombia's Borders: The Weak Link in Uribe's Security Policy*, ICG Latin America Report 9 (Quito and Brussels: ICG, September 23, 2004); and Brian Loveman, ed., *Addicted to Failure: U.S. Security Policy in Latin America and the Andean Region* (Lanham, MD: Rowman & Littlefield, 2006).

4. Christopher R. Day, "The Fates of Rebels: Insurgencies in Uganda," *Comparative Politics* 43, no. 4 (July): see especially 442.

5. Miguel Centeno, *Blood and Debt: War and the Nation State in Latin America* (University Park, PA: Pennsylvania State University Press, 2002), 9, 52–53.

6. Jeffrey Herbst, *States and Power in Africa: Comparative Lessons in Authority and Control* (Princeton, NJ: Princeton University Press, 2000), 25; see also 18–19, 104–6.

7. Ken Menkhaus and Jacob N. Shapiro, "Non-State Actors and Failed States: Lessons from Al-Qa'ida's Experiences in the Horn of Africa," in *Ungoverned Spaces: Alternatives to State Authority in an Era of Softened Sovereignty*, ed. Anne L. Clunan and Harold A. Trinkunas (Stanford, CA: Stanford University Press, 2010), 79.

8. For an overview of ties between Colombia's armed forces and paramilitary groups, see, for example, Maiah Jaskoski, *Military Politics and Democracy in the Andes* (Baltimore, MD: Johns Hopkins University Press, 2013), 245, n. 5.

9. Camilo Echandía, "Expansión territorial de las guerrillas colombianas: Geografía, economía y violencia," in *Reconocer la guerra para construir la paz*, ed. María Victoria Llorente and Malcolm Deas (Bogotá, Colombia: Cerec, 1999), 99–150; and María Alejandra Vélez, "FARC-ELN: Evolución y expansión territorial," *Desarrollo y sociedad* 47 (March 2001): 161–62, 164–65.

10. Russell Crandall, *Driven by Drugs: U.S. Policy toward Colombia* (Boulder, CO: Lynne Rienner, 2002), 72–73; and Cynthia J. Arnson, "The Peace Process in Colombia and U.S. Policy," in *Peace, Democracy, and Human Rights in Colombia*, ed. Christopher Welna and Gustavo Gallón (Notre Dame, IN: University of Notre Dame Press, 2007), 136–40.

11. Adrián Bonilla, "U.S. Andean Policy, the Colombian Conflict, and Security in Ecuador," in Loveman, *Addicted to Failure*, 116.

12. For example, see Jaskoski, *Military Politics and Democracy in the Andes*, 116–17.

13. "Colombia descuida su extensa frontera del sur," *El Comercio*, September 21, 2003; Pablo Celi, "La vulnerabilidad estructural de la agenda de seguridad ecuatoriana frente al deterioro regional andino," in *Agenda de seguridad andino-brasileña: Primeras aproximaciones*, ed. Marco Cepik and Socorro Ramírez (Bogotá, Colombia: Friedrich-Ebert-Stiftung en Colombia [Fescol], 2004), 269; and ICG, "Colombia's Borders," 5.

14. The connection between the attacks and the army's removal of the detachments was described by an Ecuadorian journalist who has specialized in the FARC in the north

and by the former helicopter pilot. See also Mariana Neira, "La narcoguerrilla: El enemigo oculto," *Vistazo* 633 (January 6, 1994).

15. Arturo Torres, *El juego del camaleón: Los secretos de Angostura* (Quito, Ecuador: Eskeletra Editorial, 2009), 179–83.

16. This anecdote was shared by a security specialist in Ecuador; for her own research, she had learned of the case from a police officer who had participated directly in the investigation in the north.

17. Jaskoski, *Military Politics and Democracy in the Andes*, 47–48.

18. David R. Mares and David Scott Palmer, *Power, Institutions, and Leadership in War and Peace: Lessons from Peru and Ecuador, 1995–1998* (Austin, TX: University of Texas Press), 38.

19. Keith Stanski, "'This Land Is Your Land / This Land Is My Land': Territory, Politics, and Irregular War Along and Across the Colombia-Ecuador Border, 1975–2003," master's thesis, University of Oxford, 2007, 68.

20. Because of a tunnel system that the commander of the Santa Rosa detachment, Second Lieutenant Moreano, had created, the army personnel under his command escaped the FARC's attack on the border post in 1987. Moreano was decorated as a hero for his bravery and as of 2009 had risen to the rank of colonel, according to the former helicopter pilot mentioned above.

21. Conflict has brought civilian Colombians into Ecuador, in addition to guerrilla fighters; Colombian applications for asylum in Ecuador increased from 362 in 2000 to more than 11,000 in 2003. Alto Comisionado de las Naciones Unidas para los Refugiados (ACNUR), unpublished statistics (Quito, Ecuador: ACNUR, 2006).

22. "Los armados multiplican sus bases de entrenamiento táctico," *El Comercio*, August 4, 2003.

23. Jaskoski, *Military Politics and Democracy in the Andes*, 158. On the international effects of this incident, especially on the relationship between Colombia and Venezuela, see chapter 6 by Harold A. Trinkunas, in this volume.

24. "Guerrilla colombiana se camufla en Ecuador," *Hoy*, August 31, 2001. Colombia and Ecuador are separated by one continuous waterway that has multiple names. The San Miguel and Putumayo Rivers border Sucumbíos; the San Juan River, Carchi; and the Mataje River, Esmeraldas.

25. "Las FARC se aprovechan de la vecindad del Ecuador," *Hoy*, June 28, 2005.

26. Anthony Faiola, "Colombia's Creeping War: Neighbors Now Fear Spillover of Violence," *Washington Post*, October 1, 2000. For other examples of assassinations of paramilitaries by the FARC and vice versa, see Juan O. Tamayo, "Ecuador Feels Fallout from Colombia's Narcotics War," *Miami Herald*, November 18, 2000.

27. Faiola, "Colombia's Creeping War."

28. Clifford Krauss, "Colombian Rebels Said to Seize 10 Foreign Oil Workers," *New York Times*, October 13, 2000.

29. Mark Peceny and Michael Durnan, "The FARC's Best Friend: U.S. Antidrug Policies and the Deepening of Colombia's Civil War in the 1990s," *Latin American Politics and Society* 48, no. 2 (2006): 107, 111.

30. ICG, "Colombia's Borders," 18.

31. "La coca se cosecha y transporta en mayo," *El Comercio*, May 8, 2005. Information in this paragraph about the steps by which cocaine is produced was obtained through an interview with a US official. Though this analysis centers on illegal drug trafficking in northern Ecuador, the country in general has been central in the cocaine trade. In 2005, Ecuador ranked third in Latin America and fifth in the world for the amount of cocaine intercepted in the country. See the United Nations Office on Drugs and Crime, 2007 *World Drug Report* (Vienna, Austria: United Nations, 2007).

32. The Colombian police reported that during those two years, it had confiscated 171,095 bullets that had come from Ecuador, 72,617 from Venezuela, and 3,514 from Panama. During that period, the police had intercepted 4,915 weapons from Venezuela, 1,632 from Ecuador, 301 from Panama, and 43 from Brazil. See "El Consejo de Guerra dará su sentencia por el robo de armas," *El Comercio*, November 29, 2003.

33. For example, see Faiola, "Colombia's Creeping War"; Observatorio Internacional por la Paz (OIPAZ), "Informe preliminar: Testimonios de frontera—derechos humanos y Plan Colombia" (Quito: OIPAZ, 2001), 33; and ICG, "Colombia's Borders," 11.

34. Policía Judicial, Ecuador, unpublished statistics (Quito, Ecuador: Policía Judicial, 2006).

35. Arie Farnam, "Colombia's Civil War Drifts South into Ecuador," *Christian Science Monitor*, July 11, 2002.

36. Observatorio Internacional por la Paz, "Informe preliminar," 32.

37. Faiola, "Colombia's Creeping War."

38. "El 70% negocia con las FARC, encuesta de Informix revela nexus con la subversión," *Expreso de Guayaquil*, August 6, 2001, referenced by Oswaldo Jarrín R., "La Junta de Seguridad Ciudadana: El caso Sucumbíos," *Nueva Sociedad* 191 (May / June 2004): 149.

39. "La guerrilla profundiza sus redes en el Ecuador," *El Comercio*, May 17, 2005.

40. Faiola, "Colombia's Creeping War"; and Tamayo, "Ecuador Feels Fallout."

41. "Las clínicas no reportan heridos de bala," *El Comercio*, May 17, 2005.

42. Some basic goods that can be bought and sold legally have been used in combat. In particular, the FARC have been known to use propane cylinders as bombs, according to army officers interviewed. See also Farnam, "Colombia's Civil War Drifts South."

43. Jaskoski, *Military Politics and Democracy in the Andes*, 127–28.

44. Jaskoski, *Military Politics and Democracy in the Andes*, 131.

45. For example, see Pablo Andrade, "Diagnóstico de la frontera Ecuador-Colombia," *Comentario internacional* 4 (2002, Semester II): 205–6. On US security assistance to Ecuador's security forces for work in the north, see Jaskoski, *Military Politics and Democracy in the Andes*, 128–29.

46. Jaskoski, *Military Politics and Democracy in the Andes*, 162–63.

47. Ibid., 126–27.

48. Ibid., 133–34, 160–61.

49. Ibid., ch. 5.

50. Stanski, "'This Land Is Your Land,'" 68–69.

51. Andrade, "Diagnóstico," 220–25.

52. "La cultura del silencio y el terror impera en la frontera: Iglesia," *El Comercio*, December 3, 2004.

53. "La guerrilla profundiza."
54. See also Faiola, "Colombia's Creeping War"; and "La guerrilla profundiza."
55. "La cultura del silencio."
56. Tamayo, "Ecuador Feels Fallout."
57. Jaskoski, *Military Politics and Democracy in the Andes*, 153–54.
58. "Un grupo armado amenazó a tres poblaciones de la frontera," *El Comercio*, September 7, 2004; and "Los grupos armados se filtran en Sucumbíos," *El Comercio*, September 8, 2004.
59. "La frontera teme un rebrote de violencia por la vuelta de los paras," *El Comercio*, July 26, 2005.
60. One officer gave the examples of a cow and salt.
61. Until the Ecuador-Peru peace agreement in 1998, there was ongoing tension surrounding the international border dispute, including a "war scare" in August of that year. See Mares, *Violent Peace*, 168.
62. On weapons scandals involving the Ecuadorian armed forces, see "Las FARC usan armas de las FF.AA.," *El Comercio*, July 11, 2000; "Seis militares con prisión por el robo de 49 fusiles," *El Comercio*, July 15, 2000; "Los cohetes Igla están bajo custodia militar," *El Comercio*, February 19, 2002; and "El Consejo de Guerra dará su sentencia."
63. For more examples of tense encounters between Ecuadorian army units and the FARC, see Jaskoski, *Military Politics and Democracy in the Andes*, 156–57, 160–61.

Chapter Ten

Making Sense of Borders

*Global Circulations and the Rule of Law
at the Iguazú Triangle*

José Carlos G. Aguiar

Neoliberalism has an ambivalent nature. On the one hand, it removes commercial barriers and intensifies the exchange of policies and flows of power across regions. On the other hand, it creates new borders and protects national markets and territories. Surveillance became a critical issue in the Global North after 9 / 11 and amid later financial crises, and this phenomenon also has been echoed in the South. This chapter examines one such case, from Brazil. The Brazilian government has launched a number of projects to reorder and "securitize" national and commercial borders at the Iguazú Triangle (frequently referred to as the Tri-Border Area), a cross-border urban conglomerate that unfolds across the national borders of Paraguay, Brazil, and Argentina.

Since the 1970s, economic and demographic booms have marked cycles of growth in the Iguazú Triangle. In the 1990s the zone reached an economic peak, mostly due to international trade and migration. The economic bonanza attracted migrants to the region, which reached a population of eight hundred thousand inhabitants in the early 2000s.[1] However, this development has a controversial aspect since most of the commercial activities are illegal. The smuggling of liquors, cigarettes, industrial products, and electronics has taken place for decades. The area has been perceived as a space where illegality is tolerated. Yet since 2001 there have been signs of renewed state intervention. Police surveillance and new tax regimes have been promoted, contravening the open market ideology and mobility on which neoliberalism is based.

Historically, diplomatic tensions and wars among the three nations have occurred at the Iguazú Triangle. In contrast, in the beginning of the twenty-first century and in the context of the neoliberal cooperation programs, the control of illegality is the source of new frictions. At stake now is not international territorial conflict, but rather the legal system defining commercial relations across borders. The model that gave rise to "free-trade zones" at the Iguazú Triangle is now countered by discourses and projects in Brazil that fence in cross-border trade and mobility. Under a new regime of legality influenced by the neoliberal ideology, traffickers are defined as microentrepreneurs driven by profit. Their position as informal agents who work outside of state control is increasingly seen as an individual choice. Since 2004, on-and-off deployments of Brazilian military police during *operações* (raids) at the international bridges suggest that a new cycle of state presence in the region has begun. The Brazilian state intervenes to reduce cross-border trafficking, implementing programs for state surveillance and launching new legal frameworks like the 2009 popularly known "*sacoleiros* law*" (baggers law), which attempts to regulate and thus legalize trafficking and in doing so generate state revenue.

Based on ethnographic material, this chapter examines the impact of neoliberal policies on cross-border trade in the urban conglomerate at the Iguazú Triangle. Increased state surveillance at the border and the sacoleiros law have been attempts to regulate trade and create new definitions of entrepreneurship in order to tax realms formerly defined as illegal. After a period of liberalization, visible in the opening of national economies, regional projects, and free-trade zones, neoliberalism now reveals its ambiguous nature; the supposedly borderless capitalism in fact depends on the securitization of national borders.

The data presented in this chapter were gathered between 2008 and 2010. Participant observations were carried out in buses, at checkpoints, in commercial areas, and at the international bridges joining the three cities that compose the Iguazú Triangle. Informants included traffickers, shop owners, importers, journalists, activists, and municipal and federal authorities. In order to protect the privacy of interviewees, pseudonyms have been used in the text.

The Neoliberal Ideology and the Definition of Illegal Markets

The notion of a world without borders where individual freedom and self-regulating market forces prevail is at the ideological core of neoliberalism.[2] Indeed, in a first stage, neoliberalism promoted a free market. Nevertheless, after the terrorist attacks of 9 / 11, the neoliberal ideology entered a second phase, with new sets of frictions and conflicts. The neoliberal ideology now increasingly emphasizes the role of the state as the guardian of the legal regime. Illegal actors are defined as antistate actors who threaten the very core of the nation state and global trade.

Since the 1980s, Latin American countries have adopted neoliberal policies. In the aftermath of military dictatorships that entailed the heavy hand of the state, governments in the region welcomed the neoliberal ideology promoted by the United States with the 1984 Washington Consensus. The structures of global governance mobilized political power and resources across national borders. The emergence of international legal bodies and structures of supranational governance eroded the autonomy of the nation-state, but at the same time it also constrained the state's monopoly over violence.

"Integration" and "modernization" projects included the creation of commercial regions. In the 1990s, Mexico joined the North America Free Trade Agreement (NAFTA) with Canada and the United States as commercial partners, and in the Southern Cone, the Mercado Común del Sur (Mercosur) was signed by Argentina, Brazil, Paraguay, and Uruguay. Differently from the trade-oriented model of NAFTA, Mercosur resembles somewhat the European model of integration, stimulating the removal of market borders, the creation of a common infrastructure, and the acknowledgment of citizens' rights in all member countries.

Neoliberal reforms in Latin America ran parallel to an ongoing process of democratization that has redefined the relations between the state and the citizenry. Yet in many Latin American countries, there is an ongoing discussion about a perceived loss of national sovereignty to international agencies and corporate power on the one hand, and the social costs of privatization and the expanding power of international capitalists, on the other.[3] Moreover, critics of neoliberalism perceive "historical continuity" between the processes of the colonial era and neoliberalism qua neocolonialism.[4]

In urban Latin America, the influence of neoliberalism becomes tangible in the definition and governance of public space. The implementation of policies to gentrify historical centers and "whiten" their users, slum upgrading, and iron-fist programs to halt criminality, have reordered the relationship among the citizenry, the (international) private sector, and the state.[5] Zero-tolerance policies and "wars" on drugs, piracy, and delinquency have mushroomed throughout the region. These programs often function to enforce the regime of legality engendered by neoliberalism.

A second major influence of the neoliberal ideology on urban spaces is visible in the transfer of accountability from the state to individual agents. Reductions in the size of the state, fiscal reforms, privatization, liberalization, and deregulation have shrunk state protections and encroached on citizens' rights. As a consequence, poverty and economic marginality are perceived as results of flawed individual choices. Citizens are urged to assume individual responsibility for the improvement of their own position or material conditions. In their analysis of the impact of neoliberalism on employment and governance in Latin American cities, Alejandro Portes and Brian R. Roberts have coined the term "forced entrepreneurship" to capture this process. In a context of growing informality, individuals are compelled to seek new opportunities and create their own employment.[6] Portes and Roberts take their analysis further and debate the relationship between neoliberalism and expanding illegality in Latin American cities: "It is probable that informal economic activities rise, but less conventional forms can also appear to face the absence of opportunities in the labor market. Delinquent activities of any sort, like drug trafficking, robbery and kidnapping can be interpreted within this perspective, as alternative sources of employment. Those engaged seek to pursue material goods that they wouldn't legally access otherwise."[7] Disfranchised, without access to the labor market or perspectives for material improvement, new generations of Latin Americans have turned to the informal market. The neoliberal ideology transfers responsibility to these individuals: they ought to become entrepreneurs and create their own sources of employment. And they do so—albeit not in the way the neoliberal state envisioned.

The Iguazú Triangle: Crossing Borders across Regimes

The Iguazú Triangle comprises an urban conglomerate that encompasses sections of the national borders of three countries. It includes three cities: Ciudad del Este (Paraguay), Foz do Iguaçu (Brazil), and Puerto Iguazú (Argentina). Each national corner is demarcated by the Iguazú and Paraná rivers, which converge at the Triangle. The urban area is connected by international bridges. The region followed the typical pattern of urban growth in Latin America: fast, unregulated urbanization that was possible with the arrival of migrants from the countryside and later from international communities. As the state played a secondary role in the process, the informal sector gained in prominence. The informal street economy became entangled in an illegality mesh, where legal / licit / informal undertakings are intertwined with criminal activities.

Cross-border economic transactions were prominent in the Tri-Border Area long before the Washington Consensus. In the 1960s, monumental works funded by international capital investments were launched in the zone. The construction of the Itaipú Dam (1974–84) marked the beginning of a demographic boom. The region, however, has profited the most from its position as a trading post. Trade in Ciudad del Este blossomed during Paraguay President Alfredo Stroessner's dictatorship, which declared the city a free-trade zone in 1960. Smuggling then became the main economic policy and source of growth in Paraguay. The arrival of international communities in the 1980s secured the position of Ciudad del Este as one of the most dynamic trading posts in the world.[8]

Since the introduction of Mercosur in 1994, the cities have been trying to position themselves as tourist and shopping paradises. Tourists come to enjoy the Iguaçu waterfalls and the biodiversity, and they stay for the shopping. Nevertheless, this image of a bonanza has another side. Promises of conspicuous consumerism and luxury in Foz do Iguaçu coexist with illegality, violence, and marginality. Due to drug violence, the city has the highest homicide rate in Brazil among young people (ages fifteen to twenty-five years) and the second highest rate among the total population.[9] There is also human trafficking, weapons smuggling, child prostitution, tax evasion, and copyrights piracy. It is believed that global crime syndicates use the Iguazú Triangle to launder money.[10] Brazilian and US authorities allegedly have evidence that funds from the zone have provided financial support to extremist groups in Islamic countries,[11] as discussed in more detail by Arie M. Kacowicz in chapter 5 of this volume.

International attention to the region has promoted punitive perspectives against illegality. Commercial integration of the region is now countered by new policies to enforce national borders. Ramón Fogel has adequately described this ambivalent operation of the free-trade ideology as simultaneous integration and disintegration.[12] As a matter of fact, the neoliberal ideology has inspired new and expanding control mechanisms to supervise and regulate the crossings of people and merchandise at the Iguazú Triangle, as the final section of this chapter will demonstrate.

Fluid Cross-Border Trade and the Sacoleiro

"O shopping" (the shopping mall, in Portuguese) has become the trademark of an increasingly urbanized Brazil. Following the American model of urbanization and economic growth, malls have turned into the space of modernity. Shops, cinema complexes, and food courts are the social playground where individuals build and exhibit their individual identities, which are based on expectations of consumption and cosmopolitanism. Here, the cultural patterns of global consumerism are materialized and visible even in remote Foz do Iguaçu. The shopping streets of Avenida Brasil and Av. Jorge Schimmelpfeng downtown and the various shopping malls built around the city, including the "fashionable" and "exclusive" Cataratas JL, are open for local buyers but also meant for *turismo de compras* (shopping tourism).

Commerce among the three cities is one of the key, if not the most important, economic sectors of the Iguazú Triangle. According to records from the city government, trade with Ciudad del Este provides employment to more than 67 percent of the population in Foz do Iguaçu.[13] Next to, or more accurately on top of, the established commerce, there is a sizable domain formed by petty smugglers that in the end provides a flow of cash into the formal sector. The illegal circulation of commodities has shaped the economy and society of the region. Smuggling across national borders in the Iguazú Triangle can be traced back to the 1960 declaration of Ciudad del Este as a free-trade zone. Once the tax system in Ciudad del Este was reformed to stimulate the input of international goods, infrastructure—in particular, the international bridge Puente de la Amistad and an international road—was created to stimulate international mobility. Commerce at the free-trade zone became Stroessner's national economic policy that ambiguously included both legal commodities and counterfeit. Trade in Paraguay was oriented toward the international arena and "complemented" Brazil and Argentina's protected national markets. Rapidly thereafter, trade blossomed, and by the end of the 1960s Ciudad del Este was known as a paradise for cheap whisky and cigarettes and had developed a pivotal function in the trade of illegal goods and counterfeit in South America.

In the 1980s Foz do Iguaçu began seeing sacoleiros ("baggers" in Portuguese), which are petty smugglers specializing in the supply, transport, and retail of goods that they later resell to shop owners or informal vendors back home.[14] The term sacoleiros is inspired by the characteristic big plastic bags (*saco*) that these smugglers carry for transporting merchandise. Sacoleiros cross from Brazil to Ciudad del Este by bus or car to make use of the monthly allowance they can import, which in 2009 was US$150, but in prior years had reached US$300. Receipt forgery is a common practice in order to import a higher value of merchandise than that allowed. The goods sacoleiros supply include items that are inherently illegal—including counterfeit, piracy, and forbidden merchandise—as well as items that become illegal during the import process when sacoleiros do not meet import tax requirements.

The appearance of sacoleiros can be explained as an alternative to the unemployment that prevailed in Brazilian cities in the 1980s.[15] The emergence of sacoleiros is linked to the urban unemployed masses that make a living out of weak state control at the Iguazú Triangle. Where do these people come from? Many were laid off once construction of the Itaipú Dam concluded,[16] while others come from different regions of Brazil. In the 1990s sacoleiros were clearly identified in the *vox populi* as a social category: transporters who skillfully play and manipulate the limits of the law. The world of the sacoleiros is defined by their ability to avoid customs or police controls and negotiate with officers when necessary. This streetwise agent resembles the *malandro*, which according to the Brazilian anthropology of urban types, communicates marginality, social stigma, and inventiveness.[17]

By the 2000s an estimated thirty thousand sacoleiros were crossing from Brazil to Paraguay every day to shop in Ciudad del Este.[18] Although there are no official records or sources on the amount or value of merchandise hauled by sacoleiros, it is known that they smuggle industrialized products, like textiles, toys, electronics, and pirated CDs and DVDs. These commodities mainly come from China and Taiwan and often are counterfeit, refurbished, or have an illegal origin. With the arrival of digital technologies, sacoleiros have become more specialized in smuggling electronics, which present various advantages. Mobile phones, video cameras, and computer hard drives are easy to store and hide, and electronics are in demand in Brazil, where tariffs on imported electronic devices are high. Minimal state control at the border facilitates the crossings with merchandise; it is believed that only 1 percent of the cars and buses in this period was controlled by customs officers at the checkpoint in Foz do Iguaçu.[19]

Sacoleiros work autonomously, but they can also be integrated into larger networks. Some of these connected smugglers travel from different Brazilian provinces, such as São Paulo, Rio Grande do Sul, or Minas Gerais. The term *o circuito sacoleiro* (the sacoleiro circuit) has been employed to capture the uncertainty, informality, and clandestineness that characterize the movement of illegal goods through this flexible organization of smugglers that integrates friends and family members.[20]

Sacoleiros are capitalists par excellence who profit from cross-country differences in prices and tax rates. They do not constitute a category fairly identifiable with entrepreneurship, nor are they organized in unions. Rather, they are traders typical of the informal sector, who act on opportunity and need. The structure in which sacoleiros work is open and liberal; agents can enter and exit, compete with one another, and mostly work on an autonomous basis. This openness provides them flexibility, allowing them to organize their travels such that they earn an income up to five times the minimum wage,[21] and accumulate some capital in the long run.

The Legal Makeover? Turning Smugglers into Entrepreneurs

The city government and the entrepreneurial elite in Foz do Iguaçu were for many years ambivalent about the sacoleiros, as these agents represent a source of revenue but also illegality. They are travelers who stay one or two nights in a city hotel, buy, and consume. Yet they are also smugglers who come to reinforce the stigma of Foz do Iguaçu as a no man's land of illegality and bad-quality products, and thus sacoleiros are perceived as criminals who nurture corruption and profit from the weak rule of law on both sides of the border.

The Iguazú Triangle might have remained a wild spot in the ambiguous geopolitics of Latin America were it not for growing international attention directed toward the region. Perhaps most notably, in 2001 the US government resumed intervention in the region in response to suspicions of terrorist activities in the region,[22] an issue addressed by Kacowicz in chapter 5 of this volume. In this context, a cycle of state control in the Iguazú Triangle commenced. The governments of Argentina, Brazil, and Paraguay have embarked on various programs to control the flow of trade in the region. The customs offices and surveillance technology have been renewed at the crossing points in Argentina and Brazil, and the Paraguayan government has been renovating its infrastructure since 2009. Influenced by neoliberal discourses of city management and gentrification, the municipal government in Foz do Iguaçu promoted new policies to diversify tourism, create new niches in the local economy, and punish illegality. The downtown area was sanitized; with the introduction of new regulations, beggars and sellers were removed from the streets to make room for shopping tourists.[23] Notions of ecotourism started to take root, and the transition from smuggling to formal trade was framed.

In 2004, 2006, and 2008, Brazil deployed military police surveillance at international bridges and checkpoints, even closing the international bridge Puente de la Amistad in 2006 for several days. These actions, called *fiscalização* (customs controls), were also carried out on roads coming from and going to Foz do Iguaçu in order to control the buses that sacoleiros ride. With these measures the Brazilian national government sought to better regulate flows of goods coming from Paraguay. These actions contributed to the negative social perception of sacoleiros as criminals, thereby supporting the iron-fist policy.

Military controls have created a climate of panic among sacoleiros that is visible as the baggers cross Puente de la Amistad. The bridge has a lane with a sidewalk for each direction. Half of the bridge is painted with the colors of the Brazilian flag, and the other half, the Paraguayan flag. By dawn there is already a long line of cars waiting to cross from Brazil to Paraguay. The traffic jam extends four kilometers from Foz do Iguaçu to Ciudad del Este's downtown. People also travel by bus, shared taxi-vans, standard taxi, or motorcycle taxi (*mototaxi*), or on foot. Between the cars, mototaxis drive dangerously fast over the bridge. The pedestrian lane is full too, and people progress slowly. The majority of walkers are Brazilian men and women, though some are Paraguayan locals and Argentine and other Latin American tourists.

At the Paraguay border, migration officers randomly halt vehicles, particularly those that are flashy or have tinted windows. Pedestrians enter Paraguay undisturbed. Once people reach Ciudad del Este, they fade into shops and commercial streets. Whereas street vending has been expunged in Foz de Iguaçu, it flourishes in Ciudad del Este. Indigenous people, the elderly, and youths immediately greet travelers with, "*¿Qué busca?*" (What are you looking for?). Up to two thousand people work in Ciudad del Este's downtown streets,[24] and in practice there is no distinction between commercial and public space; the streets, avenues, parks, corners, and roundabouts are all one large commercial zone where *quinielas* (lottery tickets), cigarettes, soft drinks, snacks, toys, clothing, electronics, and perfumes are on display. Even illegal goods—including counterfeit and pirated CDs, cocaine, marijuana, and weapons—are available. In essence, Ciudad del Este is the embodiment of the free-trade spirit, with all of its shortcomings. A vast amount of merchandise is mobilized every day in Ciudad del Este in pickup trucks, cars, and carts pulled by children, and on the shoulders of teenagers. In the boxes and black plastic bags there are electronics and novelties with destination to Brazil.

The afternoon is the peak hour of activity in Ciudad del Este and of congestion on the international bridge. As tourists continue to arrive in Paraguay, sacoleiros, having shopped at midday, are ready to make the return trip with their bags of goodies, taking the bus either directly from Ciudad del Este or from immediately after the checkpoint across the border in Foz do Iguaçu. Sacoleiros try to pass unnoticed as they enter Brazil and casually chat with the travelers around them, yet the bulky packages they carry raise customs officers' suspicions.

In order to reduce the risk of being arrested or charged fines, sacoleiros walk the bridge many times a day, transporting small amounts of merchandise each time. By crossing with a few items, they can smuggle hundreds of dollars in a single day, while limiting their loss; if officials confiscate merchandise during a given crossing, the damage to a sacoleiro's business is minimized.

Sacoleiros that use public transport to cross the border face their own set of inspection risks. Every bus that comes from Paraguay into Brazil is checked by the fiscal police. Among the passengers, the majority of whom are Brazilian, there are many laranjas ("orange" in Portuguese, used for female Brazilian smugglers of African ancestry) transporting blankets, clothing, and toys. Two police officers stop every bus and jump to look at the suitcases and bags travelers carry.

I observed on one occasion in the field an interesting dynamic aboard one of these buses. During the check, there was silence on the bus; everybody held their breath. Dark-colored bags drew the searching eyes of the officers. Even before they were asked to do so, women opened their bags to allow officers to take a look. Nobody said a word, and everybody avoided eye contact. The police carefully in-spected bags and goods in search of contraband. An officer hastily ripped away a woman's black plastic bags. This laranja was transporting three mobile phones rolled in a baby blanket. She was asked to exit the bus and go to the customs office for further investigation. She stood behind dozens of people queuing at the customs office to clear their merchandise. As the woman waited her turn, she took from her fake receipts one that listed a lower value for the products she was carrying. With luck, she would be allowed to pay import taxes based on the amount declared; otherwise her merchandise would be confiscated and destroyed.

Inside the bus, the police continued their inspection. Some people were asked about the shops they visited or the length of their stay in Paraguay. The inspection concluded once the customs officers had searched every traveler they deemed sus-picious. Finally, the police departed the bus and hit the back of the vehicle as a sign to go. As the bus resumed its trip, travelers breathed again, and laughed. For a moment, there was a collective feeling of having cleared the frontier. Some sacoleiros instantly opened their bags to review their merchandise: cameras, computer hard drives, and mobile phones hidden in handbags and between bus seats. An older woman inwardly smiled and then looked at grandson sitting next to her while she caressed the painting set she carried on her lap.

The majority of the people who walk the Puente de la Amistad Bridge in fact transport goods through some form of petty smuggling. Mototaxi drivers double-shift as *paseros* (a Spanish word for smuggler), carrying mobile phones and computer components in their helmets or in the seats or tires of their motorcycles. Mototaxis are hired by shop owners to transport computer components to Brazil; in one day they can cross the border twenty times or more, taking advantage of their mobile identity as taxi drivers to avoid border controls.

Although most smuggling in the Iguazú Triangle flows from Paraguay into Brazil, contraband moves in all directions. Restaurant owners in Foz do Iguaçu buy supplies in the supermarkets of Puerto Iguazú and profit from the low currency rate of the Argentine peso. Packages of juice, pasta, and many other groceries not available locally are smuggled from Argentina into Brazil. Agricultural products including eggs, sugar, and meat are smuggled from Brazil into Paraguay, where there is practically no agricultural industry.[25]

Smuggling has been facilitated through the discovery of new routes to avoid the international bridge and customs office. Sacoleiros make use of the Paraná and Iguazú rivers to transport goods by boat among the three cities. These smugglers, called *balseros* (from *balsa*, "boat" in Spanish), transport goods including drugs and weapons into Brazil, and agricultural products from Brazil to Paraguay and Argentina. Thus, rather than eliminating the smuggling networks, in some cases state surveillance has diverted smuggling routes, a phenomenon also true on US borders, as examined by Peter Andreas in chapter 8 of this volume.

Despite such shifts, military police surveillance and harsher controls at the Brazilian customs office in Foz do Iguaçu since 2001 have affected cross-border trade. The number of daily crossings per day on the Puente de la Amistad has dropped from ninety thousand in the early 2000s to between ten and fifteen thousand in 2009, according to the customs office in Foz do Iguaçu.[26] As a consequence, shop owners at both sides of the border have complained about plummeting sales. Some sources estimate up to a 90 percent decrease in commerce between the two cities,[27] although from my own interviews with shop owners and municipal authorities in Ciudad del Este, the estimated loss has been between 40 and 60 percent. In response, shop owners and the mayor of Ciudad del Este, Sandra Zacarías, have joined forces to protest the measures at the Brazilian border.

Moreover, as sacoleiros argue, police presence at the international bridges primarily targets small smugglers who cross by foot, while the large and powerful smuggling networks continue doing business as usual. Juan Aparicio, a smuggler I spoke to, noted the following: "What crosses over the bridge is the small stuff.

Big smugglers don't cross over the bridge. They use planes or cross with boats at the Itaipú Lake."[28] This perception of raids affecting only small-scale, autonomous agents opens up a discussion on justice and the validity of the rule of law.

In the midst of these debates, the most important project for reordering the region was launched in 2009 by the Brazilian national government. The industrial lobby in São Paulo had long urged the Brazilian state to better protect the market from smuggled goods. After years of discussion about whether sacoleiros should be prosecuted as criminals or allowed to make their living at the margins, the Brazilian congress passed the "sacoleiro law" in 2009 (number 11.898/2009). With the introduction of a simplified tax system (Regime de Tributação Unificada), the law defines sacoleiros as small entrepreneurs who, in order to operate, are to register as importers, receive accreditation, and meet tax duties. In a neoliberal fashion, this law legalizes the activities of sacoleiros by treating them as microentrepreneurs.

The sacoleiro law was implemented to facilitate the overland importation of merchandise from Paraguay into Brazil. Sacoleiros, now importers, are required to set up and register as microenterprises, declare the value of the goods at the customs office upon entrance to Brazil, and produce receipts to customs officials. The law introduces a unified tax rate of 42.25 percent on the declared price of all imported merchandise, a rate that is broken down into four different taxes: an 18 percent import tax, a 15 percent tax on industrialized products, a 7.6 percent contribution to social security, and a 1.65 percent social contribution (PIS/Pasep-Importação). Only merchandise for the final consumer is regulated by the new regime. It remains illegal to import a number of products, including weapons, ammunition, fireworks, liquor, cigarettes, cars, boats, medicine, tires, and second-hand articles. Each entrepreneur can import a maximum of US$61,000 each year in goods. The law contemplates various penalties when importers fail to follow the regulations. Sanctions include fines and the temporary suspension of import accreditations.

The law represents a new peak in the cycle of tolerance-repression-regulation to control trade in the Iguazú Triangle. Activities that for decades were tolerated in practice are now subject to regulation. Brazilian politicians, particularly those of the ruling Workers' Party (the PT), celebrated the new law. Their enthusiasm prevented them from anticipating the limitations and problems that the new system has brought. The first critical voices in Foz do Iguaçu and Ciudad del Este pointed out that the high taxes and bureaucratic red tape are too much. Sacoleiros—already at the margins of society—simply cannot make an adequate living with this new regulatory system in place.

Closing Remarks

In the cross-border urban conglomerate of the Iguazú Triangle, neoliberal principles of free trade, entrepreneurship, and liberalization clash with border surveillance and import tariffs. Moreover, the introduction of the sacoleiro law underpins the role of the nation-state in the organization of the market and creates supplementary state revenues with a fiscal system to tax cross-border smugglers. This legal project takes for granted that sacoleiros own the technical know-how to set up their own microenterprises; but this assumption does not hold, due to the circumstances of sacoleiros, who have little or no contact with the state and are not entrepreneurs but rather a link in a larger network of transport and supply.

The case presented in this chapter demonstrates the paradoxical effect of the neoliberal ideology on state policies in border regions; it stimulates trade across borders and fosters the creation of free-trade zones that in turn create new commercial barriers and regulations to control national markets. These tensions become particularly visible in cross-border trade that often consists of both legal and illegal activities. Though further research is necessary to investigate the long-term impact of the regime of legality promoted by global neoliberalism on the economy of border cities, this chapter has analyzed an important aspect of border relations—the effects of neoliberalism in regions of economic and regulatory disparity. The Brazilian state made itself felt, destabilizing the equilibrium that sacolerios enjoyed. A new equilibrium has arisen in which smugglers seek alternative mechanisms to circumvent state control in order to, oddly enough, maintain the ideology at the heart of neoliberalism: the exchange of goods without state intervention.

NOTES

1. Fernando Rabossi, "Nas ruas de Ciudad del Este: Vidas e vendas num mercado de fronteira," PhD diss., Universidade Federal do Rio de Janeiro, 2004.

2. Hastings Donnan and Thomas M. Wilson, *Border Approaches: Anthropological Perspectives on Frontiers* (Lanham, MD: University Press of America, 1994); and David Harvey, *The New Imperialism* (New York, NY: Oxford University Press, 2003).

3. Javier Auyero and Timothy Patrick Moran, "The Dynamics of Collective Violence: Dissecting Food Riots in Contemporary Argentina," *Social Forces* 85, no. 3 (2007): 1341–67; and Alejandro Grimson, "The Making of New Urban Borders: Neoliberalism and Protest in Buenos Aires," *Antipode* 40, no. 4 (2008): 504–12.

4. David J. Myers and Henry A. Dietz, eds., *Capital City Politics in Latin America: Democratization and Empowerment* (Boulder, CO: Lynne Rienner, 2002).

5. Mo Hume, "Mano Dura: El Salvador Responds to Gangs," *Development in Practice* 17, no. 60 (2007): 739–51; Kate Swanson, "'Bad Mothers' and 'Delinquent Children': Unravelling Anti-Begging Rhetoric in the Ecuadorian Andes," *Gender, Place and Culture* 14, no. 6 (2007): 703–20; and José Carlos G. Aguiar, "Nuevas ilegalidades en el orden global. Piratería y la escenificación del estado de derecho en México," *Foro Internacional* 196, no. (2009): 403–24.

6. Alejandro Portes and Brian R. Roberts, "La ciudad bajo el libre mercado: La urbanización en América Latina durante los años del experimento neoliberal," Center for Migration and Development Working Paper Series 5, Princeton University, Princeton, NJ, 2005.

7. Portes and Roberts, "La ciudad bajo el libre mercado," 15–16, author's translation.

8. Ricardo Grinbaum, "In Paraguay, Smugglers' Paradise," *World Press Review* 43, no. 1 (1996): 25–26; and Sebastian Rotella, "Jungle Hub for World's Outlaws," *Los Angeles Times*, A1, August 24, 1998.

9. Julio Jacobo Waiselfisz, *Mapa da violência dos municípios brasileiros* (Brasilia: Organização dos Estados Ibero-Americanos para a Educação a Ciência e a Cultura, 2007); and Jurandir Zamberlam and Giovanni Corso, *A emigração da Grande Criciúma na ótica de familiares–Desafios para a igreja de origem e de destino* (Porto Alegre: Solidus, 2007).

10. Rex Hudson, *Terrorist and Organized Crime Groups in the Tri-Border Area (TBA) of South America* (Washington, DC: Federal Research Division / Library of Congress, 2003); Rabossi, "Nas ruas de Ciudad del Este"; and Gustavo Lins Ribeiro, "Economic Globalization from Below," *Etnográfica* 10, no. 2 (2006): 233–49.

11. Hudson, *Terrorist and Organized Crime Groups*, 14–31; and Matthew Levitt, *Hezbollah: Financing Terror through Criminal Enterprise*, working paper, The Washington Institute for Near East Policy, 2005.

12. Ramón Fogel, "La región de La Triple Frontera: Territorios de integración y desintegración," *Sociologias* 10, no. 20 (2008): 270–90.

13. Elen Patricia de Jesús Silva Davi, "Trabalhadores na 'fronteira': Experiências dos sacoleiros e laranjas em Foz do Iguaçu–Ciudad Del Este (1990 / 2006)," master's thesis, Universidade Estadual do Oeste do Paraná, 2008, 15.

14. Sacoleiro specifically refers to a Brazilian petty smuggler, yet Paraguayans and Argentines have coined their own categories; the word *pasero* (from *pasar*, "pass" in Spanish) refers to a *contrabandista* ("smuggler" in Spanish) who illegally transports merchandise across countries. Brazilians also employ the term *camelô* ("camel" in Portuguese), although there is no clear difference in use. There are also ethnic distinctions in the use of subcategories: as noted below, *laranja* ("orange" in Portuguese) is used for Brazilian female smugglers of African ancestry.

15. Ricardo Antonio Correa and Amalia Maria Goldberg Godoy, "Políticas públicas e turismo sustentável em Foz do Iguaçu," *Revista Paranaense de Desenvolvimento* 115 (2008): 154; and Silva Davi, "Trabalhadores na 'fronteira,'" 23.

16. Lineu Franciscco Oliveira and Sonia Regina Valério do Sacramento, "Rede global de empreendedores sacoleiros alavancando exportações no Ceará," paper presented at 6th Congresso do Instituto Franco-Brasileiro de Administração de Empresas: Inovação, Cooperação Internacional e Desenvolvimento Regional, São Paulo, Brazil, May 23–24, 2011.

17. Roberto da Matta, *Carnavais, malandros e heróis* (Rio de Janeiro: Zahar Editores, 1979).

18. Fogel, "La región de La Triple Frontera," 271.

19. Eric Gustavo Cardin, "Sacoleiros e laranjas na Triple Fronteira: Uma análise da precarização do trabalho no capitalismo contemporâneo," master's thesis, Araraquara: Universidade Estadual Paulista, 2006, 81.

20. Eric Gustavo Cardin, "O circuito sacoleiro e as suas configurações: Conflitos e resistências nas três fronteiras," paper presented at XI Congresso Luso Afro Brasileiro de Ciências Sociais, Salvador, Bahia, Brazil, August 7–10, 2011.

21. Silva Davi, "Trabalhadores na 'fronteira,'" 70–71.

22. Alvaro de Souza Pinheiro, *Narcoterrorism in Latin America. A Brazilian Perspective*, Joint Special Operations University Report 06-4 (Hurlburt Field, FL: JSOU, 2006).

23. On this removal of beggars and street vendors, see Silva Davi, "Trabalhadores na 'fronteira,'" 114–26.

24. Rabossi, "Nas ruas de Ciudad del Este."

25. As I have argued elsewhere, the smuggling economies at the Iguazú Triangle are complementary and change according to the circumstances of the national markets. See José Carlos G. Aguiar, "Stretching the Border: Smuggling Practices and the Control of Illegality in South America," Global Consortium on Security Transformation: New Voices Series 6 (Santiago, Chile: Facultad Latinoamericana de Ciencias Sociales, FLACSO, 2010), http://www.securitytransformation.org/gc_publications.php.

26. Interview, June 2010.

27. Hudson, *Terrorist and Organized Crime Groups*.

28. "Lo que pasa por el puente es lo menos. Los grandes contrabandistas no cruzan por el puente. Ellos usan aviones o balsas y cruzan por el lago de Itaipú."

Chapter Eleven

Conclusions

Maiah Jaskoski, Arturo C. Sotomayor,
and Harold A. Trinkunas

In spite of the peaceful nature of interstate relations in the Americas at the beginning of the twenty-first century, borders remain sites and sources of both
tensions and harmonies. Overall, the variations and consequences of different
frontier dynamics in the Western Hemisphere in terms of cross-border flows of
persons, goods, and data have created a highly complex set of challenges for states
and nonstate actors. Democratization, regionalization, and globalization have accelerated and increased these flows within licit and illicit networks across the
Western Hemisphere's borders. The rise of NAFTA in North America and Mercosur in the Southern Cone have promoted free trade and accompanying economic
development in border regions. At the same time, other issues pertaining to security and the market have arisen, including the shifting of routes for narcotics and
human trafficking from the Andes and the Caribbean in the 1980s, into Central
America, Mexico, and the United States; changes resulting from varying patterns
of border enforcement in the last decade. This dynamic has fostered a dramatic
escalation of violence in a number of borderlands in the hemisphere.

Three main sets of conclusions can be drawn from the evidence presented in
this volume. The first is that territorial boundaries have an enduring role in defining states and create limits that continue being contested. However, the way in
which conflicts over boundaries are pursued by states has changed over time,
from the more traditional war-making dynamic of the nineteenth century to the
currently prevalent judicial and diplomatic approaches to settling borders.

The second set of conclusions focuses on the implications of the success and failure of border control policies and the administrative structures that support them. These structures define state jurisdictions, regulate flows across borders, and determine the legality of these movements. The intersection of this administrative-policy border complex among states can be a site for misperception, collaboration, and friction, often simultaneously. Moreover, the interaction of border policy and administration themselves is an important area through which domestic, political, and organizational structures influence the conduct of foreign policy.

The third set of conclusions is drawn from the role of border populations, including both licit and illicit actors, in influencing border policies and the actual operation of borders. This chapter ends by reviewing the challenges that these three sets of issues pose for the state and for the goal of maintaining safe, peaceful borders, and by recommending policies to address those challenges.

The Geopolitics of Borders

The dominant literature on geopolitics and international relations finds that territorial border disputes are the most common underlying cause of war between states. According to this literature, control over territory has an intrinsic strategic value for the state. Territory contains minerals, energy sources, and water. Similarly, territorial holdings can provide access to key canals, oceans, straits, and dominions. Sovereignty over a piece of land also symbolizes power over populations within delineated borders.[1] Territorial control thus plays a primary role as it shapes and conditions key state policies. Given the importance of such control, it is not surprising that conflicts over territorial boundaries and maritime frontiers are more likely to involve military force and escalate to war than are disputes about other issues.[2] In fact, territorial and boundary issues have been present in more than one-quarter of all militarized disputes and accounted for more than one-half of wars throughout the world between 1816 and 1992.[3]

We can derive two key components of territoriality and international border conflict. First, territorial issues influence the levels of conflict and cooperation between bordering states. Highly sensitive and vulnerable territorial and maritime borders in dispute can yield serious interstate tensions. Second, state resources and capabilities increase as governments aim to control borders and expand territorial boundaries. Charles Tilly summarized both war-making and state-making processes in his famous statement, "states make wars and wars make states." Implicit in this argument is the notion that states need to fight wars for territorial consolidation, and in the process, war making supports the institutional development of the state.[4]

The relationship among territories, borders, and conflict is the focus of the first section of this volume. The cases analyzed, drawn from Latin America, suggest that the relationship between territory and borders is in fact more complex than the dominant findings in the literature. While Latin America exhibits evidence of war and state capacity forming together, conflicts short of war, as well as cooperation, have taken place between states with enduring territorial and boundary disputes. Furthermore, variations in available resources and institutional development exist even among the most bellicose nations examined.

In his chapter, Cameron G. Thies provides a broad picture of territorial conflict in the region and its impact on state making and regional order. Thies considers that a geopolitical vision of borders and territory has been widely present in the region. Conflicts over territorial resources and boundaries have been salient and contentious, and have caused wars, especially in nineteenth-century South America.[5] But even with major interstate conflicts (such as the Paraguayan war, involving Argentina, Bolivia, and Brazil), the levels of war making in Latin America have remained relatively low compared to those in Europe.

Ultimately, territorial and border conflicts did not fundamentally shape the nature of war in the region. For Thies, the development of *uti possidetis juris* (the principle that post-independence boundaries should match those of the colonial period), enabled the territorial demarcation of newly created Latin American states after decolonization, and reduced the levels of violence among contiguous countries. War as a means of acquiring new territory had almost entirely vanished in the region in the twentieth century. But rivalries between states prevailed and persisted. The implementation of *uti possidetis juris* did create serious problems of interpretation regarding how territory was demarcated. Conflict over interpretation became the norm, as every former colony had a contested boundary dispute emanating from treaties and colonial settlement. These unresolved territorial issues stimulated interstate rivalries and shaped schooling, public opinion, foreign policy, and military training and doctrine. Thies uses Chile and Argentina to demonstrate how border disputes can nurture intense rivalries between neighbors and yet do not necessarily result in full-scale war. Thus, while territory and control over disputed borders remain significant for most countries in the region, the existence of boundary disputes does not, in itself, lead to war as an outcome.

Is war making necessary for state making? Here the evidence is more nuanced and not completely consistent with most theoretical assumptions—grounded in evidence from other regions—about war and the state. Latin Americans by and large have refrained from engaging in full-scale wars, creating a condition that Thies describes as "negative peace."[6] In the absence of war, political leaders could not rely on a "rally around the flag" appeal to extract resources (taxes) from citizens. Hence, in most cases state bureaucracies and political institutions remained underdeveloped. And yet interestingly, war and rivalry apparently do not explain why some Latin American states achieved stronger institutions than others, with Argentina, Brazil, Chile, and Mexico having stronger state institutions than Bolivia, Paraguay, and Central American countries.

Exemplifying that border cooperation can take place amid rivalry, Kristina Mani and Arturo C. Sotomayor each trace the processes by which several Latin American states peacefully settled common boundaries and resolved territorial disputes during democratization. Since the 1990s, two models of border dispute settlement have emerged in Latin America, one involving bilateral confidence-building measures and a second involving judicial arbitration. The mechanisms of operation of the two models are different, but the motivations are quite similar. In both cases, amid domestic pressures for political liberalization, governments implemented dispute settlement at least in part to demilitarize border policy and weaken military political power.

In her chapter on security cooperation in South America, Mani analyzes an unusual case for bilateral dispute resolution between two archrivals: Argentina and Chile. The two countries share the second longest border in the world and historically have had profound differences over frontiers, passages, and sovereignty rights. In 1978 they narrowly escaped war over the Beagle Channel, and while a papal mediation the following year preempted direct military confrontation, brinkmanship and blackmail persisted through the 1980s. By the early 1990s, when both states were undergoing democratization and economic liberalization, their twenty-three unresolved boundary disputes stood squarely in the way of new opportunities for bilateral trade and investment. The armed forces in both countries had played a key role in shaping political developments and had de facto control of territorial settlements. In fact, the military was the most active veto player, resisting efforts of civilians to settle border disputes. As Mani explains, territorial settlement was complicated by military opposition and demarcation flaws, in that the governing treaty that defined the lines of international separation contained contradictions when considering geographic reality. That is, the treaty established the boundary based on faulty topographical surveys, resulting in two different formulas, each of which favored a different country.

Cooperation emerged when Argentina and Chile began their reconciliation through regular, formal and informal debates and dialogues between foreign affairs and defense ministry representatives (the so-called 2 + 2 mechanism). Trust and mutual confidence slowly developed as diplomats and technical experts generated political coalitions that favored peaceful settlement. At a critical period in 1997–1998, diplomacy prevailed politically and became the preferred strategy for resolution. Slowly but surely, the military was isolated and separated from the decision-making process. The dispute over the sovereignty of the Patagonian Ice Fields was effectively depoliticized as a border issue and eventually demilitarized, allowing elected civilians to not only settle the issue, but also impose their leadership over foreign and defense policies.

Two findings can thus be drawn from Mani's analysis. First, the Argentina-Chile case reveals that cooperation can in fact emerge surrounding serious territorial and border disputes. Second, we find a path to achieve interstate cooperation that differs from avenues identified in mainstream research on international relations. For theorists such as Robert O. Keohane, systematic and regular coordination requires institutionalized and formalized cooperation in the form of international organizations.[7] By contrast, Mani describes a logic of cooperation and harmony that involved informal networks between policy makers without the assistance of formal organizations, and in which domestic variables (such as civil-military relations) assisted governments in identifying common interests and goals. Indeed, in the Argentina-Chile example, trade and international institutions were irrelevant in determining the final peaceful border settlement of 1999.

Few Latin American states have followed the bilateral settlement path established by the Argentina-Chile precedent. Instead, countries in the region are increasingly relying on the arbitration of high international tribunals, such as the International Court of Justice, to settle unresolved territorial, maritime, and boundary disputes. In fact, Latin America has the highest propensity for territorial arbitration processes when compared to other regions, with as many as nine cases documented in the highest international court at The Hague in the past two decades. The reasons for and implications of judicialization are analyzed in Arturo C. Sotomayor's chapter, in which he tests different international, legal, normative, and international variables to explain the predominance of international courts and tribunals in the region's dispute settlements.

Sotomayor finds that democratization in Central and South America provided strong incentives to demilitarize border conflict and disempower the armed forces, a dynamic similar to the one identified by Mani. In the Peru-Chile maritime dispute, democratically elected civilians found it increasingly tempting to rely on international judicial means to gradually transfer some policy decisions from military organizations to diplomatic bureaucracies where lawyers tend to dominate.[8] Furthermore, judicialization is a means by which domestic authorities delegate a degree of authority to an international court that is relatively isolated from geopolitics and domestic politics, and therefore more capable of implementing a neutral and impartial ruling on the contested territory.

While judicial intervention by international tribunals has successfully demilitarized previously contested borders and de-escalated bilateral conflict between bordering states, Sotomayor also raises a note of caution about unintended effects of judicialization. Diminished interstate conflict caused by territorial disputes can come at the expense of increased border trafficking, smuggling, and domestic violence. As borders have become demilitarized and are subject to legalistic dispute resolution, they have also turned into open spaces for illicit activities that are no longer monitored by the armed forces (an observation shared by Arie M. Kacowicz and José Carlos G. Aguiar in their chapters in this volume). In some countries, such as Ecuador, the armed forces have abandoned border posts and operated according to constrained rules of engagement, resulting in a security vacuum within the borderlands, analyzed in greater depth in Maiah Jaskoski's chapter.

In sum, war over territorial disputes is rare in the Western Hemisphere, even as interstate rivalries persist. Moreover, there is a spectrum of state response to border issues, ranging from conflict, to rivalry and negative peace, to peaceful settlement. Across the region, border disputes evolve in response to domestic trends that include democratization, civil-military tensions, and internal security challenges. But against most liberal expectations, new sources of border tension and conflict have emerged in the Americas even as states have demilitarized and pursued peaceful dispute settlements.

National Border Control Policies

Borders are much more than geopolitical boundaries delimiting sovereignty. They also function as areas of administrative organization and state control. As such, they entail specific state practices, such as customs, passport control, and policing, that organize political and public life and define the scope and domain of sovereignty.[9] Borders delimit state jurisdiction over individuals and territories, and often determine the limits of legality. As the essays in this volume suggest, the difference between an imported good and a trafficked item, or between a legal immigrant and an illegal one, is often determined by how the person or item crossed the border. The chapters in part II focus on the interaction between economic and security policies along borders and offer insight into how effective the state has been at improving cross-border security while facilitating legal flows of people, goods, and capital.

The authors examine three distinct and fundamentally different border zones of the United States and Mexico, Colombia and Venezuela, and the Triple Frontier in Argentina, Brazil, and Paraguay. These cases nonetheless share two noteworthy similarities. First, while territorial disputes in all three zones have been settled and pacified, illegal trafficking and crime have become an issue of concern. Second, as economic liberalization took off in the early 1980s, the flows of trade and finances dramatically increased in the three cases. In fact, most of the trade that takes place in the Americas passes through four main borders, including the three analyzed in this section of the volume.[10]

For all three cases, the authors demonstrate that there has been limited state control over actors on and near the border, with implications for the effectiveness of national border policies. Key elements have been lack of state capacity to deal with the problems that they perceive on the border, and the state's relative tolerance for the evasion of border policies by individuals and organizations. This compounds the lack of legitimacy of border policies within local and national society and further decreases voluntary compliance with border policies.

Adam Isacson's chapter on the United States–Mexico case describes two different but mutually reinforcing and intriguing border dynamics. He first identifies a number of policy misperceptions about security issues, in which public opinion and political attitudes in both countries, dominated by fears emanating from 9 / 11, increasingly portray the border as anarchic, affected by drug cartel violence in Mexico, and uncontrolled by massive migration flows; this perception was sharpened by the crisis of unaccompanied minors from Central America reaching the US border in the summer of 2014. Isacson argues that this view in fact is not matched by the reality on the US side of the border, where incidents of terrorism have never been reported, and homicide and crime rates have reached historically low levels. The only potential security threat to the US border is the one posed by increased drug trafficking and cartel activity, which in actuality have not brought a spillover of violence from Mexico. To some extent, misperceptions about United States–Mexico border security reveal an implicit failure in US policies. Legislators continue to support enlarged border patrols, militarized interdictions, and intelligence gathering without having performed any real assessment of the effectiveness of these measures. That is, state resources are often poured into the wrong areas—border patrol and defense—while other areas, including the reduction of drug trafficking and consumption, remain largely neglected. That is, there are substantial differences between national border policies defined in Washington and actual border imperatives.

What explains the mismatch between reality and perception at the national level when it comes to the border zone? Isacson argues that border security policies have acquired a life of their own. The United States–Mexico border has become an arena for political maneuvering around budgets for border security technologies, which greatly benefit both the security agencies and their private sector suppliers. Border issues are moved out of the local political arena and presented as existential threats, thereby validating extreme national policies in response and generating a securitizing move in which trade, migration, and law enforcement on the border have been framed as "national security" issues.[11]

The second dynamic addressed by Isacson is the relative improvement in security conditions on the United States' southern border, even as national perceptions about the border itself continue to deteriorate. Isacson suggests that tougher border policies and buildups—fortifying walls, deploying troops, and criminalizing immigration—may have improved security negligibly, as exemplified by decreasing homicide rates on the US side of the border and an absence of terrorist incidents. As an alternative, he hypothesizes that Mexico's economic recovery and shifting conditions in the US labor market could be transforming patterns in transborder migration. Furthermore, cartels may find it profitable to engage in criminal behavior in Mexico, but have few incentives to do so in the United States; this is partly because the drug market consists of wholesale operations in Mexico and retail in the United States.

Harold Trinkunas also examines a border that exhibits an unexpected economic-security dynamic. In the Colombia-Venezuela case, high economic interdependence has frequently coincided with significant interstate conflict. Like its United States–Mexico counterpart, the border between the two Andean countries is not just a single port of entry, but a series of sectors and areas, where state control varies substantially from one transborder community to another. Similar to other borders analyzed in this book, the lack of full state control over sectors has prompted contraband, insurgency, and narcotrafficking. While there is a long history of militarized conflict on the border, the flow of commerce has increased substantially in the past two decades. Economic reforms in the early 1990s stimulated trade liberalization in both countries, and Colombia became Venezuela's most important South American trading partner. An intertwined but asymmetric marriage of convenience soon emerged as Bogotá benefited from a trade surplus with Caracas, and Venezuela became an informal supplier of cheap gasoline and subsidized goods smuggled into Colombia's border regions.

Conventional theory on interdependence would predict a decrease of military action and conflict as economic and commercial ties increase between states.[12] Conversely, Trinkunas points out that Colombian President Álvaro Uribe and Venezuelan President Hugo Chávez were preparing for war just as bilateral commerce experienced a boom. Between 2005 and 2010 the two governments downgraded their diplomatic relations, and troops were mobilized to the border in response to various diplomatic crises and incidents, including Venezuela's support for the FARC insurgency and Colombia's aircraft attack against an insurgent camp in Ecuador.

Trinkunas embraces a two-level approach to explain the puzzle of war preparation amid increased trade liberalization. He finds that foreign policy making follows a double-edged diplomatic logic;[13] war preparedness belongs squarely to the foreign and defense policy arena, and presidential imperatives, executive branch preferences, and US security policy affect outcomes. Indeed, the process of ideological polarization in Colombia and Venezuela at the presidential level made political accommodation difficult, as both presidents promoted opposite national policies (statism in Venezuela and liberalization in Colombia). United States policy in the area aggravated the crisis by contributing to Venezuelans' perceptions of military escalation—especially that produced by deepened United States–Colombian security and military ties in the aftermath of 9/11—which in turn provoked Chávez to acquire additional weapons from Russia.

In contrast, bilateral trade policy was driven by domestic actors and interests. The economic liberalization phase of the 1990s routinized bilateral trade, generating long-lasting economic coalitions that included state and private political actors in both countries. The protrade coalitions intensified on the border even as national politics in Colombia and Venezuela grew more polarized. When conflict and escalation emerged, the business community in Colombia, Venezuela's state-led oil sector, border communities, and even insurgents, drug traffickers, and some segments of the military, informally coalesced in favor of bilateral trade. Pressures from these actors helped keep the borders open to commerce and dissuaded the presidents from declaring full-scale war.

Although to a greater extent than in the United States–Mexico case, we also find that in Colombia and Venezuela, state and national politics exercise little control or influence over local border dynamics. While Uribe and Chávez dictated opposing foreign policy strategies, they were unable to control economic processes on the border. In short, Trinkunas finds that the nature of Colombia and Venezuela's relationship is such that war is unlikely because of border interdependence, particularly when driven by the dynamics of local actors who depend on their ability to cross the border for their economic advantage and survival.

Kacowicz, in turn, analyzes the Triple Frontier or Tri-border Area (TBA, also known as the Iguazú Triangle) where Argentina, Brazil, and Paraguay converge on the Paraná and Iguazú rivers. Unlike the Andean case, the TBA has been transformed from a conflictive or negative peace zone into a peaceful area, where its core members cooperate intensely at the national level. At one point, the border became the economic powerhouse of the Mercosur integration process, in which free trade and low import tariffs drove decisions about economic transactions. The case also provides an interesting contrast to the US southern border, since flows of trade in the TBA have taken place without a concomitant increase in border security measures. Indeed, the stability based on predictable relations among the three national governments contrasts with the anarchy that prevails inside the TBA, where contraband smuggling, organized criminal activity, and increased violence are highly noticeable.

For Kacowicz, the illegality and illicitness that dominate the Triple Frontier are directly linked to the processes of regional integration (via Mercosur) that followed a rapprochement between Argentina and Brazil in the 1970s. The impulse for economic liberalization and increased regionalism generated the expected boom in trade and financial transactions across South America's borders while also creating incentives for informality, and thereby yielding unintended consequences. Free-trade zones and ports of entry were established on previously contested borders, making it extremely difficult to monitor illicit activity. The common border thus provided a safe haven for, and an environment conducive to, organized crime.

Limited state control of border dynamics is front and center in Kacowicz's analysis. The author notes that poor regulatory structures impede the efficient control of organized crime. Moreover, high levels of corruption in the police and other law enforcement agencies hamper antinarcotic and counterterrorism efforts. Militarizing the TBA border is not an option since its member states are constitutionally barred from deploying soldiers to conduct law enforcement or antinarcotic operations (part of the demilitarization process described by Mani and Sotomayor in their respective chapters). While the TBA has witnessed a rise in criminal activity, Kacowicz still cautiously observes that, within the TBA, the degree of "limited statehood" varies from one border community to another. Ciudad del Este on the Paraguayan side of the border is more vulnerable to illicit activities than its counterparts Foz de Iguaçu in Brazil and Puerto Iguazú in Argentina. The end result of this variation is a mixture of harmonies and tensions in the borderlands, where the success of regional peace is counterbalanced by poverty, illegality, and the expansion of organized crime.

Together, these cases provide a rich array of conclusions about border control and state policy. One finding is that both cooperation and conflict coexist with increased trade and regionalization. Furthermore, in spite of differences in state capacity and levels of economic development, the cases reveal that states often exercise little control over borders. Attempts by states to increase policing and reduce illicit activity in fact often yield more illegal activity as local actors react by finding ways to evade increasingly onerous state control.

Licit and Illicit Behavior by Borderland Actors

The essays in part III delve still deeper into understanding illicit actors in borderlands. They focus on explaining and understanding the behavior of varied nonstate border actors, and in doing so point to the limitations of mainstream, state-centered approaches.[14]

From smugglers to insurgents, illicit borderland actors adapt to and often outsmart state agencies, and they even have an impact on state organizations. Through their actions on the borders and in borderlands—trafficking, training, crossing, buying, and supplying goods—they can tacitly and sometimes unintentionally provide meaning to, or even assume, state functions. The profitability of their ventures creates incentives for the state to tax and police, their transactions create monetary enticements for legal and black markets, and their services can fill state gaps or challenge public functions in the borderlands. The state sometimes interacts and cooperates with these border actors through various means, including neglect, when the state ignores them; fiscalization, when the state attempts to tax or regulate their behavior; and/or institutional corruption, when state agents accept bribes. As a result, illegal borderland actors and state structures are interdependent, mutually implicating, and coconstitutive.[15]

The chapters in the final section of this volume question the claim that illicit border actors—be they traffickers or insurgents—can be fully controlled, showing how nonstate actors have proven highly successful in crossing and using borders and borderlands for illegal purposes in spite of varying state development and capabilities. As Peter Andreas demonstrates in his essay about smuggling in North America, illegal trafficking has been a permanent feature in the hemisphere for centuries; attempts to eradicate traffickers have continuously failed. At best, the state can aim to manage smuggling, but this is often achieved inefficiently and with unintended consequences. In turn, Aguiar demonstrates in his chapter on petty smugglers in the Iguazú Triangle that attempts by Brazilian authorities to tax and legalize smugglers have been challenging for the state and costly for both the state and borderland residents. Similarly, Jaskoski's chapter on the Colombia-Ecuador border suggests that limited state presence in some areas of the Ecuadorian borderlands provides substantial incentives for guerrillas to establish territorial control.

The three analyses address a number of key questions about nonstate actors, their relationships to the state, and the interaction between state policies and borderland actors. Traffickers have played a fundamental role in contributing to political development in North America, as Andreas argues. Echoing Charles Tilly, Andreas claims that trafficking supports state making and states promote trafficking, and shows how efforts to regulate illicit border crossings have expanded the reach of central government authorities, ultimately stimulating the development of border enforcement infrastructure and capacity. Moreover, the nature of trafficking, involving different forms of commodities and services, has shaped the way the United States deals with its neighbors across the borders, sometimes eliciting cooperation from them and at times escalating conflict in an effort to limit illicit transactions.

Even as border enforcement capabilities improve, trafficking in licit and illicit commodities continues to expand. For Andreas, there is a direct relationship between legal trade and illicit trafficking. Licit and illicit actors alike are intimately intertwined because they use the same trade regimes—routes, highways, modes of transportation, and currencies—to exchange goods and services across borders. Thus, as long as there is a market, there will be economic incentives for legal and illegal transactions in common frontiers. As a result, the amount of illegal trafficking will necessarily surge if the flows of legal trade increase because of economic liberalization and open societies.

Andreas shows how attempts at detection, deterrence, and interdiction of illicit economic activities have had limited success and dangerous effects. Prohibition and the opium war provide valuable historical analogies for the current "war on drugs," which is producing devastating effects on northern border communities in Mexico. Legalizing traffickers, the way distillers were once legalized after prohibition, may temporarily appease them, but new types of commodities will continue to challenge border enforcers. Marijuana and cocaine might become legal one day, only to be replaced by newer and more processed types of drugs, such as amphetamines and methamphetamines.

Aguiar describes a similar phenomenon of sequential reactions among state border control efforts and smugglers' tactics. When the national economies of Argentina, Brazil, and Paraguay were in decline, trafficking propelled expansive growth in the border zone (the Iguazú Triangle) by contributing to, for example, urbanization, migration, and tourism. The type of economy generated in the area was mostly informal (see also Kacowicz in this volume). Disorganized development generated massive shantytowns along the borders, and corruption became the modus operandi. Aguiar believes that most of these unintended effects can be attributed to the neoliberal approaches undertaken by governments during the process of economic liberalization, which in turn generated large ungoverned spaces.[16] This dynamic resembles Kacowicz's explanation, which highlights the effects of regionalization.

Aguiar focuses on petty traffickers—*sacoleiros*, or "baggers" in Portuguese. These merchants operate in the borderlands, trading and transporting goods, most of which are legal, without paying customs fees. They profit mainly by this evasion of customs duties. Although the sacoleiros have existed for many decades, it was not until very recently that governments imposed measures to regulate them. That is, Mercosur and the expansion of legal trade have brought increased duties and higher bureaucratization on borders. Just as in the North American case, attempts to tax these actors in the Mercosur area have prompted an expansion of deviant behavior; routes have been modified, counterfeit goods from China are on the rise, trafficking of illegal products (mostly weapons and drugs) has increased, new smuggling techniques have appeared, and bribery is rampant.

To reduce smuggling, states in the TBA have relied on legalization paired with taxation by imposing additional fiscal duties and customs to actors once engaged in illegal trafficking. However, illicit merchants have reacted to this new fiscal environment by focusing on transporting smaller, high-technology items, such as mobile phones and tablets, which can be more easily hidden in handbags and are not as readily detected by authorities; these items also have a higher value on the black market.

Like Aguiar and Andreas, Jaskoski examines unintended consequences of state practices in borderlands, especially with regard to effects on illicit behavior of nonstate actors. She finds that, in response to weak state presence, the Colombian FARC insurgency not only challenges state policy, but also shapes the borderlands when it assumes varying postures vis-à-vis bordering states and local communities. The rebels fight against the armed forces on the Colombian side of the border, but have overtly refrained from staging militarized attacks on Ecuador's armed forces in order to use Ecuadorian borderlands for resting, resupplying, and training. The Ecuadorian state has reciprocated by avoiding engagement.

Jaskoski demonstrates that the presence of trade, populations, and a weak state have created incentives for guerrilla forces to seek refuge in Ecuador's northern borderlands. The guerrillas wield influence on the Ecuadorian borderline and on state actors—namely, the Ecuadorian army—through activities such as buying supplies, hiring services, interacting with border communities, and even enforcing public order. The irony is that instead of blurring borders, the insurgents have contributed to maintaining the borderline separating the two Andean nation-states. This dynamic creates a strange reversal of geopolitics whereby conflict between Ecuador and Colombia—which almost caused a war in the Andes in 2008, as described in Trinkunas' chapter—is due not to a territorial border dispute, but to insurgent activity and the state responses it generates. The FARC thus shape border dynamics and in so doing have affected interstate behavior.

The three chapters suggest that understanding the limitations of state border practices is the first step in providing an accurate diagnosis of border dynamics. Though as Andreas finds, even the US border has never been a "hard" border, fully controlled by the state; we expect even greater border porosity in the present context in which states increasingly share power with subnational, international, and transnational actors. This issue may be particularly true in the Western Hemisphere, where the spread of democracy, free trade, and insecurity have intensified social and economic interactions in borderlands.

Going Forward: Implications for Policymaking in the Americas

This volume has sought to understand how border policies affect and are affected by international, national, and subnational dynamics. Particularly striking is the variety of conflictive and cooperative behaviors and unintended consequences that arise as states and nonstate actors attempt to formulate and implement policies for American borders and borderlands. This book is grounded in the observation that there are important differences between the borders and borderlands in the Americas and those in other regions of the world, such as Western Europe. For example, the evolution of war, militarized conflict, integration processes, state making, and trafficking is patently different in the Western Hemisphere borders than in the European Union.[17] This final section seeks to translate these insights about borders into concrete policy strategies both for fostering peaceful borders—in terms of safety for residents and legal commerce and international relations—and for achieving state capacity to accomplish this. The discussion is based on the normative standpoint that harmonies are preferable to conflicts on borders and in borderlands, and that states should have autonomy to seek out and protect public interests, independent of private influence.

One set of recommendations pertains to addressing conflict that arises with international border disputes. Sotomayor identified at least eleven cases of unresolved territorial and maritime boundary disputes in Latin America, and other chapters examine in detail two longstanding disputes—those between Argentina and Chile, and Colombia and Venezuela.

Where border conflict and rivalry prevail, we envision three main policy options. One is to maintain the status quo, minimizing accidents and misperceptions in the contested borders so as not to incite either side. This strategy will not resolve the underlying border issues, but it may allow states to coexist without the escalation to militarized conflict and even war. The Falklands/Malvinas dispute fits this situation. Another possibility, suggested by Mani's chapter, entails confidence-building measures such as those implemented in Argentina and Chile in the 1990s through the 2 + 2 mechanism, which regularly gathers two deputy ministries (foreign affairs and defense) from its two member states. This approach will not resolve the fundamental domestic differences that separate, for example, Colombia and Venezuela, but at least it might allow them to better navigate the waters of political polarization and politicization. A 2 + 2 mechanism could allow bilateral issues to be handled by bureaucrats and technocrats in specialized agencies that are better able to focus on shared border threats than more politicized national-level actors. Such a collaborative approach requires compromise and a deep commitment by all governments involved to understand and respect their counterparts' different border policy agendas. This option is merely a mechanism to enhance mutual confidence, especially when the domestic political context signals uncertainty. A final alternative is to seek a third-party mediator, such as an international court. While this avenue has been appealing to a number of Latin American countries, it only transfers militarized conflict to the legal domain where tensions can persist (as has been the case in the El Salvador-Honduras-Nicaragua and the Bolivia-Chile border disputes).

States that have settled their boundary disputes face a different set of challenges and problems for achieving peaceful borders and for supporting state capacity. In terms of economic border dynamics, we identify increasing challenges posed by trade liberalization. Throughout the 1990s borders were seen predominantly through the prism of free trade. Trade liberalization may be undermining the rationale for conflict in once high-risk areas, such as Central America and the Southern Cone. However, while increased trade may improve economic exchange and raise the costs of war, improved trade relations at the national level should not be considered a panacea for reducing tension and illegal transactions in borderlands. States should be aware that when they foster free trade they are simultaneously creating conditions for increased illicit trafficking.

Hard-line policies to eradicate smuggling are likely to fail. Instead, state policies should focus on minimizing, not eliminating, the externalities caused by free trade. Economic liberalization can create winners and losers, since more open trade policies tend to prompt competition that rewards successful entrepreneurs in positions to make risky investments. In this context, activities in the informal economy that range from petty smuggling to organized crime can be particularly appealing alternatives for many groups and individuals. Domestic social policies that make it more attractive and more possible for people to participate in legal economic activities may thus serve as better deterrents of crime than more aggressive controls in the borderlands. From this perspective, the overall improvement of Mexico's development indicators—including higher quality education, an expanded middle class, and better healthcare—could minimize the security concerns that NAFTA has unintentionally created for both sides of the border. Similarly, the response by the governments in Central America's Northern Triangle, the United States, and the Inter-American Development Bank to the unaccompanied children crisis in 2014 focuses in part on creating better development and security indicators with the aim of reducing emigration.

Turning to security on borders, we find worrying signs of "fortress mentality" in the wake of 9/11, and draw conclusions similar to those regarding hardline antismuggling policies. This fortress mentality is seen mostly in the form of securitization along the United States–Mexico border (fear of terrorism and migration), increased fiscalization in the Tri-Border Area (fear of smuggling), and militarization in the Andean region (fear of insurgency). The implicit danger in pursuing such an approach is the possibility of reversing previous efforts to open and liberalize borders by then imposing security burdens on legal trade. Moreover, border securitization often encourages unilateralism and mistrust among neighbors. For example, the United States and Brazil frequently act without substantial consultation with Mexico or Paraguay, respectively. A fortress strategy ultimately has the potential of inciting interstate tensions, evidenced in the United States–Mexico, Colombia-Venezuela, and Ecuador-Colombia cases.

Not only can securitizing borders ignite international tensions, but at a fundamental level it may even fail to establish safe borderlands. For example, increasing the number of border patrol agents, as has occurred along the United States–Mexico border, will not necessarily detect or detract illicit traffickers and migrants, as suggested by Isacson's chapter.

International collaboration could result in both safer borders and more peaceful international border relations. A new approach to border control and security would aim to reduce the burden on security agencies by shifting the focus from patrolling thousands of miles of border to managing the border "in depth," using shared intelligence, analysis, and methodologies to identify the areas, transit routes, and persons posing the greatest risk, and by also devoting more resources away from the border to target these threats before they reach the borderline. The "21st Century Border Initiative," agreed to by Presidents Peña Nieto and Barack Obama in 2013 in regard to the United States–Mexico border, contains some elements of this approach; these include its focus on secure flows and coordinating investigative strategies by agencies on both sides of the border. The initiative has not been fully implemented, and it could go much farther toward establishing a collaborative approach to border management. The eventual goal of collaborative border management is to create confidence on both sides that the security agencies of each will enforce policies, identify threats, and develop responses at a similar level of effectiveness.

Indeed, despite the existence of such international collaboration on border policies, the fact that we observe the two opposing forces of securitization and economic liberalization affecting borders suggests there is substantial room for improvement when it comes to policy convergence and coordination. There are varied definitions across the region of what many policymakers consider "the border problem." There are even serious divergences in this regard between states that share a common border. For example, the US government defines borders in the wake of 9 / 11 as being predominantly about security and law enforcement, whereas for its neighbor, Mexico, borders are mainly about economic development and trade. Venezuela's leaders present their border with Colombia as a security or even ideological problem, when in fact trade drives the actual border policies of both governments. While Brazil, Argentina, and Paraguay agree that the triple frontier region should be understood primarily in terms of economic transactions and tourism, other international actors see the zone as posing a significant security problem.

These divergences have implications for how states talk to or past each other about managing common borders. As a result, it is imperative to increase interstate collaborative efforts to improve outcomes across diplomatic, development, and security dimensions. This is not to suggest that the Western Hemisphere should follow the Schengen model in Europe, which eliminates passport and other related border controls within the EU area. However, making a modest investment into multilateral training, capability development, information sharing, and institution building can pay handsome dividends. Most US border security and law enforcement relationships in the hemisphere are managed on a bilateral basis; the possibility of multilateral or plurilateral institutions should be explored. This would help to address the threats that affect multiple borders simultaneously, such as transnational crime, and avoid the possibility that success in one bilateral effort will simply shift the activities of illicit actors toward jurisdictions less prepared to address them, resulting in the so-called balloon effect.

Moving beyond international coordination questions, local policy changes can also be considered for borderlands. The local level, and specifically the legitimacy of border policy in borderlands, has a significant impact on the effectiveness of state border policies and thus on the very autonomy and legitimacy of the state itself. In a sense, borders are not just fixed lines, installations, systems, or institutions; they also exist in the minds of people. Local support in borderlands may be particularly critical for the effectiveness of a national government's border policy. Resident knowledge of how to navigate borders (and how illegal border-crossers navigate borders) is frequently superior to that of national authorities. Borderland residents are naturally better at identifying those who do not "belong" in border communities. Alternatively, where border policies are considered illegitimate, border populations have superior knowledge of the means to evade border authorities and controls, and therefore can actively undermine national-level border policies.

Unfortunately, governments have a poor historical record of consulting and incorporating the preferences of local populations or local border-control authorities. Increases in state capacity can provoke a reaction by local communities that makes them more opaque to the state. Likewise, greater national efforts by militaries and national police forces to improve border security may undermine capabilities and authorities at the local level, fostering competition between local and national bureaucracies.

Finally, nonstate actors also benefit from well-managed and secured borders, especially when it comes to minimizing political risks associated with security failures. There are everyday examples, such as airport security, where the private sector benefits enormously from the public provision of security for the air transportation system. One way to strengthen state capabilities is by relieving border agencies of the burdens of routine border operations, such as inspections and the processing of border shipments. These functions could be outsourced, allowing states to focus their capabilities more closely on intelligence, enforcement, and regulation efforts that target the ringleaders of major illicit networks. Another way of improving the capabilities of states is by levying taxes or fees on the private-sector actors who derive the greatest benefit from efficient border regimes; these taxes or fees would help defray the cost of operating border crossings and airports, performing customs inspections, and monitoring for security threats.

These suggested measures may have limited utility, in that they address problems in a fairly general sense. This limitation is foreseen by Etel Solingen and Alexander George, who in their respective works observe that causal analysis is often more capable of conceptualizing and framing puzzling questions than formulating detailed policy plans.[18] Nonetheless, we do believe that the insights from this volume provide ideas and suggest preliminary steps that would build on existing approaches to borders in the Americas. These ideas could help to facilitate cross-border trade, provide security on borders and in borderlands, and resolve international border disputes, while potentially limiting associated material and human costs. Crucially, the volume's findings and implications underscore that borders in the Western Hemisphere simultaneously exhibit conflicts and harmonies. Existing border policies and border politics reinforce the general trend toward interstate peace and increased trade, but they also produce negative externalities, particularly in the realm of illicit flows and their associated impact on security.

NOTES

1. For a discussion on the relevance of territory, see Paul F. Dielh, "Territory and International Conflict: An Overview," in *A Road Map to War: Territorial Dimensions of International Conflict,* ed. Paul F. Diehl (Nashville, TN: Vanderbilt University Press, 1999), viii–xii.

2. Diehl, "Territory and International Conflict," ix–x.

3. See John A. Vasquez, *The War Puzzle* (New York, NY: Cambridge University Press, 1993); and Boaz Atzili, *Good Fences, Bad Neighbors: Border Fixity and International Conflict* (Chicago, IL: Chicago University Press, 2012), 11, 51.

4. Charles Tilly, *Coercion, Capital, and European States, A.D. 990–1992* (Oxford, UK: Blackwell, 1993).

5. For an analysis of the impact of geopolitical thinking in South America, see Jack Child, *Geopolitics and Conflict in South America: Quarrels Among Neighbors* (New York, NY: Praeger, 1985); and João Resende-Santos, *Neorealism, States, and the Modern Mass Army* (New York, NY: Cambridge University Press, 2007).

6. Negative peace is often contrasted with the term positive peace, which is identified by the presence of confidence and trust, and exists in states that have ruled out war as an instrument and have developed expectations of peaceful change. See Emanuel Adler and Michael Barnett, eds., *Security Communities* (New York, NY: Cambridge University Press, 1998); Karl W. Deutsch, *Political Community and the North Atlantic Area* (Princeton, NJ: Princeton University Press, 1957); and Arie M. Kacowicz, *Zones of Peace in the Third World: South America and West Africa in Comparative Perspective* (New York, NY: State University of New York Press, 1998).

7. Robert O. Keohane, *After Hegemony: Cooperation and Discord in the World Political Economy* (Princeton, NJ: Princeton University Press, 1984).

8. For a theoretical discussion on how democratization incentivizes participation in international organizations, see Kenneth W. Abbot, Robert O. Keohane, Andrew Moravcsik, Anne-Marie Slaughter, and Duncan Snidal, "The Concept of Legalization," *International Organization* 54, no. 3 (2000): 401–19; Beth Simmons and Lisa Martin, "Theories and Empirical Studies of International Institutions," *International Organization* 52, no. 4 (1998): 729–57; and Edward D. Mansfield and John C. Pevehouse, "Democratization and International Organizations," *International Organization* 60, no. 1 (2006): 137–67.

9. See, for example, Hastings Donnan and Thomas M. Wilson, *Borders: Frontiers of Identity, Nation and State* (New York, NY: Berg, 1999); and George Gavrilis, *The Dynamics of Interstate Boundaries* (New York, NY: Cambridge University Press, 2008).

10. The fourth is the United States–Canada border.

11. For an analysis of securitization, see Barry Buzan, Ole Waever, and Jaap de Wilde, *Security: A New Framework for Analysis* (Boulder, CO: Lynne Rienner, 1998).

12. See Robert O. Keohane and Joseph S. Nye, *Power and Interdependence* (Boston, MA: Little Brown 1977).

13. For a theoretical analysis of double-edge diplomacy see Peter B. Evans, Harold K. Jacobson, and Robert D. Putnam, *Double-Edged Diplomacy: International Bargaining and Domestic Politics* (Berkeley, CA: University of California Press, 1993).

14. A statecentric approach conceives of the state as the main actor defining borders. Since the state is a structure of political authority with a monopoly on the legitimate use of organized violence, states are often (and perhaps erroneously) seen as the ultimate tool of control and regulation of borders. For a critique of statecentric approaches, see Alexander Wendt, *Social Theory of International Politics* (New York, NY: Cambridge University Press, 1999), 8–10.

15. This interdependence links directly to the structure and agent relationship, per Alexander Wendt. Wendt, "The Agent-Structure Problem in International Relations Theory," *International Organization* 41, no. 3 (1987): 335–70.

16. For a discussion of ungoverned spaces, see Anne L. Clunan and Harold A. Trinkunas, eds., *Ungoverned Spaces: Alternatives to State Authority in an Era of Softened Sovereignty* (Stanford, CA: Stanford University Press, 2010).

17. For an analysis of the European model, based on a different culture of borders that emphasizes supranational institutions and challenges long-established conceptions of sovereignty and territoriality, see Ruben Zaiotti, *Cultures of Border Control: Schengen and the Evolution of European Frontiers* (Chicago, IL: Chicago University Press, 2011).

18. See Etel Solingen, *Nuclear Logics: Contrasting Paths in East Asia and the Middle East* (Princeton, NJ: Princeton University Press, 2008), 289; and Alexander L. George, *Bridging the Gap: Theory and Practice in Foreign Policy* (Washington, DC: US Institute of Peace, 1993).

Contributors

José Carlos G. Aguiar (PhD, University of Amsterdam, 2007) is an urban anthropologist who specializes in cultures of illegality, borders, commodity chains, security policies, and minority issues. He is an assistant professor in the Department of Latin American Studies at Leiden University. Aguiar has conducted extensive fieldwork in Latin America and China, particularly in Mexico, Peru, and the Iguazú Triangle, the urban cluster at the borders of Paraguay, Brazil and Argentina. He has published widely in edited volumes and journals such as *Political and Legal Anthropology Review*, *Etnográfica*, and *Iconos*.

Peter Andreas is the John Hay Professor of International Studies at Brown University. Previously, Andreas was an academy scholar at Harvard University, a research fellow at the Brookings Institution, and an SSRC–MacArthur Foundation Fellow on International Peace and Security. He holds an MA and PhD in government from Cornell University and a BA in political science from Swarthmore College. Andreas is the author, coauthor, or coeditor of nine books. He has also written for a wide range of scholarly and policy journals. Other writings include congressional testimonies and op-eds in major newspapers. His latest book, on the politics of smuggling in American history, is *Smuggler Nation: How Illicit Trade Made America* (Oxford University Press, 2013).

Adam Isacson joined the Washington Office on Latin America (WOLA) in 2010 after fourteen years working on Latin American and Caribbean security issues with the Center for International Policy. At WOLA, his Regional Security Policy Program monitors security trends and US military cooperation in the Western Hemisphere. He has published and cowritten articles, reports, and book chapters for his own organizations, as well as in *Foreign Policy*, *Current History*, *LASA Forum*, *Americas Quarterly*, *Foreign Affairs en Español*, and several university presses. He has testified before Congress eight times, and led seven congressional delegations to the Americas. He holds an MA in international relations from Yale University. Before WOLA and CIP, he worked for the Arias Foundation for Peace and Human Progress in San José, Costa Rica.

Maiah Jaskoski is an assistant professor in the Department of Politics and International Affairs at Northern Arizona University. She specializes in environmental politics, borders, military missions, civil-military relations, and security privatization in Latin America. Jaskoski is author of *Military Politics and Democracy in the Andes* (Johns Hopkins University Press, 2013). Her research has also been published in *Armed Forces and Society, Latin American Politics and Society, Latin American Research Review, Studies in Comparative International Development*, and *World Development*. She holds a PhD in political science from the University of California, Berkeley, and a BA in political science from Swarthmore College.

Arie M. Kacowicz (PhD in politics, Princeton University, 1992) is the Chaim Weizmann Chair in International Relations and associate professor in the Department of International Relations at the Hebrew University of Jerusalem, Israel. He is the author of *Peaceful Territorial Change* (University of South Carolina Press, 1994), *Zones of Peace in the Third World: South America and West Africa in Comparative Perspective* (SUNY Press, 1998), *The Impact of Norms in International Society: The Latin American Experience, 1881–2001* (University of Notre Dame Press, 2005), and *Globalization and the Distribution of Wealth: The Latin American Experience, 1982–2008* (Cambridge University Press, 2013). His areas of interest include international relations theory, peace studies, international relations of Latin America, globalization and global governance, and the Arab-Israeli conflict.

Kristina Mani (PhD in political science, Columbia University, 2004) is an associate professor of Politics at Oberlin College. Her research interests center on military and security issues in Latin America, civil-military relations, and the political economy of the military. Dr. Mani's publications include *Democratization and Military Transformation in Argentina and Chile: Rethinking Rivalry* (Lynne Rienner, 2011) on the development of security cooperation and its impact on the militaries of Argentina and Chile, as well as articles on military entrepreneurship in *Armed Forces and Society, Bulletin of Latin American Research*, and *Latin American Politics and Society*. She has served as a consultant to Transparency International and the United Nations Development Programme on projects related to defense industry integrity and the armed forces' role in economies undergoing political transition. She is currently writing a comparative study of military entrepreneurs in Latin America since 1930.

Arturo C. Sotomayor is an associate professor in the Department of Political Science and Geography at the University of Texas at San Antonio. Most recently, he was associate professor in the National Security Affairs Department at the Naval Postgraduate School (NPS), in Monterey, California. His areas of interest include civil-military relations in Latin America, UN peacekeeping participation by South American countries, Latin American comparative foreign policy, and nuclear policy in Argentina, Brazil, and Mexico. He is the author of *The Myth of the Democratic Peacekeeper: Civil-Military Relations and the United Nations* (Johns Hopkins University Press, 2014) and coeditor of *Mexico's Security Failure* (Routledge, 2011).

Cameron G. Thies is professor and director of the School of Politics and Global Studies at Arizona State University. He is the author of *The United States, Israel, and the Search for International Order: Socializing States* (Routledge, 2013) and *Intra-Industry Trade: Cooperation and Conflict in the Global Political Economy* (Stanford University Press, 2015). His work has also appeared in journals such as *World Politics, International Studies Quarterly, Comparative Political Studies, American Journal of Political Science,* and *Journal of Politics.*

Harold A. Trinkunas is the Charles W. Robinson Chair and senior fellow and director of the Latin America Initiative in the Foreign Policy Program at the Brookings Institution. His research focuses on Latin American politics, particularly on issues related to foreign policy, governance, and security. He is currently studying Brazil's emergence as a major power, and Latin American contributions to global governance on issues including energy policy, drug policy reform, and internet governance. He authored *Crafting Civilian Control of the Military in Venezuela* (University of North Carolina Press, 2005) and coedited and contributed to *Ungoverned Spaces: Alternatives to State Authority in an Era of Softened Sovereignty* (Stanford University Press, 2010).

Index

Page numbers in *italics* indicate maps and tables.